JONATHAN BATE, King Alfred Professor of English Literature and Leverhulme Research Professor at the University of Liverpool, is well known as a critic and essayist. His most recent books are the highly acclaimed *The Genius of Shakespeare* and a novel, *The Cure for Love*, both published by Picador.

Also by Jonathan Bate in Picador

The Song of the Earth

Jonathan Bate

PICADOR

First published 2000 by Picador

First published in paperback 2001 by Picador
an imprint of Macmillan Publishers Ltd
Pan Macmillan, 20 New Wharf Road, London N1 9RR
Basingstoke and Oxford
Associated companies throughout the world
www.panmacmillan.com

ISBN 978-0-330-37269-5

A CIP catalogue record for this book is available from
the British Library.

Typeset by SetSystems Ltd, Saffron Walden, Essex
Printed and bound in Great Britain by
Mackays of Chatham plc, Chatham, Kent

for Tom

Therefore all seasons shall be sweet to thee,
Whether the summer clothe the general earth
With greenness . . .

Preface

This is a book about why poetry continues to matter as we enter a new millennium that will be ruled by technology. It is a book about modern Western man's alienation from nature. It is about the capacity of the writer to restore us to the earth which is our home.

The argument begins from certain prose works – novels by Jane Austen and Thomas Hardy, the philosophy of Jean-Jacques Rousseau, Mary Shelley's *Frankenstein*, the writings of the naturalist W. H. Hudson – but is then concentrated upon a group of early nineteenth-century English poets who meditated deeply on the complex relations between humankind, nature and society: William Wordsworth, Samuel Taylor Coleridge, John Keats, Percy Bysshe Shelley, Lord Byron and John Clare. They are chief among those who have come to be called the 'Romantics'. In the twentieth century some of their concerns were reawakened by a more geographically widespread array of writers. Among the small but powerfully representative selection discussed are the Americans Wallace Stevens and Elizabeth Bishop, the West Indian Edward Brathwaite, the Northumberlander Basil Bunting, the Australian Les Murray, the middle-Europeans Rainer Maria Rilke and Paul Celan, and the Anglo-Welsh Edward Thomas.

In the first three chapters I establish some contexts. Why do we value literary works with rural settings? How can we reconcile 'culture' and 'nature', two forces which are traditionally opposed to each other? What indeed do we mean by 'nature'? How and why do we dream of living in unity with 'her'? Then in the book's middle chapters I ask with respect to a range of poems some of the questions which ecologists ask of biological organisms. How are they influenced by climate? In what kind of landscape do they flourish? What are their modes of creating shelter, their relations with other species?

Human beings are not, however, like other species: there are spiritual, linguistic, historical, regional and national aspects to our senses of identity and belonging. In meditating on these in the closing two chapters, I have found myself drawn to the work of the German philosopher Martin Heidegger – but I have also felt the need to speak of that about which Heidegger remained notoriously silent.

Contents

List of Illustrations

The poetry of earth is never dead . . .

(John Keats)

But there remains the song that names the earth.

(Martin Heidegger)

1

Going, Going

And that will be England gone,
The shadows, the meadows, the lanes,
The guildhalls, the carved choirs.
There'll be books; it will linger on
In galleries; but all that remains
For us will be concrete and tyres.

(Philip Larkin, 'Going, Going')

AT THE END OF the twentieth century, the two most popular English writers of the nineteenth century were Jane Austen and Thomas Hardy. Year in, year out their books have gone on selling in paperback in quantities undreamed of by their modern-day successors. The agency which calculates the number of books borrowed from British libraries, for the purpose of paying the modest Public Lending Right fee to living authors, publishes a record of annual borrowings of dead authors: Austen and Hardy are consistently at or near the top. In the United States, Austen's stock was massively inflated in the 1990s as the result of a series of highly successful film adaptations.

What is the source of their enduring appeal? There is a cynical answer to this question, which could be summarized as *frocks and smocks*. Austen stands for a lost world of elegance, of empire-line dresses, of good manners, of ladylikeness and gentlemanliness in large and beautiful houses. Hardy, meanwhile, represents nostalgia for a simple, honest rustic way of life among hedgerows, haystacks and sturdy English oak trees. Together they stand for the imagined better life of both the higher and the lower classes in a world where there is no place for the motor car.

They represent the spirit of Philip Larkin's England of shadows, meadows and lanes that are gone.

The cynic will say that nostalgia for the old southern shires is a cultural disease. If that is so, then the popularity of Austen and Hardy suggests that our culture is in the grip of an epidemic. Our longing for the imagined health of the past must be a sign of the sickness of the present.

Jane Austen went to the small medieval cathedral city of Winchester to die. To get there now you drive through the deep scar – it feels like a wound upon the very earth – which the motorway has cut through the ancient chalk downland of Twyford. Stand on Hardy's Egdon Heath and you will be deafened by the roar of low-flying Air Force jets, while far above the blue of the sky will be broken by the white ribbons of condensed water vapour in the exhaust gases of the Jumbos on their path into Heathrow – the visible remnant of the thousands of gallons of fossil fuel consumed by each flight. For Austen's characters and for Hardy's, a journey to the nearest town is an event, a trip to London an adventure. Now we can fly from London to New York in about the time it takes Hardy's Jude to get to Oxford.

Already, though, in Hardy the possibilities of mobility are being opened up by the advent of the railway. His novels document rural customs of great antiquity even as they represent a world standing on the brink of modernity. We usually read his novels in the text which he revised for the Wessex edition of 1912, just two years before the first international war of technologically engineered mass destruction. Born in 1840, the son and grandson of master stonemasons who performed in the band of the local parish church, Thomas Hardy died in 1928 with a knowledge of the automobile, the aeroplane, the gramophone record and the radio. We may take a measure of the changes through which he lived if we contemplate the difference between two kinds of inscription. First, think of the words chiselled with slow care on stone by a master mason, words on a gravestone, let us say, which only disappear through the inexorable but imperceptible erosion of time and weather in the passing of – a phrase from one of Hardy's best poems – 'the years, the years'. Then think of the values printed on a banknote in Weimar Germany or a stock market listing in Wall Street, 1929, inscriptions which lose their meaning almost before the ink is dry.

Our instinct about Hardy is this: he values a world – for him vanishing, for us long vanished – in which people *live in rhythm with nature*. Presumably we value such a world because we are not entirely happy with our own modernity, with speed, with noise. We sense that there is something wrong about our comfortable insulation against the rhythms of the seasons, something alienating about the perpetual mediation of nature through the instruments of culture, whether radio and canned food, which Hardy lived to see, or television and genetically modified crops, which he would have had grave difficulty in imagining.

On first reflection, the attraction of Jane Austen would seem to be very different, to be bound up with the rhythms not of nature but of a supremely poised culture. A battle between the country (customarily regarded as the sign of nature) and the city (the sign of civilization) has been fought almost since literature began. Austen's anatomy of social relations and the high value which she places upon civility would seem to place her on the side of the city. But she is not. Like Hardy, she is suspicious of mobility and of the city. A lack of rootedness and a metropolitan brashness are associated with modernity and with corruption. The immoral Crawfords come from London to disrupt the harmony of Mansfield Park. The nouvelle riche Mrs Elton barges into the closed community of Highbury, bringing with her the smell of slave-port Bristol.

This suggests that the association of Hardy with 'nature' and Austen with 'culture' is erroneous. The error is, I believe, bound up with the changing meanings of the word 'culture'. *The New Shorter Oxford English Dictionary* offers seven different definitions of 'culture' as a noun, dividing them into two semantic categories. The earliest meaning of 'culture', which endured from the middle English period to the end of the eighteenth century, was 'a cultivated field or piece of land'. In late middle English, the primary sense shifted from cultivated land itself to the action of cultivation: the word referred to tillage, the working over of the soil. In the early seventeenth century, it was extended to other forms of farming: one could speak of the cultivation not only of crops, but also of fish, oysters and bees, even of silk. The only remnant of this range of meanings associated with organic growth is the scientific sense, emerging in the late nineteenth century, which refers to the action which causes bacteria or tissue to grow in a prepared medium, as when one speaks of a cancer culture. The word's path from common currency in the context of agricultural subsistence to technical usage in biological research is itself a little allegory of the march to modernity.

The second range of meanings goes back to the early sixteenth century. It was originally figurative: as the soil is improved and made productive by tillage, so the mind and manners may be improved by education and training. The word is thus removed from the earth and linked to the advance of society. It is, if you will, removed from the country to the city – cultivation comes to mean civility, a word which has its root in the Latin *civilis*, meaning 'of, or pertaining to, the city'. William Shakespeare and his wife came from rural families who cultivated the land, whereas he himself underwent the cultivation of a grammar school education and moved to London, where he became a professional anatomist of mind and manners.

From Shakespeare's time to Jane Austen's, the old and the new senses of 'culture' existed side by side. But in the nineteenth century, with the diminution of the proportion of the population involved in tillage and the rapid growth of industrialization and urbanization, the old sense died and the new one was further developed. Early in the century, the word was applied to the aesthetic sphere: it came to mean 'refinement of mind, tastes, and manners; artistic and intellectual development; the artistic and intellectual side of civilization'. It is in this sense that we speak of Shakespeare, Jane Austen and Hardy as part of 'our cultural inheritance'. Then in the mid-century the word was given an anthropological spin: 'A particular form, stage, or type of intellectual development or civilization in a society; a society or group characterized by its distinctive customs, achievements, products, outlook'. As Darwin and his successors developed the sciences of evolution and ecology, so there emerged a parallel science which studied the variations and the development of human social behaviour; it is in this sense that we speak of 'cultural relativism'. By the end of the nineteenth century, a sociological variant was emerging, whereby one might speak not only of, say, 'Mayan culture' but also of 'working-class culture' and, later, of the arts and the sciences as 'two cultures'.

The key development for our purposes was the association of 'refinement of mind, tastes, and manners' with 'the artistic and intellectual side of civilization'. For it was here that a division between culture and nature was made explicit. Consider the *Shorter Oxford Dictionary*'s two exemplary quotations for this sense: 'The great men of culture' (Matthew Arnold, inspector of schools) and 'Of what use is culture to a labourer' (Manny Shinwell, Socialist politician from the East End of London). Originally 'culture' *was* the work done by a labourer in the fields, whereas for Arnold and his successors culture is intellectual, even spiritual, work which serves the moral needs of a society and is set in opposition to the very idea of physical labour.

In Jane Austen, however, this division has not yet been opened up. Here is Emma Woodhouse, surveying the view from the grounds of Donwell Abbey, the home of George Knightley:

> The considerable slope, at nearly the foot of which the Abbey stood, gradually acquired a steeper form beyond its grounds; and at half a mile distant was a bank of considerable abruptness and grandeur, well clothed with wood; – and at the bottom of this bank, favourably placed and sheltered, rose the Abbey-Mill Farm, with meadows in front, and the river making a close and handsome curve around it.
>
> It was a sweet view – sweet to the eye and the mind. English verdure, English culture, English comfort, seen under a sun bright, without being oppressive.

The knightly Mr Knightley takes his Christian name, George, from England's patron saint. He embodies a value-structure which remains profoundly Christian, but which has shifted from pious observance to secular virtue. His house is on the site of a former abbey. A place that was once consecrated to the spiritual good life, to the vertical relationship between humankind and God, it is now consecrated to the social good life: it has become an emblem of productive and harmonious rural being. Instead of being drawn upward to the heavens, the eye looks out horizontally to the well-ordered environment.

The abbey occupies a safe middle ground, below a hill and above a river. It is surrounded by mature woodland that signifies Knightley's willingness to take the long view of profit – potential timber is an investment for future generations. The farm is below the abbey in the landscape, as the gentleman farmer Robert Martin is below Mr Knightley in the social order, but it is protected by its environment, as the interests of Martin are cared for by Knightley. The weather – 'a sun bright, without being oppressive' – is made one with the social structure. Here Austen is inheritor of a long tradition of European thought which associated a temperate climate with a liberal society and excessive heat with oriental despotism.

'English verdure, English culture, English comfort' are thus embedded in a particular landscape. What Austen regards as authentic national identity is derived not from a set of political institutions based in London – monarchy, parliament and so forth – but from the harmonious play, suggested by the verbal euphony, of 'verdure' and 'culture'. Verdure is natural greenness, the product of England's wet weather, while 'culture' is intended to imply the mixed farmland of traditional English farming methods. The presence of 'meadows' is crucial here. Meadow is grassland mown for hay, which serves as winter feed for cattle. It is the supreme example of culture working together with nature: the grass grows naturally (it is not sown in the manner of arable crops), but it needs to be maintained artificially (if not mown, it would revert to wildwood). Larkin wrote 'Going, Going', a poem commissioned by the Department of the Environment, in 1972. He was prescient about the loss of England's flower-rich hay meadows: since the Second World War, no less than ninety-seven per cent of their acreage has gone. England no longer offers many 'sweet views' of the chequered fields that are charac-teristic of mixed farmland. Instead, most of the country is now covered by vast unbroken tracts of intensive cereal crop and a monoculture of artificially fertilized perennial ryegrass. As for winter feed, the consequence of replacing hay with a compound including ground-down animal carcasses has been BSE, or 'mad cow disease'.

For Austen, then, 'culture' is located in a landscape and a mode of agriculture, not merely in manners and aesthetics. Her ideal England is one in which social relations and the aesthetic sense – that sweetness to the eye and the mind – are a function of environmental belonging. But she is also acutely aware of change. William Cobbett, the son of a farm labourer, was born in 1763 in Farnham, Hampshire; Jane Austen, the daughter of a village clergyman, was born two years later in Steventon, in the same county. Chawton, where she wrote her mature novels, is just ten miles from Farnham. Raymond Williams noted this proximity in his classic study, *The Country and the City*. He then quoted a famous passage from *Rural Rides*, in which Cobbett distinguished between

> a resident *native* gentry, attached to the soil, known to every farmer and labourer from their childhood, frequently mixing with them in those pursuits where all artificial distinctions are lost, practising hospitality without ceremony, from habit and not on calculation; and a gentry, only now-and-then residing at all, having no relish for country-delights, foreign in their manners, distant and haughty in their behaviour, looking to the soil only for its rents, viewing it as a mere object of speculation, unacquainted with its cultivators, despising them and their pursuits, and relying, for influence, not upon the good will of the vicinage, but upon the dread of their power.

Attitudes to the soil and to those who work the soil are seen by Cobbett to be implicit in one another. He believes that both the community and the earth are served better by stay-at-home Tory paternalists than by mobile Whig arrivistes. Jane Austen explores exactly the same distinction between good stewardship and absenteeism, though by example and not by polemic. And she is more discriminating in her judgements: whereas Cobbett flails indiscriminately at all the representatives of new money – financial speculators, nabobs and negro-drivers, generals and admirals – Austen is doubtful about some (Sir Thomas Bertram, the bad father who has bought Mansfield Park on the proceeds of his sugar plantations in Antigua) but robustly defensive of others (Admiral Croft, the good husband who in *Persuasion* rents Kellynch Hall on the proceeds of his successes during the Napoleonic Wars). Knightley is her prime example of the 'resident *native* gentry, attached to the soil'. Henry Crawford in *Mansfield Park* is the very image of the second kind of landowner. He has no relish for his Norfolk estate, where in his absence worthy tenants have nearly been evicted as a result of the underhand dealing of his agent. In a crucial passage Fanny Price makes him choose between returning there or going to London; he opts for London, a road which leads to elopement with Maria and the loss of Fanny.

*

Sense and Sensibility begins with a higher-level eviction. The novel opens as follows:

> The family of Dashwood had been long settled in Sussex. Their estate was large, and their residence was at Norland Park, in the centre of their property, where, for many generations, they had lived in so respectable a manner, as to engage the general good opinion of their surrounding acquaintance.

This is Cobbett's resident native gentry, long settled through the generations. Respect emanates from the central point of the great house in an environing circle that embraces the community and the soil. But a complex set of testamentary provisions forces the surviving Dashwood women away from their patrimonial home and into rented accommodation in the West Country. The estate falls into the hands of Mr John Dashwood, who has only ever made occasional visits to Norland and has no feeling for the place. Having expelled his stepmother and half-sisters, he rides roughshod over the bond of reciprocal responsibility he owes to the local commoners and small farmers. He encloses and he engrosses:

> The inclosure of Norland Common, now carrying on, is a most serious drain. And then I have made a little purchase within this half year; East Kingham Farm, you must remem-

ber the place, where old Gibson used to live. The land was so
very desirable for me in every respect, so immediately adjoining my own property, that I felt it my duty to buy it. I could
not have answered it to my conscience to let it fall into any
other hands.

(Gibson of East Kingham Farm would, like Robert Martin of
Abbey-Mill Farm, have been a yeoman, or gentleman farmer with
a freehold on a small parcel of land.) The old Dashwood family
knew their obligations to the place; that 'general good opinion of
their surrounding acquaintance' would have been earned by the
performance of duties to tenants and neighbours. Austen turns
her ironic glare on John by means of the twist on 'duty' and
'conscience': it can only be hypocrisy for him to use such words,
since he has failed in his duty even to his own family and has
shown scant conscience as his wife has talked him out of leaving
them a reasonable annuity. When he turns his attention to the
land, the language of harmonious reciprocation is again replaced
by that of greedy appropriation.

Lack of respect for neighbours is accompanied by lack of
attachment to the soil. On the next page we learn that a greenhouse is to be built upon the knoll behind the house:

The old walnut trees are all come down to make room for it.
It will be a very fine object from many parts of the park, and
the flower-garden will slope down just before it, and be
exceedingly pretty. We have cleared away all the old thorns
that grew in patches over the brow.

Old English trees are felled to make way for the exotic plants of
the hothouse. The history of the greenhouse is bound up with
that of empire. Originally 'nothing more than a room or building
to keep oranges and other tender "greens" (hence the name) over
the winter, with provision for a small stove or even an open fire
to keep the keenest frosts at bay', the greenhouse developed
into a much more elaborate and heat-efficient structure during
the last two decades of the seventeenth century as a result of
the increased cultivation of exotic plants brought back from the
empire in the East and West Indies. Austen's youth, a century

later, was the heyday of the imported exotic, as may be seen from a passage in her favourite poem, William Cowper's *The Task*:

> Who loves a garden, loves a greenhouse too.
> Unconscious of a less propitious clime
> There blooms exotic beauty, warm and snug,
> While the winds whistle and the snows descend.
> The spiry myrtle with unwith'ring leaf
> Shines there and flourishes. The golden boast
> Of Portugal and Western India there,
> The ruddier orange and the paler lime,
> Peep through their polish'd foliage at the storm,
> And seem to smile at what they need not fear.
> Th' amomum there with intermingling flow'rs
> And cherries hangs her twigs. Geranium boasts
> Her crimson honours, and the spangled beau,
> Ficiodes, glitters bright all winter long.
> All plants, of ev'ry leaf, that can endure
> The winter's frown if screen'd from his shrewd bite,
> Live there and prosper. Those Ausonia claims,
> Levantine regions these; th' Azores send
> Their jessamine; her jessamine remote
> Caffraria: foreigners from many lands,
> They form one social shade, as if convened
> By magic summons of th' Orphean lyre.

For Cowper, the greenhouse provides the opportunity to display the trophies of empire; he regards it as his role as poet – wielder of the Orphean lyre – to celebrate a shared exoticism of place-names and plant-names.

The hothouse flowers and trees of *The Task* tend to have smoothly polished surfaces, a veneer analogous to that social slickness which characterizes the morally dubious newcomers to Austen's communities. That geranium boasting its crimson honours and the 'spangled beau' ficiodes are horticultural equivalents of the red-coated seducer Wickham in *Pride and Prejudice*. To judge therefore from the activities of Mr John Dashwood, in the matter of greenhouses Jane Austen for once did not share the sensibility of her admired Cowper. Her allegiance was to the rough old walnut tree, a species originally imported by the Romans but so fully naturalized as to be classed in Austen's time as native rather than exotic.

Though Cowper and Austen differ over the greenhouse, they share a scepticism about the principal 'improving' activity of the new landowners of the late eighteenth century: the work of landscape gardening. Later in book three of *The Task*, Cowper attacks 'Capability' Brown for altering houses and landscapes that had for generations been integrated with their local environment. Brown is presented as a dangerous magician who subverts the course of nature: 'The lake in front becomes a lawn, / Woods vanish, hills subside, and valleys rise.' The employment of his arts is seen as characteristic of new money and the loss of the old order in which 'Mansions once / Knew their own masters, and laborious hands / That had survived the father, served the son'. Improvement goes hand in hand with the selling of old woodland and with short-term commercialism: 'Estates are landscaped, gazed upon awhile, / Then advertised, and auctioneer'd away.'

Instead of having a responsible, nurturing relationship to the soil, the improver has a purely aesthetic one. He regards his estate as a pleasure-garden rather than as land which needs to be managed with care and consideration. John Dashwood clears the old thorn patches simply in order to improve the view. In so doing, he erases one of the enduring links between English culture and English nature, for the hawthorn was

> the ancestor of the Maypole, the source of May Day garlands and the decorations of Jacks-in-the-Green and Green Georges, and one of the models for the foliage which wreathes the faces of Green Men carved in churches and inns. . . . Isolated hawthorns [have traditionally been] treated with respect, too, and though often little more than bushes, are the most frequent trees mentioned in Anglo-Saxon boundary charters. The thorn is also the tree after which the Anglo-Saxon runic letter þ is named.

Where hawthorn summons up a whole folk-history and a communal way of life, improvement bespeaks the tyranny of the nouveau riche landowner's eye. Landscaping is, then, a symptom of the growing division between the aesthetic and the agricultural senses of the word 'culture'.

Elinor is thankful that Marianne is not present to hear of the clearing of the thorns and the felling of the walnuts. Had the younger sister of tender sensibilities been there, she would no doubt have quoted Cowper, as Fanny Price does upon hearing that an avenue of trees must come down in the name of Mr Rushworth's improvement of his estate, a result of his faddish obsession with the landscape designs of Humphrey Repton:

> 'Cut down an avenue! What a pity! Does it not make you think of Cowper? "Ye fallen avenues, once more I mourn your fate unmerited."'

Fanny's quotation is from a passage in book one of *The Task* concerning Sir John Throckmorton's enclosure and improvement of his estate at Weston Underwood, near Cowper's village of Olney. 'The Poplar-Field', one of Cowper's best-known lyrics ('The poplars are felled; farewell to the shade, / And the whispering sound of the cool colonnade!'), was a further lament occasioned by the gentleman improver's changes to his local environment. Fanny's instinctive reaction to landscape 'improvement' is sympathy for the felled tree expressed through an apposite line of poetry. Austen wishes us to register it as a mark of her heroine's sensitivity that she should regard the figure of the poet as the spokesman for nature.

In making these connections, Austen comes closer to the sensibility of Romanticism than we usually allow her to be. Her more sensitive heroines read Cowper rather than Wordsworth, but they would be broadly in sympathy with the argument of the preface to *Lyrical Ballads* that the poet has a special bond with rustic life because it is in the country that the essential passions of the heart 'find a better soil' and in the rural condition that 'the passions of men are incorporated with the beautiful and permanent forms of nature'. William Blake said that the tree which moves some to tears of joy is to others nothing but a green thing that gets in the way. Poets and Jane Austen heroines are alike in being troubled by the moment when an ancient tree ceases to be permanent, when it is uprooted not because it is diseased but because it gets in the way.

Jane Austen was writing about rooted (I use the word advisedly) communities during the period when Wordsworth, following in the footsteps of Cowper, was arguing that the increasing accumulation of men in cities was a cause of what we now call the 'alienation' of the human spirit. In the next few generations, the Victorians had a proud sense of their own 'progress', but they also worried profoundly about their loss of 'place'. No writer had a deeper sense of that loss than Thomas Hardy.

*

When Hardy gathered together his works in 1896, he grouped the most celebrated of them together under the rubric 'Novels of Character and Environment'. I have suggested that Jane Austen was also interested in the influence of 'environment' on character, but, interestingly, the word was barely available to her. 'Environment' does not appear in Dr Johnson's dictionary. The modern meaning of the word emerges in the course of the nineteenth century, in parallel contexts of social and biological analysis: 'The set of circumstances or conditions, especially physical conditions, in which a person or community lives, works, develops, or a thing exists or operates; the external conditions affecting the life of a plant or animal.' *The Oxford English Dictionary*'s earliest example of the word in the context of physical or geographical setting is Thomas Carlyle writing in 1830 of the 'picturesque environment' around Bayreuth (I will argue in a later chapter that the emergence of the term 'picturesque' was crucial to the whole question of the growth of environmental consciousness).

I suspect that the word 'environment' began to be applied to social contexts exactly because of the feeling of the alienation of city-dwelling which was identified by Wordsworth and others. That is to say, prior to the nineteenth century there was no need for a word to describe the influence of physical conditions on persons and communities because it was self-evident that personal and communal identity were intimately related to physical setting. The influence of, for instance, the climate and the soil was taken for granted. But from the late eighteenth century onwards, there was an increasing awareness of industry's tendency to alter the quality of our surroundings, even to affect the air we breathe. In several passages of *The Task*, Cowper noted with alarm the effects of smoke on the health of city-dwellers. The most often quoted line of *The Task*, 'God made the country, and man made the town', is famously false – historians of the countryside have demonstrated that, especially in a crowded island such as Britain, most rural landscapes (felled, planted and ploughed) are influenced by the hand of man every bit as much as all urban ones – but Cowper nevertheless registers an enduring intuition that the country offers a natural environment, the town an artificial one. The word 'environment' emerges as a sign of that difference.

The Reverend T. R. Malthus's *Essay on the Principle of Population*, which appeared in its first edition in 1798, the same year as the first edition of Wordsworth and Coleridge's *Lyrical Ballads*, was among the first works to predict environmental catastrophe. Malthus's infamous argument was that population grows geometrically, but the means of subsistence arithmetically, so some form of social engineering is required in order to forestall mass starvation. Independently, Charles Darwin and Alfred Wallace each read Malthus and came to the conclusion that his principle held the key to evolution: natural selection operates through a species' fitness to its *environment*. By the end of the nineteenth century, this biological principle had filtered back into the Malthusian realm of human society by way of the 'Social Darwinism' which sought to naturalize rampant capitalism on the grounds of – Herbert Spencer's variant on 'natural selection' – 'the survival of the fittest'.

It is in this context that we must understand Hardy's conception of 'Character and Environment'. Where Social Darwinism was a gospel of change and the new, Hardy – who acknowledged Darwin, Thomas Huxley and Herbert Spencer as three of the thinkers who had most influenced him – found true fitness in stability and the old. He placed mobile new men and advanced ideas in opposition to rooted types and traditional ways. The irreconcilable clash between the forces of tradition and of innovation is at the core of his tragic vision. The opposition between

Giles Winterbourne and Edred Fitzpiers in *The Woodlanders*, published in 1887, provides a perfect example.

The novel begins with the image of an old coach-road cutting a line from Bristol to the south coast, skirting extensive woodlands interspersed with apple orchards. The immediate suggestion is of a mixed rural economy – timber and fruit-growing – linked by the artery of the road to a city that is strongly associated with trade. Hardy frequently figures the landscape as a human body. Here the *face* of the country has been changed by the road, but the process has been slow, the balance between dwelling and trading thus remaining relatively stable. But the road is now forsaken: in place of an economy of local connections between country and town, the railway has brought national and potentially international forms of commerce which have no need to respect geographical particularity.

The contest between the old and the new is dramatized in the traditional form of a love-triangle. Grace Melbury, the daughter of a prosperous timber merchant, belongs to the locality, but has been educated abroad. She is 'flexible': she will either be drawn back down to her roots or aspire upward towards social improvement and mobility. She is first seen returning from her 'finishing' school, wearing a pair of new gloves which insulate her hands from the soil. She is met by her childhood sweetheart, Giles Winterbourne, who – to her embarrassment as a newly made 'lady' – is standing in the middle of the market place holding a ten-foot high apple tree, a specimen of his produce which brings the 'suggestion of orchards into the heart of the town'. A green man in a green shade, he is a woodlander in the most literal sense.

As Giles drives Grace home in his gig, her mental distance from her native environment becomes apparent:

'They had a good crop of bitter-sweets; they couldn't grind them all.' He nodded towards an orchard where some heaps of apples had been left lying ever since the ingathering.

She said 'Yes,' but looking at another orchard.

'Why, you are looking at John-apple trees! You know bitter-sweets – you used to well enough?'

'I am afraid I have forgotten, and it is getting too dark to distinguish.'

Winterbourne did not continue. It seemed as if the knowledge and interests which had formerly moved Grace's mind had quite died away from her.

She has lost that intimate awareness of the particularities of her immediate surroundings which Hardy describes in a crucial phrase later in the chapter as 'local knowledge'.

Winterbourne's perception of the world is shaped by the local environment, whereas Grace is at this moment remembering 'a much contrasting scene: a broad lawn in the fashionable suburb of a fast city, the evergreen leaves shining in the evening sun'. Suburbia is a new kind of living space, a simulacrum of the quiet country within the bounds of the 'fast' city, where manicured lawns and imported ornamental evergreens stand in for meadows and productive native broadleaf woodland. The suburbanization of Grace's sensibility enacts the nineteenth-century change in the meaning of the word 'culture':

> It was true; cultivation had so far advanced in the soil of Miss Melbury's mind as to lead her to talk of anything save of that she knew well, and had the greatest interest in developing: herself. She had fallen from the good old Hintock ways.

The association of cultivation with the metaphorical soil of the mind obliterates the old root of the word in the literal earth. The move from the state of nature to that of civility is likened to the fall of man.

'The good old Hintock ways' are intended to be evocative of communal obligations rooted in locality. Grace abnegates these in the name of a modish self-cultivation which denies the true self. She has developed the capacity to imagine herself in a place other than the one where she is. A few pages later we hear of Edred Fitzpiers, who embodies scientific progress as opposed to local knowledge. Grace sees a strange light in the night, caused by his scientific experiments. According to old Grammer Oliver, Fitzpiers believes that 'Everything is Nothing', that 'There's only Me and Not Me in the whole world'. He is a disciple of the transcendental philosophy – originated by Kant, schematized by Fichte – which thinks not of a symbiosis between human community and natural environment, but of two opposing realms, interior and exterior, mind and world, self and not-self. Grace's commitment to imagination as opposed to observation, and to a fashionable other world as opposed to a native community, mark her out as an embryonic transcendentalist bound for the arms of Fitzpiers.

Whereas Hardy brings Giles and Grace together beneath a tree, he has Fitzpiers first spy the girl from a distance through an eyeglass. The doctor is an outsider who always looks to mediate nature through technology. For the very reason that he has no commitment to environment, that he rejects local knowledge in the name of the Germanic metaphysic which prefers the ideal to the real, Fitzpiers does not belong among the woodlanders. He is 'like a tropical plant in a hedgerow, a nucleus of advanced ideas and practices which had nothing in common with the life around'. The 'alchemist-surgeon' is concerned only with the future, not the past; he exists in an ironic relation to his own origin as a member of an ancient local family whose name is linked to the most traditional of English trees: the Fitzpierses of Oakbury-Fitzpiers. The character to whom the name of Oak should belong, for he is the equivalent of Gabriel in *Far from the Madding Crowd*, is of course Giles:

> He had a marvellous power of making trees grow. Although he would seem to shovel in the earth quite carelessly there was a sort of sympathy between himself and the fir, oak, or beech that he was operating on; so that the roots took hold of the soil in a few days.

At the end of the novel, it is Marty South, not Grace Melbury, who stands over the dead woodman's grave and possesses his memory because she is the only one who 'had approximated to Winterbourne's level of intelligent intercourse with Nature'. The spirits of Giles and Marty ultimately belong together because they have planted, coppiced and felled together, they have shared the language of the wood, 'the tongue of the trees and fruits and flowers themselves'.

Giles represents the acceptance of limits. His thoughts are

'coterminous with the margin of the Hintock woodlands'. Fitzpiers, on the other hand, is bored because the place has no *presence* to him. Because he is a professional man who has dropped down into the rural place 'by mere accident', he has no sense of the embeddedness of a community's history in its environment. Without this sense, he is told upon by loneliness. Those who truly dwell in the place are never lonely because they are attuned to collective memory, to 'old association – an almost exhaustive biographical or historical acquaintance with every object, animate and inanimate, within the observer's horizon'. For Hardy, to belong in a place means to know its history, to

> know all about those invisible ones of the days gone by, whose feet have traversed the fields which look so grey from his windows; recall whose creaking plough has turned those sods from time to time; whose hands planted the trees that form a crest to the opposite hill; whose horses and hounds have torn through that underwood; what birds affect that particular brake; what bygone domestic dramas of love, jealousy, revenge, or disappointment have been enacted in the cottages, the mansion, the street or on the green. The spot may have beauty, grandeur, salubrity, convenience; but if it lacks memories it will ultimately pall upon him who settles there without opportunity of intercourse with his kind.

For the old woodlanders, there is no division between human intercourse and local environment. The presence of memory means that the countryside is inhabited rather than viewed aesthetically. The condition of the modern man, with his mobility and his displaced knowledge, is never to be able to share this sense of belonging. He will always be an outsider; his return to nature will always be partial, touristic and semi-detached. Fitzpiers is never without his eyeglass; he peers fitfully at his environment instead of dwelling steadily within it.

Grace's tragedy is that her realization that she wishes to be a native who returns comes too late. At the pivotal point of the novel – the end of chapter twenty-eight – the motions of the plot are dramatized in the landscape. Fitzpiers disappears on the high ground as he rides away in the direction of his mistress, and in the next instant Giles 'arise[s] out of the earth' below, looking and smelling 'like Autumn's very brother',

> his face being sunburnt to wheat-colour, his eyes blue as corn-flowers, his sleeves and leggings dyed with fruit-stains, his hands clammy with the sweet juice of apples, his hat sprinkled with pips, and everywhere about him that atmosphere of cider which at its first return each season has such an indescribable fascination for those who have been born and bred among the orchards.

The man beneath the apple-tree is now covered with the signs of his trade. We could almost say that he has become cider and that Grace is drawn to drink him in:

> Her heart rose from its late sadness like a released bough; her senses revelled in the sudden lapse back to Nature unadorned. The consciousness of having to be genteel because of her husband's profession, the veneer of artificiality which she had acquired at the fashionable schools, were thrown off, and she became the crude country girl of her latent early instincts.

In a moment which vividly anticipates D. H. Lawrence, Grace revolts 'against social law' and in 'her passionate desire for primitive life' her face seems to welcome Giles, who reaches out and gently caresses the flower she is wearing between her breasts. But where in Lawrence this would herald the beginning of a passionately earthy illicit affair in the manner of Lady Chatterley and Mellors, in *The Woodlanders* the force of the social law is such that Giles and Grace manage no more than a single kiss. It is essential to Hardy's honesty as a writer that he recognizes that once we have left our native home and been educated into gentility, we can never return, save in the brief moment of blind passion, to the world of latent early instinct.

In this sequence, the new sense of the word culture has fully taken over from the old. The apple-spattered Giles represents 'Nature unadorned', whilst Grace's education into fashionable society represents a modern 'culture' which is seen at an extreme of anti-Nature in Fitzpiers – with his eyeglass, his microscope, his chemistry apparatus, his phrenological studies, his use of the railway and his German idealist philosophy which sets the interior life of the mind above the day-to-day motions of the seasons and the body.

As a professional man of letters, Hardy himself could not help being a representative of that same modern culture. Unlike his father, he was not a stone-mason making music in the village church. First an architect who went west to find work (where he found a wife as well), then a writer drawn to the London world of publishing houses and high culture, he physically returned to his native Dorset but lived a life of the mind and the word that was always elsewhere. He built a grand townhouse in Dorchester, not a humble hut in the woods, like that of Henry David Thoreau in Walden. His study is a dark indoor place a world away from the light and space of his imagined Egdon Heath.

Giles Winterbourne surrounded by the atmosphere of cider, his eyes blue as cornflowers, is an image of man as part of nature. Thomas Hardy, inventing Giles Winterbourne in his imagination, is a man apart from nature. Winterbourne is at one with the song of the earth, yet he is rendered in language, by means of the skilled control of rhythm and rhetoric, arts that are of culture not nature. As readers of Thomas Hardy, we are inevitably closer to the position of the writer than that of the cider-maker. We are more Fitzpiers than Winterbourne. We do not *know* cider. In our imagination, it is a powerful sign of lost nature – it conjures up an orchard in southern England, a pub in which locally produced 'scrumpy' is served from ancient casks once turned by a local cooper, a boy's sexual initiation under a hay-wagon at harvest time (the nostalgia-fest of Laurie Lee's *Cider with Rosie*) – but in our reality cider is the smell on the breath of the homeless in concreted city shopping precincts. We read *The Woodlanders* to remind ourselves of the world we think we have lost, but the fact that we are reading it at all is a symptom of the very loss.

In the early 1930s, the years immediately after Hardy's death, the young Cambridge literary critic F. R. Leavis and his school-master friend Denys Thompson became obsessed with *The Wheelwright's Shop* and *Change in the Village*, two books by George Sturt which documented the decline of the old village crafts, the old way of life based on what Hardy had called 'local knowledge'.

Leavis and Thompson were fired into the publication of a jeremiad in the form of a textbook for English students in schools,
entitled *Culture and Environment*. They vented their spleen upon
the whole apparatus of modernity: advertising, mass production,
standardization, 'levelling-down' and, above all, 'suburbanism'.
Sturt had convinced them that 'we have lost the organic community with the living culture it embodied'. They argued that it
was the mission of a literary education to fill the gap left by that
loss:

> Many teachers of English who have become interested in the
> possibilities of training taste and sensibility must have been
> troubled by accompanying doubts. What effect can such
> training have against the multitudinous counter-influences –
> films, newspapers, advertising – indeed, the whole world
> outside the class-room? Yet the very conditions that make
> literary education look so desperate are those which make it
> more important than ever before; for in a world of this kind
> – and a world that changes so rapidly – it is on literary
> tradition that the office of maintaining continuity must rest.

Organicism, tradition, continuity: these are the conservative values which were so eloquently expounded by Edmund Burke in
that archetypal jeremiad against modernity, the *Reflections on the
Revolution in France*, published in 1790. If modernity is defined by
'improvement', by the project of social engineering and the march
of culture away from nature, then the apologist for the supposed
naturalness of the old ways must speak the language of heritage
and of conservation. The Larkin who anatomized the vulgarity of
the masses and longed for the dying England of guildhalls and
carved choirs was, notoriously, deeply Conservative in his politics.

In *Culture and Environment* Leavis and Thompson also quoted
a key passage from D. H. Lawrence on the ugliness of the
suburbanized environment and the process whereby 'The industrial England blots out the agricultural England. One meaning
blots out another. The new England blots out the old England.
And the continuity is not organic, but mechanical.' Lawrence's
resistance to industrial modernity, his search for something primitive, strong and organic, led him in some troubling directions.

His novel *Kangaroo*, published in 1923, took a robust interest in an Australian fascist leader who preached the return to nature. Lawrence's lifelong wandering in rebellion against 'the new England' eventually led him to the far south-west of the United States. He ended his life in New Mexico, where the values of the old frontier still endured. By the end of the twentieth century, this same American West had become the home of both radical environmentalists fighting to protect the receding wilderness at any cost and that anti-modern, anti-culture, anti-centralizing fringe of survivalists whose atavism was epitomized by the bombing of the Federal Building in Oklahoma City.

As for F. R. Leavis and Denys Thompson in 1933, they only had to look across to Germany to see the politics of organicism in action – back to the land and out with the Jews. Being good liberals in the tradition of Matthew Arnold, they would have been horrified at any imputation of continuity between their values and those of Nazism, but the synchronicity should not go unnoticed. Indeed, it gives us the opportunity to ponder a choice.

Let us assume that the desire to live closer to nature, whether in the wilds of the American West or the gentler green world of Austen and Hardy, is an instinct that is in us for a reason. Let us suppose that it is a mechanism of admonition, that it serves to make us pause, as Larkin pauses in the third stanza of 'Going, Going':

> Things are tougher than we are, just
> As earth will always respond
> However we mess it about;
> Chuck filth in the sea, if you must:
> The tides will be clean beyond.
> – But what do I feel now? Doubt?

The choice, then, is as to what we do with our doubt about the capacity of the earth to go on sustaining all we throw at it, our fears about diminishing resources and increasing pollution, our nostalgia for Hardy's 'good old Hintock ways' – which is in part nostalgia for our own past (Larkin recognizes that it may be merely 'age' he is feeling). Do we hitch our sense of crisis directly to the bandwagon of an atavistic politics? Or do we, in the words of Raymond Williams, begin by acknowledging 'that recognition of the crisis, and almost all possible ways of resolving it, are functions of consciousness'? The choice of those who make a commitment to writing and reading must be the latter. The question of consciousness comes first; the political consequences which may flow from a different kind of consciousness should not be anticipated too readily. D. H. Lawrence was over-hasty in this respect.

For Leavis and Thompson the function of a literary education was to develop critical awareness, to resist the blandishments of the mass media shouting their breathless praise of 'progress' and of everything shiny and new. The business of literature is to work upon consciousness. The practical consequences of that work – social, environmental, political in the broadest sense – cannot be controlled or predicted. They will be surprising, haphazard, indirect, long-term. William Wordsworth could not have known that one effect of his writing on the consciousness of later readers would have been the establishment of a network of National Parks, first in the United States and then in Britain.

My aim in this opening chapter has *not* been to advocate a return to the values of Jane Austen's English gentry or to propose that we should renounce our metropolitan modernity and become cider-makers. I am interested in the way in which an imaginative entry into the fictive worlds of Austen's Donwell and Hardy's Wessex – places which have some kind of historical origin, but which are ultimately quasi-mythic – may serve as an analogy for the human capacity, in Thoreau's phrase with regard to his time in Walden woods, 'to live deliberately'. To live, that is to say, with thoughtfulness and with an attentiveness, an attunement to both words and the world, and so to acknowledge that, although we make sense of things by way of words, we do not live apart from the world. For culture and environment are held together in a complex and delicate web.

2

The State of Nature

With painful nostalgia we yearn to return as soon as we have begun to experience the pressure of civilisation and hear in the remote lands of art our mother Nature's tender voice.

(Friedrich Schiller, 'On Naïve and Sentimental Poetry')

AT THE BEGINNING OF the third millennium of the Christian era, the state of nature is parlous. The litany of present and impending catastrophes is all too familiar. Carbon dioxide produced by the burning of fossil fuels is trapping the heat of the sun, causing the planet to become warmer. Glaciers and permafrost are melting, sea levels rising, rainfall patterns changing, winds growing stronger. Meanwhile, the oceans are overfished, deserts are spreading, forests shrinking, fresh water becoming scarcer. The diversity of species upon the planet is diminishing. We live in a world of toxic waste, acid rain and endocrine disrupters – chemicals which interfere with the functioning of sex hormones, causing male fish and birds to change sex. The urban air carries a cocktail of pollutants: nitrogen dioxide, sulphur dioxide, benzene, carbon monoxide and more. In intensively farmed economies, the topsoil is so eroded that the growth of cereal crops is entirely dependent on artificial fertilizers. The feeding of dead poultry to living cattle has bequeathed us bovine spongiform encephalopathy ('mad cow disease'), which causes the collapse of the central nervous system and is transmissible to humans.

We are bound to ask again the old question, but in changed circumstances: where did we begin to go wrong? With pesticides and post-war 'factory farming'? With the advent of the automobile? With consumerism, capitalism and the extinction of the 'organic community'? With the industrial revolution and mass production? But where in history do we fix the origin of these latter phenomena? Economic historians seem to spend most of their time changing the dates of the industrial and agricultural revolutions, or arguing that they never really happened.

For Philip Larkin in the 1970s, rural England was vanishing under concrete and tyres. But if Leavis and Thompson were right about the 'organic community' having disappeared by the 1930s, one would have thought that by the 1970s the meadows and lanes would have been not 'Going, Going' but long Gone. And wasn't Hardy gauging the same loss of the old ways in *The Woodlanders* in the 1880s? What about Cobbett in the time of Jane Austen, fulminating about the rise of the new rentier class with their exploitative relationship to the environment? But then Oliver Goldsmith in his *Deserted Village* of 1770 was blaming modern consumerism for the desolation of the land.

Raymond Williams reflects on exactly this problem of historical perspective in his book *The Country and the City*: the better life is always just behind us, 'over the last hill'. We imagine that there was an 'organic community' in the time of our parents (perhaps) or our grandparents (for sure), but they in turn look back to the 'good old ways' and sun-drenched idylls of their own childhood. Williams portrays rural nostalgia as an escalator reaching further and further back into the past. 'Where indeed shall we go, before the escalator stops?' he asks. To which 'One answer, of course, is Eden'.

Where did we begin to go wrong? Where do we begin in even attempting to grasp such a question? In prehistory, perhaps, or in myth? Eden seems a good place to start. Telling stories is the characteristically human way of humanizing the big questions.

Idealization of the supposed organic communities of the past, like idolization of the aboriginal peoples who have supposedly escaped the ills of modernity, may often serve as mask for the oppressions of the present. But the myth of a better life that has gone is no less important for being myth rather than history. Myths are necessary imaginings, exemplary stories which help our species to make sense of its place in the world. Myths endure so long as they perform helpful work. The myth of the natural life which exposes the ills of our own condition is as old as Eden and Arcadia, as new as Larkin's 'Going, Going' and the latest Hollywood adaptation of Austen or Hardy. Its endurance is a sign of its importance. Perhaps we need to remember what is 'going, going' as a survival mechanism, as a check upon our instinct for self-advancement.

A child playing with building bricks, learning how to balance them, could be a young chimpanzee. A child listening to a story could not. Once we have language, we soon want narratives. Our being is always in time, and our perception of time is dependent on a conception of beginnings. 'Once upon a time', the child's story begins. All human communities have myths of origin, stories which serve both to invent a past which is necessary to make sense of the present and to establish a narrative of humankind's uniqueness and apartness from the rest of nature. For instance: we were the chosen ones whom God created last and whom he made lord and master of the earth. Or: we were the chosen ones on whom the gods bestowed the Promethean gift of fire, which is to say of technology. The danger in such progressive narratives is hubris. The inadequacy of them is their failure to account for, let us say, war, slavery, suicide, social oppression and environmental degradation. To understand these ills, we need darker narratives, stories of our fall into knowledge and death, of the expulsion from Eden and the opening of Pandora's box.

The Graeco-Roman counterpart to the story of Eden is that of the lost Golden Age. It is a story which has had an extraordinarily long and fertile history as a mythic and literary archetype. It tells of how all beasts had horizontal backbones and a gaze that looked down towards the earth, until there came Prometheus who 'Upended man into the vertical', and 'tipped up his chin / So to widen his outlook on heaven'. Once man looked away from where he walked, the earth became vulnerable. The desire for transcendence, the aspiration to higher realms, was predicated upon a denial of biological origin, a departure from *ground*.

The earliest surviving version of this ancient Greek myth of origins is the *Theogony* of Hesiod. It tells of how the original

Golden Age declined to Silver and thence to Bronze and finally to the Iron of the present. From Hesiod and his Greek successors, the myth passed to Ovid, who gave it definitive Latin form in the first book of his *Metamorphoses*. From the Renaissance onwards, Ovid has been the poets' favourite classical poet. He has been well served by his translators, from Arthur Golding, whose 1567 version of the *Metamorphoses* was well known to Shakespeare, to Ted Hughes, whose flagging reputation was revived by his remarkable *Tales from Ovid* of 1997.

The poetry of Hughes graphically presents a nature that is, in Tennyson's phrase, 'red in tooth and claw'. Yet whilst relishing the violence of nature's own processes, Hughes in his later years became increasingly angry about the violence wrought by man upon nature. He cared deeply about the pollution of the country-side and the decimation of Britain's wildlife population. In 1970, in the first number of a new journal called *Your Environment*, he reviewed *The Environmental Revolution* by Max Nicholson, one of the earliest books to enumerate the full extent of our ecological crisis. Here the future Poet Laureate declared his hand as a card-carrying Green. He wrote of the need to salvage 'all nature from the pressures and oversights of our runaway populations, and from the monstrous anti-Nature that we have created, the now nearly-autonomous Technosphere'. He advanced a sweeping argument in which 'The story of the mind exiled from Nature is the story of Western Man'. He castigated modern capitalism for its expoitative attitude to the earth:

> While the mice in the field are listening to the Universe, and moving in the body of nature, where every living cell is sacred to every other, and all are interdependent, the Developer is peering at the field through a visor, and behind him stands the whole army of madmen's ideas, and shareholders, impatient to cash in the world.

A biological scientist would not be entirely happy with Hughes's spiritual claims about the mice and the cells – but the poet would reply that the reductive method that predominates in modern science is itself a big part of the problem. Where Hughes finds hope is in the relatively new science of ecology, which emphasizes the interconnectedness of all things. The ecologist builds a model which shows us the wholeness of the living globe, shows us 'the extreme intricacy and precision of its interconnected working parts – winds, currents, rocks, plants, animals, weathers, in all their swarming and law-abiding variety'. At the same time, he shows us 'the extreme smallness' of the earth, 'its finiteness and frailty'. 'Moreover, with this model the ecologist puts the whole globe into our hands, as something now absolutely in our care.' For Hughes, this vision binds the ecologist to the poet.

On turning to Ovid some twenty-five years later, Hughes found his mythic paradigm for the crisis of Western Man's self-exile from Nature. In translating the 'Four Ages' sequence, he gives it a profoundly ecological spin:

> And the first age was Gold.
> Without law, without law's enforcers,
> This age understood and obeyed
> What had created it.
> Listening deeply, man kept faith with
>   the source.

The Golden Age precedes the arrival of the social law. It is imagined as a time in which natural processes are acknowledged and limits are accepted. At first the translation stays close to the original. But with the line 'Listening deeply, man kept faith with the source', Ovid is given a distinctly Hughesian idiom. One senses the implication that the Poet is a seer who, alone in our Iron Age, is still capable of listening deeply and keeping faith with the source. After all, in his own original work Hughes had always written of pike, crow and fox in a style which sought to keep faith with nature's own cycle of creation and destruction.

The fall from the Golden Age comes with deforestation (the lofty pine gives way to the axe), with empire (timber is hauled to shipyards, and soon other lands are glimpsed 'from the lift of the ocean swell'), with the building of cities, with war, agriculture, mining, property and money. By the time of the Iron Age, mankind has ceased to listen deeply 'To the harmony of the whole creation'. Instead, 'The inward ear, attuned to the Creator, / Is underfoot like a dog's turd' and 'Mother Earth' is left 'blood-fouled'. The image of the earth as a violated woman may strike a chord with the feminist critics who – their eyes riveted to the corpse of Sylvia Plath – have made so much of the aggression and masculinity of Hughes's poetry, but here the modern translation is only being true to the original. Language which identifies all-conquering humankind as male and the ravaged earth as female is as old as Hesiod. The more telling respect in which the ancient narrative of the Four Ages is, so to speak, ecologized in its Hughesian retelling is revealed by that reference to the 'inward ear': the Hughes version consistently heightens the notion that harmonious dwelling with the earth is a matter of *staying put* and *listening in*, whereas the rapacious drive of 'progress' is towards *travelling out* and *making claims* – the claims of knowledge, of conquest and of possession. In contrast to Seamus Heaney, who began as a poet of turf, bog and locality, but has become ever more cosmopolitan in his interests, Hughes dug himself in on a smallholding in the far west of England. In his later poetry, he is always driving away from London, back to the farm. He rarely went abroad, and when he did the places which inspired him were the Australian outback and the wilderness of Alaska.

The example of Ted Hughes's *Tales from Ovid* shows that classical myth can still serve a poet's sense of where he belongs and what we have done to the earth. But we no longer believe that Eden or the Golden Age are true stories of our origin and our break from 'the state of nature'. We look for more tangible things: names, dates, inventions, facts. The demand for historical explanations as well as, or instead of, mythical ones is one of the characteristics of 'modernity'.

The notion that we are 'moderns' who possess a rational set of explanations for our condition, explanations which were not available to our forefathers, is another of Raymond Williams's escalators. The story of the loss of the imagined organic community plays out in miniature the bigger story of humankind's departure from nature. 'The emergence of modernity' is a term of shorthand for that bigger story. Being a bigger story, it has a longer timescale. As the miniature story places the loss a generation or two ago, so the bigger one places its great change a cycle or two back in the grand narrative of the march of ideas. Thus it was the general consensus among the intellectuals of the last century of the second millennium that the key period for the emergence of modernity was the so-called Enlightenment of two centuries before. Myth, magic, the idea that Nature was a sacred book written by God: these ancient and closely interrelated ideas were called into question by the new science and new philosophy of the seventeenth century. According to this narrative, the intellectual life of the eighteenth century was characterized by processes of secularization, rationalization and codification which decisively inaugurated the era of modernity – with its magnificent progress in human knowledge, its technological and medical advances, but also its accompanying alienations.

Even within the Enlightenment, though, there was a critique of Enlightenment. The old story of the fall of man and the loss of the Golden Age was given new forms.

*

In 1754 the Academy of Dijon proposed the following question for an essay competition: 'What is the origin of inequality among men and is it warranted by natural law?' Five years earlier a fiery young man from Geneva named Jean-Jacques Rousseau had won the annual Dijon prize for his discourse on the sciences and the arts. He did not repeat his success on this second occasion, but the essay which he submitted, *Discourse on the Origin and Foundations of Inequality among Men*, has continued to haunt Western man's thinking about nature.

Creatures of all species have natural inequalities of age, health, physical strength, and, in the case of higher mammals, temperament. But human beings also have political inequalities – of wealth and power, command and service. Rousseau's discourse sought to 'pinpoint the moment in the development of events when right replaced violence and nature was subjected to law, and to explain by what sequence of marvellous events the strong could resolve to serve the weak and the people to purchase a semblance of peace at the price of true felicity'. Natural inequality leads to the rule of the physically strong, as among other species, whereas human societies are ordered according to other kinds of law, which sustain a political inequality whereby it is not the strong who rule over the weak but the rich who rule over the poor.

In order to find the origin of the law of political inequality, we need to imagine a 'state of nature' in which that law is absent. We need to ask what unsocialized man might look like. In his preface, Rousseau hedges his bets as to whether the 'state of nature' is a heuristic model or a real lost condition: it 'no longer exists and *perhaps* never did and probably never will' (my italics). Either way, we must have an accurate conception of it 'in order to judge our present state properly'. The second discourse is a thought experiment, a piece of hypothetical reasoning which asks us to imagine a state of nature as a way of critiquing the state of society. In this sense, it is in the tradition of Sir Thomas More's *Utopia*, with the difference that instead of an imaginary better *place* it envisions an imaginary better *time*.

That time is one in which we are imagined to be in touch with our instincts. Rousseau addresses mankind: 'I shall, as it were, describe the life of your species, in light of the characteristics you once received which your education and habits could corrupt but not entirely destroy'. According to this argument, to be in touch with instinct – to be in touch with nature – is to be at liberty. Our original freedom is compromised by the necessity to live under the rule of institutions, that is to say, compromised by education, by government, by the rule of civil law.

The critic Jean Starobinski summarizes the object and scope of Rousseau's social analysis as follows:

> his protest is directed against society insofar as society is contrary to nature. Society, which *negates* nature (or the natural order), has not eradicated nature. Society and nature remain, rather, in permanent conflict, and it is this conflict that gives rise to all man's ills and vices. Rousseau's critique thus begins a 'negation of the negation.' He *accuses* civilization, which is characterized by its *negativity* with respect to nature. The established culture denies nature: this is the dramatic claim put forward in the two *Discourses* and *Emile*. Civilization's 'deceptive lights' do not illuminate man's world but veil the transparency of nature, separate men from one another, give rise to special interests, destroy all possibility of

mutual confidence, and substitute for true communication between souls a factitious commerce, devoid of sincerity.

Society is the negation of nature. The work of the thinker is to negate the negation, to accuse civilization, which is characterized by its negativity with respect to nature. Insofar as he held such beliefs, Rousseau may be characterized as a proto-Green thinker.

The word 'nature' is notoriously difficult to define. Rousseau uses it in two principal senses, which are best understood in relation to their opposites. One sense is that of innate disposition or inherent constitution, though for Rousseau this includes not only that with which we are born but also that which we develop in response to our infant and childhood environment. Nature in this sense is opposed to that which we learn through the processes of socialization. The opposition is spelt out in _Emile_, Rousseau's treatise on education:

> We are born with the use of our senses, and from our birth we are affected in various ways by the objects surrounding us. As soon as we have, so to speak, consciousness of our sensations, we are disposed to seek or avoid the objects which produce them, at first according to whether they are pleasant or unpleasant to us, then according to the conformity or lack of it that we find between us and these objects, and finally according to the judgments we make about them on the basis of the idea of happiness or of perfection given us by reason. These dispositions are extended and strengthened as we become more capable of using our senses and more enlightened; but constrained by our habits, they are more or less corrupted by our opinions. Before this corruption they are what I call in us _nature_.

Emile is a variation on the second _Discourse_, in that its temporal location of the 'state of nature' is the infancy of the individual rather than that of mankind. Its argument is that the institutionalizing processes of education constitute a denial of the natural child. Hence the dilemma: 'Forced to combat nature or the social institutions, one must choose between making a man or making a citizen, for one cannot make both at the same time.' So it is that 'nature' is made into the opposite of 'society' or, as we would now say, of 'culture'.

Imagine a world without human 'society' or 'culture' and you get Rousseau's second sense of 'nature', which corresponds broadly to the meaning of the word in common usage today, especially in contexts referring to the environment. *The New Shorter Oxford English Dictionary* comes to this definition in the following way:

> The creative and regulative physical power conceived of as operating in the material world and as the immediate cause of all its phenomena (sometimes, especially Nature, personified as a female being); these phenomena collectively; the material world; specifically, plants, animals, and other features of the earth itself, as opposed to humans or human creations or civilization.

The paradox of man and the dilemma of environmentalism are here in a nutshell. The definition begins with 'nature' as the immediate cause of the entire material world, of all phenomena including humankind, but it ends with an opposition between 'nature' and 'humans or human creations or civilizations'. We are both a part of and apart from nature.

Given the dictionary's definitional slide from *all* the phenomena of the material world to 'features of the earth itself' *as opposed to* those associated with humanity, it will be helpful to hold in mind not only Rousseau's two senses of 'nature' but also the threefold distinction of a modern philosopher, Kate Soper:

1. Employed as a metaphysical concept, which it mainly is in the argument of philosophy, 'nature' is the concept through which humanity thinks its difference and specificity. It is the concept of the non-human, even if . . . the absoluteness of the humanity–nature demarcation has been disputed, and our ideas about what falls to the side of 'nature' have been continuously revised in the light of changing perceptions of what counts as 'human' . . .

2. Employed as a realist concept, 'nature' refers to the structures, processes and causal powers that are constantly operative within the physical world, that provide the

objects of study of the natural sciences, and condition
the possible forms of human intervention in biology
or interaction with the environment. It is the nature to
whose laws we are always subject, even as we harness
them to human purposes, and whose processes we can
neither escape nor destroy.

3. Employed as a 'lay' or 'surface' concept, as it is in much
everyday, literary and theoretical discourse, 'nature' is
used in reference to ordinarily observable features of the
world: the 'natural' as opposed to the urban or industrial
environment ('landscape', 'wilderness', 'countryside',
'rurality'), animals, domestic and wild, the physical
body in space and raw materials. This is the nature of
immediate experience and aesthetic appreciation; the
nature we have destroyed and polluted and are asked
to conserve and preserve.

Throughout this book, when I talk about 'the question of
man's place in nature' or 'nature versus culture/society', I am
using the word 'nature' primarily in the first of these senses: 'the
concept of the non-human'. When I talk about biological and
ecological processes, and about 'truth to nature' as a criterion of
aesthetic judgement, I am using the word 'nature' primarily in the
second: 'the structures, processes and causal powers that are
constantly operative within the physical world'. When I talk about
'environmental' questions – the appreciation of 'landscapes', the
preservation of 'wilderness', the valuation of 'green spaces', the
extinction of great apes – I am using the word 'nature' primarily
in the third sense: 'the nature of immediate experience and
aesthetic appreciation'.

But it is impossible to hold the three senses fully apart. What
are commonly supposedly to be 'natural' landscapes, such as the
fells of the English Lake District, look as they look not only
because of millions of years of geological activity, but also because
of thousands of years of human agricultural and arboricultural
activity. Then again, the evolution of a conception of the human
as apart from 'nature' (sense 1) was itself a mechanism in our
species' struggle for survival, which is itself a prime example of
'the nature to whose laws we are always subject' (sense 2).

The 'dilemma of environmentalism', as I have termed it, stems from the way in which sense 3 is the inevitable consequence of sense 1. Once you invent the category of the 'human', you have to make 'nature' its Other. Sense 3 is needed as a register of what has been lost as a result of the advances forged by sense 1. Once nature is Other, man can advance with scant regard for it. Or do we say 'for her'? Ecofeminists have argued that the traditional personification of nature as female ('Mother Nature') yokes the exploitation of Her to the oppression of woman. Ted Hughes made this link in his 1970 essay on 'The Environmental Revolution': 'The subtly apotheosized misogyny of Reformed Christianity is proportionate to the fanatic rejection of Nature, and the result has been to exile man from Mother Nature'.

Until very recently, debates about sense 1 have tended to speak not of 'human' and 'nature' but of 'man' and 'nature'. Furthermore, 'man' has usually been taken to mean 'civilized (i.e. white, typically European) as opposed to savage (i.e. black, typically African, native American or aboriginal Australian) man'. This has resulted in 'woman' and 'black' also being regarded as Other. Hence the common association of 'woman' and 'black' with closeness to nature, with instinct and biology, of 'man' and 'European' with rationality and with transcendence of nature. In the next chapter I will ask why the recovery of the repressed 'Others' of woman and black in cultural criticism since the 1960s has not generally been accompanied by a recovery of 'nature', the original Other.

Rousseau said that 'conscience' was the 'voice of nature' working within us. Most of us do seem, at least sometimes, to feel either guilt or fear about what the advance of 'civilization' has done, and continues to do with ever more drastic consequences, to nature (sense 3). We value nature (sense 3) for the very reason that we are destroying it; the more we 'tame' nature in our everyday lives, the more we value 'wild' nature in our leisure time. Prosperous Americans, Germans, Britons and Japanese make up the bulk of those who like to watch wild animals in Africa. Perhaps Rousseau's 'conscience', the voice of nature which calls to us from within, is itself a regulative mechanism of nature (sense 2) that will eventually lead to a necessary reversal. After all, if we destroy the earth we will destroy ourselves.

But where is the voice of nature calling us? *Back* to a pre-modern age? Or *forward* to a saner future? There are dangers in the psychological mechanism which attracts us to places which seem to be purer than the cities in which the majority of moderns spend their working lives – a 'natural' landscape, a 'harmonious' village community, a 'primitive' wilderness. The urge to go 'back to nature' may lead us into nostalgia for an historical era when, we suppose, humans were less alienated from nature. Theodor Adorno warns us that 'As long as the face of the earth keeps being ravished by utilitarian pseudo-progress, it will turn out to be impossible to disabuse human intelligence of the notion that, despite all the evidence to the contrary, the pre-modern world was better and more humane, its backwardness notwithstanding.'

As I suggested at the end of chapter one, the danger lies in what we do with the nostalgia. Perhaps we will seek to return to the old values. One thinks here of a German chicken farmer of the 1920s who argued that corruption and cowardice came from the cities, purity and virtue from traditional Bavarian village life. His name was Heinrich Himmler and his programme for bringing back the old ways involved the extermination of millions of those who had no place in traditional Bavarian village life (Jews, Slavs, gypsies, homosexuals).

Alternatively, we may regard the supposed simplicity and naturalness of the old ways as an *allegory* that is necessary to our psychological and social health. According to this way of thinking, we will be in error if we try to translate the *images* into reality, but at the same time we must attend to the admonitions of Rousseau's 'voice of nature'. Adorno's analysis of this issue, to which I will return in chapters three and five, offers a hope as well as a warning: 'Natural beauty is myth transposed into imagination and thus possibly redeemed'.

Thinkers from Rousseau to the late-twentieth-century Greens have proposed that man's presumption of his own apartness from nature is the prime cause of the environmental degradation of the earth. Green thinking is not, however, a uniform phenomenon. Among both theorists and practitioners, there are deep divisions. It has become customary to draw a distinction between what might be thought of as 'light Greens', known as 'environmentalists', 'dark Greens', known as 'deep ecologists'. Environmentalists are those who believe that the degradation of nature may be reversed by a combination of regulation, restraint, less toxic and wasteful modes of production, and various forms of technologically engineered – including genetically and bioengineered – intervention. But since the intervention of technological man is the cause of the problem, can a 'technological fix' also be the solution? 'Deep ecologists' are those who think not. They believe that our only salvation from impending environmental apocalypse is to return to the state of nature. They say that we must renounce the idols that have set us apart from nature – idols variously identified as technology; civilization; Enlightenment; patriarchy (this is the ecofeminist variant); the quest for economic growth; capitalism and militarism (this is the ecological socialist variant); materialism; the consumer society; and so forth.

The true deep ecologist is a utopian who forgets that 'utopia' literally means 'nowhere', a primitivist who forgets Rousseau's wry admission that the state of nature 'no longer exists and perhaps never did and probably never will'. How can a world so crowded with cities, with 'civilization', possibly be returned to the state of nature? And, besides, would we want to return it there? Life in the state of nature, Thomas Hobbes reminded readers of *Leviathan* in 1651, is solitary, poor, nasty, brutish and short. It may be necessary to critique the values of the Enlightenment, but to reject enlightenment altogether would be to reject justice, political liberty and altruism.

Central to the dilemma of environmentalism is the fact that the act of identifying the presumption of human apartness from nature as the problem is itself a symptom of that very apartness. The identification is the product of an instrumental way of thinking and of using language. It may therefore be that a necessary step in overcoming the apartness is to think and to use language in a different way. Let us begin by supposing that we cannot do without thought-experiments and language-experiments which imagine a return to nature, a reintegration of the human and the Other. The dream of deep ecology will never be realized upon the earth, but our survival as a species may be

ıcity to dream it in the work of our
.ook will be a testing of these supposes.
.id *Discourse* is a foundational paradigm for my
.ut the majority of my examples will be – for reasons
.ll become apparent – poems in the 'Romantic' and 'post-
.antic' tradition.

Starobinski's summation of the project of Rousseau's social criticism could as well be an account of that broad cultural movement which we call Romanticism. Like Rousseau, Romanticism negates the negation. Typically, it defines civilization as alienation from nature, and accordingly idealizes both childhood and imagined lost ways of dwelling in oneness with the earth. And, like Rousseau, the Romantics explored three possible ways of returning to nature.

The first of these three paths was the dream of a transformation for all humankind, through the overthrow of that very institutionalized despotism which defines society as the opposite of nature. This was the way from Rousseau's *Social Contract* to the storming of the Bastille to the Romantics' initial enthusiastic welcoming of the French Revolution. It is the model for that brand of green thinking known as 'social ecology': the social ecologist argues that capitalism and militarism are the sources of environmental degradation and that it will therefore be impossible to harmonize humankind with nature until we remake society in a more compassionate and less competitive mould. Social ecology is Marxism with ecology added on.

But the legacy of Jacobinism and Marxism is not an entirely happy one. In the closing section of the second *Discourse*, Rousseau anticipated where the way of social liberation would eventually lead:

> This is the final stage of inequality, the extreme point that closes the circle and links up with the point from which we set out. Here, all individuals become equal again because they are nothing, here subjects have no law save the will of the master, nor the master any rule save that of his passions . . . Here, everything is brought back solely to the law of the strongest, and hence to a new state of nature differing from

the one with which we began in that the one was the state of nature in its pure form and the other the fruit of excessive corruption.

The *Social Contract* had proposed the substitution of the 'general will' for the will of the tyrant, but after every revolution in history the law of nature has always reasserted itself. The fittest survive, might rules over right, Napoleon and Stalin rise to power from the ashes of the dream. Rousseau recognizes that to frame a government according to the law of nature may ultimately mean submission to the will of a strong master.

Recent critical historians of Green thinking such as Anna Bramwell and Luc Ferry have demonstrated that the attempt to derive politics from 'ecology' has often been yoked disturbingly to a Führer principle. If Green thinking's myth of origins (of Fall) is Rousseau's second *Discourse*, its myth of ending (of Apocalypse) is Thomas Malthus's *Essay on the Principle of Population*, written forty-four years later. Greens have consistently proposed that draconian social control is the only action possible in the face of the inexorable Malthusian ratio whereby population grows by geometric progression and food production does not. But can the general will include the will to self-restraint? Is it not more likely that a Leader will be called upon to decide who is to reproduce and who is not to? Perhaps the Leader will say that the people of the Third World must restrain themselves. Or perhaps he will say that the limitations set by nature upon his people's Lebensraum are best addressed by race laws, by eugenics, by genocide.

The theory of evolution had antecedents in the late eighteenth and early nineteenth centuries, notably in the work of Erasmus Darwin and Jean Lamarck. Charles Darwin's innovation was the law of natural selection. As was noted in the previous chapter, this was a law he learnt from Malthus. When that law was reappropriated into politics by Social Darwinism, the rule of the Master prevailed. The buzzwords remain familiar: 'struggle for existence', 'will to power', 'survival of the fittest', and, of course, the Übermensch. In the 1890s, however, the anarchist Peter Kropotkin argued to the contrary that the politics of mastery rested on crude simplifications of Darwin, and that 'mutual aid' was as important a factor as competition in the complex web of interrelations which constitutes evolutionary process. That both the competitive Social Darwinism of Herbert Spencer and Kropotkin's alternative model of cooperation, community and self-sacrifice can be derived from the law of natural selection according to fitness to environment demonstrates that there is no straightforward path from scientific to political ecology. Rousseau's argument suggests that there cannot be, if only for the reason that the institutional structures which constitute the political – government, law and so forth – are the negation of nature.

The first path thus proving to be a dead end, Rousseau and the Romantics followed two other tracks back to nature, those of the small group and the self. Rousseau dedicated the second *Discourse* to his birthplace, the independent republic of Geneva. His ideal community was one of a manageable size; he argued that if we see and know our fellow-people, the love of country will 'take the form of love of its citizens rather than of its soil'. His novel *La Nouvelle Héloïse* begins with an opposition between society (represented by the difference in rank between Julie and Saint-Preux) and nature (represented by their love for each other, which is first realized by a kiss in the rural setting of a grove). But in its second half, the novel acknowledges the possibility of a sociable good life through the model of the enlightened administration of Wolmar's and Julie's compact and well-managed rural estate at Clarens on the shores of Lake Geneva. So too for the Romantics, the small-scale republic of free men living amidst the untamed forms of nature was a compelling ideal of society. William Wordsworth thought he had found such a society among the yeomanry of the English Lake District; Samuel Taylor Coleridge and Robert Southey sought one with their plan to establish a 'pantisocratic' agrarian commune beside the banks of the Susquehanna River.

If Saint-Preux, the embodiment of 'sincerity' or passionate sentiment, were to be assimilated into the community at Clarens, he would have to be cured of his love. By book four of *La Nouvelle Héloïse*, Julie is married, which is to say socially contracted, to Wolmar. In the famous boating scene, a storm forces her to shelter with Saint-Preux on the shore opposite to that of the estate. The associations of wild place and rough weather bring them close to a final relapse into passion, but Julie's disciplined will prevails. Hereafter, Saint-Preux can only be a shadow of his true self. The exclusion of the impassioned self from society, the sense that sincerity, passion and liberty of spirit require solitude, preferably in a stormy and mountainous setting, represents the third – and most characteristic, most intense – Romantic route back to nature.

In Rousseau, it is seen most fully in his final work, *Les Rêveries du promeneur solitaire* ('Reveries of the solitary walker'). The self, now set in reaction against society, takes refuge in reverie; through memory, through imagination, through the reorganization of his mental and emotional world, Rousseau creates his own interior 'state of nature'. At the same time, when he walks and then dreams in solitude, he allows himself to be absorbed into an unpeopled external nature. In the first of his *Dialogues*, Rousseau, dramatizing himself as Jean-Jacques, had written of himself thus: 'I have seen him travel two leagues daily almost throughout the spring to listen to the nightingale at Bercy. He needed water, greenery, solitude, and woods to make the bird's song touching to his ear.' In the seventh promenade of the *Rêveries*, this kind of journey into nature is extended and a state of complete absorption is achieved:

> The more sensitive the soul of the observer, the greater the ecstasy aroused in him by this harmony [of the great pageant of nature]. At such times his senses are possessed by a deep and delightful reverie, and in a state of blissful self-abandonment he loses himself in the immensity of this beautiful order, with which he feels himself at one. All individual objects escape him; he sees and feels nothing but the unity of all things.

But the price of this intoxication with the spirit of things is a definitive break from the human community. Pantheism displaces philanthropy, communion with nature stands in for social awareness. William Hazlitt constantly harried Wordsworth and the other Lake Poets because he believed that this was the story of their development – from Hazlitt's own liberal perspective, it was a story of political apostasy.

Updating the terminology, we might say that the Rousseau-istic motions of reverie, of solitude and of walking are conducive to what I shall call 'ecopoetic' consciousness but not necessarily to 'ecopolitical' commitment. They are motions which may well lead to environmentalism – the desire to conserve green spaces (parks, wilderness areas) in which to walk, dream and find solitude – but their connection with radical ecology's project of wholesale social transformation is more abstruse.

Indeed, there is a fundamental problem in making that con-nection, since poetic and practical language have very different purposes. Reverie, solitude, walking: to turn these experiences into language is to be an ecopoet. Ecopoetry is not a description of dwelling with the earth, not a disengaged thinking about it, but an experiencing of it. By 'poetry' here I mean *poiesis*, *making*, the medium of which may as well be, say, painting as writing. Thus the philosopher Maurice Merleau-Ponty on the experience of looking at a painting: 'When I see the bright green of one of Cézanne's vases, it does not make me *think* of pottery, it presents it to me.' Ecopoetry is not synonymous with writing that is pragmatically green: a manifesto for ecological correctness will not be poetic because its language is bound to be instrumental, to address questions of doing rather than to 'present' the experience of dwelling. We will, then, need to hesitate over the complex of intersections and contradictions between ecopoetics and eco-politics.

*

Rousseau's *Discourse on the Origin of Inequality* is, as I have said, modernity's founding myth of the 'state of nature' and our severance from that state. Its narrative is based upon a similar series of falls or ruptures to those identified in the classical myth of the Four Ages. Rousseau traces an accumulation of disasters, among them the fall into deforestation, the fall into meat-eating, the fall into language and the fall into property.

Part one of the discourse begins with an image of man in the state of nature. He subsists, he is contented, he is at one with an environment that is virgin, that has not yet been colonized: 'The earth, left to its natural fertility and bespread with immense forests never hewn by an axe, everywhere offers storehouses and shelter for animals of every species'. In one of his long footnotes, Rousseau acknowledges the source of this image of natural plenty – of the life-cycle which sustains ecosystems – in the 'Theory of the Earth' of the great naturalist (and keeper of the King's garden), Georges-Louis Leclerc, Comte de Buffon:

> Because plants get for their nourishment much more sub-stance from air and water than they get from the earth, it happens that when they rot, they return more to the earth than they have taken from it; furthermore, a forest keeps the waters of the rain by preventing evaporation. Thus in a wood left untouched for a long time, the layer of soil that supports vegetation would increase considerably; but because animals return less to the earth than they draw from it, and men consume enormous quantities of timber and plants for fires and other uses, it follows that in an inhabited country the layer of vegetative soil must always diminish and eventually become like the soil of Arabia Petraea, and so many other provinces of the Orient, which is in fact the area of most ancient habitation, where today we find only salt and sand; for the fixed salts of plants and animals remain, while all the other particles are volatilized.

Rousseau adds a specific link between deforestation and the progress of civilization: 'history tells us about the huge forests all over the earth which had to be cut down as it became populated and civilized'. A key principle in scientific ecology is then articulated: 'the destruction of the topsoil – that is, the loss of the substance suited to vegetation – must accelerate in proportion to the earth's degree of cultivation and to the consumption of its products of every kind by its more industrious inhabitants'. In such passages as this, we have the beginnings of a green history of the world.

The second *Discourse* tends to be read by political theorists in relation to a tradition of natural rights philosophy going back to Hobbes, Pufendorf and Burlamaqui, but an examination of

Rousseau's footnotes – and footnotes are, after all, the traditional place for the enumeration of key sources – reveals that the first two substantial quotations are from the Comte de Buffon's encyclopaedic *Natural History*. Rousseau's political theory is mediated via natural history. There is one later substantial quotation from Locke on civil government, but much more frequently Rousseau turns to eighteenth-century voyage narratives, for instance when he reproduces a long passage concerning the orang-utan in support of the argument that *Homo sapiens* is a natural vegetarian. We have the teeth and intestine of a frugivore. According to Rousseau, whereas carnivores fight over their prey, orang-utans – and humans in the state of nature – eat fruit and nuts, and therefore live at peace. Two generations later, Percy Shelley, in his 'Vindication of the Natural Diet', developed a similar argument about how the eating of red meat creates bloodthirstiness and leads to war.

By becoming omnivorous, our species improved its prospects of survival over those of the apes, rendering itself capable of adapting to different environments. But at the same time, the argument goes, the formation of groups and the division of labour necessary for the hunting of big game led to violence and inequality. Meat-eating is thus added to deforestation as a second fall on the sorry road to civilized inequality.

Rousseau does not idealize the state of nature into a pure golden age. He recognizes that it has its own inequalities: as in the animal world, the fittest survive, while weak infants and the elderly quickly die. But such deaths are from natural causes; Rousseau contrasts them with the physical and psychological illnesses brought about by progress – socially induced stress, sexually transmitted diseases, the effects of gluttony, alcoholism, and so forth. The paradox of humankind is that we are free to destroy ourselves by these means. The difference between man and animals is that we may act according to free will, as opposed to instinct.

It is not his understanding that constitutes the distinctive characteristic of man among all other animals, but his capacity as a free agent. Nature commands every animal, and the beast obeys. Man experiences the same impulsion, but he recognizes that he is free to comply or resist; and it is above all the awareness of this freedom that reveals the spirituality of his soul.

Man is also distinguished by the faculty of self-improvement: 'an animal at the end of a few months already is what it will remain all its life, and its species will be at the end of a thousand years what it was in the first of those thousand years'. But our perfectibility – by which Rousseau means the capacity perpetually to improve, not the real prospect of reaching a utopian goal – brings with it the concomitant potential for degeneration. For Rousseau, the paradox of the human condition is that our very freedom to transform and transcend the state of nature is the source of our enslavement. He was the first to articulate what Theodor Adorno and Max Horkheimer were to call the *dialectic* of Enlightenment, an idea to which I will return in the next chapter. We are born free, but we are enchained by a society which we try and fail to transform, so we seek instead to return romantically to the state of nature.

Man's improvement consists in altering the face of nature but failing to make himself happy. We have few natural predators, so we suffer hardly any evils save those we inflict upon ourselves:

> When we consider, on the one hand, man's colossal achievements, so many sciences developed, so many arts invented, so many forces exploited, chasms filled over, mountains pulverized, rocks broken up, rivers made navigable, land cleared, lakes carved out, swamplands drained, enormous buildings erected on land, the sea bespread with ships and sailors; and when, on the other hand, we search with a little meditation for the real advantages that have accrued from all this for the happiness of the human race, we cannot fail to be struck by the stunning disproportion between these things, or fail to deplore man's blindness, which to feed his lunatic vanity and I know not what undue self-admiration, makes him fervently chase after all the miseries of which he is capable, and which a beneficent nature had painstakingly kept from him.

The progress catalogued here is built upon exploitation – slaves and workers clear the land and raise the buildings; ships go to build empires, colonization destroys virgin lands. 'Admire human society as you will, it is no less true that it necessarily leads men to abominate each other to the degree that their interests conflict, and to pretend to render each other services while in fact doing each other every imaginable harm'. 'Savage man,' by contrast, 'when he has eaten, is at peace with all nature and the friend of all his fellows'. Perhaps, after all, it is the primitive who is truly free. So it is that modern Greens reawaken the image of the noble savage, idealizing native Americans, indigenous Australians and the last peoples of the Amazon.

Rousseau argues that social man is not at peace because he has moved from necessities to superfluities, to a pursuit of pleasure and wealth that inevitably depends on the subjection and slavery of others. Advanced society brings with it not only inequality, but also 'mental agonies' (it is hard to imagine a savage committing suicide) and 'epidemic diseases generated by the bad air in places where masses of men are gathered together'. Density of population leads to natural disasters – floods and landslips, say – whereby nature makes us pay for the contempt we have shown towards its lessons. Civilization also inevitably brings war and 'the numbers of unwholesome trades that shorten lives or destroy men's vigour – trades like working in mines, processing metals and minerals, especially lead, copper, mercury, cobalt, arsenic, realgar'.

At one level, Rousseau is contributing to a well-established debate in eighteenth-century social and economic theory. Bernard de Mandeville, for instance, had argued that luxury was a public benefit, an encouragement to universal prosperity and growth. More or less contemporaneously with Rousseau, Oliver Goldsmith devoted his poem *The Deserted Village* to the contrary argument that luxury, and in particular the conspicuous consumption of exotic goods imported from the colonies, led only to rural depopulation and degradation. At another level, though, Rousseau is raising the stakes in a manner that makes him into one of the first prophets of ecocide: 'I fear that it will occur to someone to answer that men wisely invented all these great things – the arts, sciences, and laws – as a therapeutic plague to preclude the excessive increase of the species, for fear that this world might in the end become too small for its inhabitants'. A darkly Malthusian deep Green might argue just this.

An assault on the plague of modernity – largely undertaken in the footnotes – is secondary to the main interest of the *Discourse*, which remains the question of origins. When and why did man depart from the state of nature? Was it with the invention of language? Rousseau writes, in a famous phrase, picked up by the Scottish Jacobin John Oswald for the title of his animal rights manifesto of 1791, that man's first language was 'the cry of nature' (*'le cri de la nature'*). Primal language is regarded as equivalent to the cry of the animal in pain or the baby expressing fear or a desire for nutrition. But with socialization comes the need to refer to things. A gestural language emerges. Then, in order to refer to absent or invisible things, sounds are substituted for gestures and names attached to things. According to this theory, language is a means by which humans *represent* the objects of nature. It is a sophisticated tool designed to further the instrumentalization of our relationship with nature. Rousseau is not sure whether society is necessary for the invention of language or language for the invention of society, but, either way, in the division between nature and society, language is firmly on the side of society. Romanticism often insists that language is a prison house which cuts us off from nature, but simultaneously the poet strives to create a special kind of language that will be the window of the prison cell.

For Rousseau, the final fall from nature to society is the invention of property. He marks the break within the structure of his *Discourse*: part one has idealized man in the state of nature, while part two is a narrative of loss. The second part begins with the memorable words:

The true founder of civil society was the first man who, having enclosed a piece of land, thought of saying, 'This is mine', and came across people simple enough to believe him. How many crimes, wars, murders and how much misery and horror the human race might have been spared if someone had pulled up the stakes or filled in the ditch, and cried out

> to his fellows: 'Beware of listening to this charlatan. You are
> lost if you forget that the fruits of the earth belong to all
> and that the earth itself belongs to no one!'

Nascent man is like Karl Marx's unalienated labourer, 'scarcely
profiting from the gifts supplied him by nature, much less imagining he could wrest anything from it'. But everything changes
with the advent of various forms of instrumentality: the use of
fire and of tools leads to a perception of *relations*, of things that
are different from the self. This leads to reflection, to subjectiv-
ism, to affirmation of the primacy of the species and thence to
the claim for the primacy of the individual, the claim which
creates the conditions of political inequality.

Agriculture and metallurgy lead to the division of labour:
'from the moment one man needed help from another, and as
soon as they found it useful for one man to have provisions
enough for two, equality evaporated, property was introduced,
and work became mandatory'. For Rousseau, what we would
now call ecological exploitation is always coordinate with social
exploitation: 'vast forests were transformed into sunny open
country that had to be watered with the sweat of man, and where
slavery and adversity were soon seen to germinate and ripen with
the crops'. With the cultivation of land come custom and law:

> Everything begins to take on a new appearance. Men who
> had once roamed the woods, having taken up a fixed loca-
> tion, slowly came together, gathered in various clusters, and
> in each region eventually formed a particular nation, united
> by customs and character ... The cultivation of the land
> necessarily led to its division, and the recognition of property
> led to the first rules of justice ... the division of land had
> produced a new sort of right, that is, the right to property,
> which is different from the right derived from natural law.

Agriculture and law have thus emerged together; the law of
property and the law of inequality are one. Within societies, civil
law comes to replace the law of nature; between societies, the
law of nature – the survival of the strongest – continues to
operate. So it is that territoriality initiates the spiral that eventually leads to war.

In the first promenade of his *Solitary Walker*, Rousseau, set firmly in opposition to civilization's inevitable progress towards property and war, describes himself as a 'monster'. To make claims for the natural man was to question the value-structure of society, and in so doing to adopt the stance of the outsider. I want to turn now to two literary reworkings of the Rousseau-esque model of 'the state of nature'. The first of them is English literature's primary myth of how the spirit of Enlightenment or modernity creates an image of the natural man as a sign of its own alienation, but having created that image can only condemn it to exile and mark it with monstrosity.

*

Mary Shelley's *Frankenstein* begins with the Enlightenment quest to master nature. The narrator, Robert Walton, is sailing north in the direction of the magnetic pole. Late eighteenth-century science had yielded new knowledge about two invisible forces which, it was speculated, might be keys to the secret of life itself: magnetism and electricity. The first of Mary Shelley's questers is in pursuit of the former force, the second of the latter. It is the sight of the effect of an electrical storm which inspires Victor Frankenstein to become a scientist.

For Walton, knowledge of the earth is also a means to con-quest on behalf of his nation. The second motivation for his journey is the desire to break through the north-eastern passage in the hope of facilitating British colonization and trade. That such an ambition brings with it the destruction of nature is signalled to the reader not only by the fact that Walton trains for his expedition by getting himself hired on a whaler, but also by the identity of the role-model whom he self-consciously adopts. He admits that he has derived his passion for polar exploration from Coleridge's Ancient Mariner. He jokes to his sister that he will return home safely, since he will not go so far as to kill an albatross. The Mariner negates the Coleridgean principle that there is one life within us and abroad: his arbitrary act of shooting the albatross is the archetypal crime against nature. The killing of the bird breaks man apart from the rest of nature, so that even after his act of atonement in blessing the water-snakes the Mariner remains an outsider. He will always be a wanderer, an alien, a creature of knowledge and of language who will never be allowed to rest at home, to dwell upon the earth. Walton and Frankenstein suffer a similar fate.

Walton is witness to the last titanic struggle between Frankenstein and his creation. The Creature is first seen through Walton's eyes from a distance of half a mile: he appears to be 'a savage inhabitant of some undiscovered isle'. The next day, Frankenstein appears: he, by contrast, is identified as 'an European' with a 'cultivated' mind. The Creature is thus identified with primitivism, with the state of nature, Frankenstein with cultivation, the state of Enlightenment.

Frankenstein's narrative of his own life confirms his role as a son of the Enlightenment intent on the conquest of nature's secrets. After a Rousseauesque childhood in which he is at one with his Swiss environment, he falls into scientific knowledge. He shares the ambition of Sir Humphry Davy, whose 1802 *Discourse, Introductory to a Course of Lectures on Chemistry* Mary Shelley read before writing the novel. Chemistry, writes Davy, has given to man

> an acquaintance with the different relations of the parts of the external world; and more than that, it has bestowed upon him powers which may be almost called creative; which have enabled him to modify and change the beings surrounding him, and by his experiments to interrogate nature with power, not simply as a scholar, passive and seeking only to understand her operations, but rather as a master, active with his own instruments.

Frankenstein's education re-enacts the history of European science, as he progresses from alchemical fancy to sceptical Enlightenment (embodied in the figure of his first university teacher, Krempe) to modern chemistry (embodied in his ideal teacher, Waldman, who, unlike Krempe, grants that the older alchemical theories must still be respected because they laid the foundations for the modern quest to understand the origins and nature of life).

The onset of Frankenstein's higher education into the mastery of nature coincides with the death of his mother and his departure from home. Science is thus set in opposition to the female principles of maternity and natural landscape. The bond with both biological mother and mother nature is broken. I would suggest that Mary Shelley makes Frankenstein a Genevan because of that city's associations with Rousseau, whose example had powerfully yoked together the idea of childhood, the bond with nature and the environment around Lake Geneva, where Shelley was writing her novel. When Frankenstein is far away in Ireland, he speaks of his 'devouring *maladie du pays*', an allusion to what was regarded as a national characteristic of the Swiss: their pathological longing for the homeland. The word nostalgia, with all its Rousseauesque associations, entered the English language in the late eighteenth century as a translation of German *Heimweh*, the technical term for Swiss homesickness.

Frankenstein cuts himself off from the natural environment of the Swiss Alps and encloses himself in his laboratory. There, like a genetic engineer a century and a half before the discovery of DNA, he pursues his dream of becoming, as the subtitle of the novel has it, 'the modern Prometheus': 'a new species would bless me as its creator and source; many happy and excellent natures would owe their being to me'. But the attempt to create a new nature is a transgression against nature. Frankenstein frequently uses a language of light-bringing – of Enlightenment – in describing his task, but the accomplishment of his deed occurs on a dark and dreary night of November; the Creature's first motion is the opening of a 'dull yellow eye' seen 'by the glimmer of the half-extinguished light'. Enlightenment proves to be endarkening. Once Frankenstein brings the Creature to life, his own eyes become 'insensible to the charms of nature'. His nightmare immediately after the creation is of the destruction of the feminine principle of nature: he imagines that on kissing his beautiful beloved Elizabeth, she is transformed into the corpse of his dead mother. By going against the natural process of generation, by making a child of his own without submission to the fecundity of a woman's womb, he symbolically kills mother nature. His subsequent story veers wildly between moments of restoration to and by nature in its pure mountain form and further severances of environmental belonging.

Where Frankenstein is the representative of Enlightenment man, the Creature is an embodiment of the state of nature. His autobiographical narrative tells the familiar Rousseauesque story – mediated via the English Rousseau, Mary Shelley's father, William Godwin – of a fall from natural benevolence to misery and fiendishness.

On being deserted by his father Frankenstein, the Creature retreats to the forest where, like Rousseau's natural man, he eats berries and shades himself under the foliage of the trees. The order of his life replicates the history outlined in Giambattista Vico's *The New Science*: 'This was the order of human institutions: first the forests, after that the huts, then the villages, next the cities, and finally the academies'. But because the Creature is created from the last of these institutions, from the knowledge of the academies, he is foredoomed to degeneration. It is Enlightenment man who invents the natural man; like Rousseau's second *Discourse*, Frankenstein uses the state of nature as a heuristic device to critique both Ancien Régime tyranny and the enlightened aspirations of the present.

As in the *Discourse*, the differentiating process initiated by the learning of language is a key stage in the fall. Language, property and institutionalization bring about the fall from nature into history, learned by the Creature as he overhears Felix's readings from Volney's *Ruins of Empire*: 'While I listened to the instructions which Felix bestowed upon the Arabian, the strange system of human society was explained to me. I heard of the division of property, of immense wealth and squalid poverty; of rank, descent, and noble blood.'

When Frankenstein first re-encounters his Creature in the sublime natural setting of Chamounix, he says 'There can be no community between you and me'. Frankenstein's crime, committed in the isolation of his laboratory, has been to deny the principle of community. Like Coleridge's Mariner, he breaks the contract of mutual dependency which binds species in a network of reciprocal relations. The attempt to cheat death through knowledge instead of intercourse is the novel's original sin. The second crime is that against the Creature, which drives him into exile and turns him to malignancy. This crime could be called 'speciesism'. The blind old man De Lacy is prepared to help the unknown stranger, eliciting from him the delighted reply, 'I shall not be driven from the society and sympathy of your fellow-creatures'. But with the entrance of the sighted – the Enlightened – Felix, Safie and Agatha, the Creature is regarded as Other, as alien. He is driven out. On the lonely night that follows, all of nature seems to him harmonized whereas he alone is alone. When he returns to the De Lacy family's cottage of pastoral retreat two days later, he finds that 'My protectors had departed, and had broken the only link that held me to the world'. Once that link is broken, he proceeds to turn against the ecosystem in which the De Lacys had eked out their living: 'I placed a variety of combustibles around the cottage; and, after having destroyed every vestige of cultivation in the garden, I waited with forced impatience until the moon had sunk to commence my operations.' Here the Promethean knowledge of the instrumentality of fire is returned upon man with a vengeance.

The Creature's request for a mate comes from a desire to regain some form of community, to 'become linked to the chain of existence' once again. Movingly, he swears 'by the earth which I inhabit' that he will do no harm to any other species. He dreams of returning to the state of nature with a beloved partner, going off to live as a vegetarian in America every bit in the manner of Coleridge and Southey's ideal pantisocratic community:

> If you consent, neither you nor any other human being shall ever see us again: I will go to the vast wilds of South America. My food is not that of man; I do not destroy the lamb and the kid to glut my appetite; acorns and berries afford me sufficient nourishment. My companion will be of the same nature as myself, and will be content with the same fare. We shall make our bed of dried leaves; the sun will shine on us as on man, and will ripen our food. The picture I present to you is peaceful and human, and you must feel that you could deny it only in the wantonness of power and cruelty.

The idea of the wilds of South America as a place where one might recover the lost state of nature is one to which writers returned throughout the nineteenth and early twentieth centuries, as we will see.

Frankenstein initially denies the Creature's request on the grounds that the 'joint wickedness' of the monster and his partner 'might desolate the world'. Later, he relents, but then changes his mind again, for fear of creating a race of destructive supermen. But in reality it is he himself, the Enlightenment scientist, who is desolating the world. It is he who refuses to give his Creature any name but Monster, who by treating him as a monster turns him into one. The Creature, we may say, is the repressed nature which returns and threatens to destroy the society that has repressed it.

The close of *Frankenstein* offers an image of nature's continuing power to resist the human quest for mastery. Enlightenment mastery is based on *division*. Knowledge is divided into categories, as in that archetypal enterprise of the eighteenth century, the encyclopaedia. Chemistry, as Davy suggests, breaks nature down into its constituent parts. Frankenstein's creation begins from bits and pieces of body part. Mary Shelley's narrative ends in the Arctic, which is, by contrast, *a place where divisions do not hold*.

The Creature does finally return to the state of nature: he is swallowed up among the ice-floes of the north. Perhaps the quest for human mastery began at the moment in the Genesis narrative when God divided the land from the waters. But on the shifting pack ice of the Arctic, there is no division between land and sea. The phenomenology of dualism cannot function. As Barry Lopez has demonstrated in his wonderful book, *Arctic Dreams*, the Arctic makes you see differently: time, season, light and spatial relations do not operate in the ways that we who know only the temperate zones regard as 'natural'. Like Coleridge's Mariner, crossing and recrossing the equatorial line, seeing the sun rise first one side then the other, temperate man is disoriented in the Arctic:

> The idea that the sun 'rises in the east and sets in the west' simply does not apply. The thought that a 'day' consists of a morning and a forenoon, an afternoon and an evening, is a convention . . . The pattern is not the same here.

But this is a healthy disorientation, for to acknowledge it is to realize that Western man may not after all be the master of all things. As Lopez shows, we are still remarkably ignorant about many northern wonders – the habits of polar bears, migration patterns, the life cycle of narwhals. You cannot fix or predict life in the Arctic: ice is both land and sea, so in the far north (and south) maps, those markers of human mastery, can only ever be provisional. If only Walton had known that the North Magnetic Pole itself does not stay in one and the same place.

*

Frankenstein begins to create the female partner for the Creature, but dismembers it before it (or she) is completed. By repressing the female, with its associations of benign nurture, Frankenstein – the man who wishes to create a life without the assistance of a womb – unleashes the destructive power of nature. The Creature, I have suggested, is the repressed which returns and destroys its maker. More specifically, we may say that its destructive force is lodged in its maleness. Having examined a female author's representation of the degeneration of the natural *man*, let us now consider a male author's representation of the state of nature as female.

William Henry Hudson (1841–1922) is a writer who has dropped out of the literary canon, partly because of a certain Edwardian purpleness that robes his prose, but principally because he defies generic categorization. He was at once a naturalist (in particular an ornithologist and a founding father of the Royal Society for the Protection of Birds), a travel writer, an English countryman, a romancer and a memoirist. He is unlikely to be much read in an age which regards the natural history essay as an unliterary, or at least a marginal, form. But I would like to suggest that what was in its own time his most successful romance will repay fresh attention a century after its first appearance. It is one of the few English literary works of the past to speak to the greatest ecological catastrophe of the present, the destruction of the tropical rainforest of South America. Written in 1904, partly in reaction against the vogue for stories of Africa as the 'dark' continent (Conrad's *Heart of Darkness* being the most eminent example), it is entitled *Green Mansions: A Romance of the Tropical Forest*.

Before turning to this novel, both the flavour of Hudson's prose and a sense of his spiritual allegiances may be suggested by a pair of passages from other works. First, from *Hampshire Days*:

> The blue sky, the brown soil beneath, the grass, the trees, the animals, the wind, and rain, and sun, and stars are never strange to me; for I am in and of and am one with them; and my flesh and the soil are one, and the heat in my blood and in the sunshine are one, and the winds and tempests and my passions are one. I feel the 'strangeness' only with regard to my fellow-men, especially in towns, where they exist in conditions unnatural to me, but congenial to them. . . . In such moments we sometimes feel a kinship with, and are strangely drawn to, the dead, who were not as these; the long, long dead, the men who knew not life in towns, and felt no strangeness in sun and wind and rain.

And secondly from *The Purple Land*, Hudson's first novel, a narrative of an Englishman journeying through South America and undergoing a conversion from patriotism to love of untamed nature:

> Ah yes, we are all vainly seeking after happiness in the wrong way. It was with us once and ours, but we despised it, for it was only the old common happiness which Nature gives to all her children, and we went away from it in search of another grander kind of happiness which some dreamer – Bacon or another – assured us we should find. We had only to conquer Nature, find out her secrets, make her our obedient slave, then the Earth would be Eden, and every man Adam and every woman Eve. We are still marching bravely on, conquering Nature, but how weary and sad we are getting! The old joy in life and gaiety of heart have vanished, though we do sometimes pause for a few moments in our long forced march to watch the labours of some pale mechanician seeking after perpetual motion and indulge in a little, dry, crackling laugh at his expense.

Here we see how the line from Rousseau to Romanticism runs on into the twentieth century. The themes are familiar: the enervation of the human spirit under the rule of technology and industry; retreat from the town as return to a natural life in which the human spirit is integrated with its environment; the imagining of a lost tribe of humans in the state of nature; a reference to nature's 'children' which implies that in childhood we might approximate to the condition of that lost tribe; critique of the Baconian–Cartesian dream of mastery, together with its politics of oppression (Nature as violated and enslaved female); an implicit condemnation of orthodox religion for its abnegation of the energies of natural life ('pale mechanician' neatly twists a famous phrase in Swinburne's assault on Christianity as extinguisher of the spirit of classical pantheism: 'Thou hast conquered, O pale Galilean; the world has grown grey from Thy breath').

But Hudson stands slightly apart from the mainstream of late Victorian and Edwardian Romanticism by virtue of his familial origins. He spent his childhood on an *estancia* in Argentina. Born in 1841, he only came to England in 1874. His memoir of his Argentinian childhood, possibly his best book, is entitled *Far Away and Long Ago*, while the original title of *The Purple Land* was *The Purple Land that England Lost*. A gringo on the pampas has a very different sense of the relationship between self and environment – a very different 'spiritual geography', to use Hudson's own phrase – from that of a smallholder on the English Downs. Hudson is an intriguing figure because he reverses Darwin's journey, going from Patagonia to southern England. The key word in the passage from *Hampshire Days* is 'strangeness': Hudson felt alienated not just from urban man, but from the tameness of the English pastoral landscape. He writes so well about English rural life because it seems strange to him, because he sees it with the unsentimental eyes of an outsider. He is only at home in a land that is lost. The year after *Green Mansions*, he published a children's story entitled *A Little Boy Lost*, about an orphan who wanders alone through pampas, sierra and rainforest. Such a tale is firmly in the Rousseauesque tradition of narratives concerning children who do not just survive but flourish when they are alone with nature – the tradition which runs from Bernardin de St Pierre's *Paul et Virginie* through Rudyard Kipling's *Jungle Book* and R. M. Ballantyne's *Coral Island*, and which is then unravelled in William Golding's *Lord of the Flies*.

Hudson knew the pampas with the intimacy of a field naturalist, but he also knew that in order to create a *myth* of the return
to nature, he would have to evoke the primeval forest. *Green
Mansions* is, accordingly, set not in the Argentina of his childhood,
but in the Guianan rainforest, known to Hudson from travel
books rather than experience. It begins in reaction against the
Baconian dream of conquering nature so that the earth is again
Eden 'and every man Adam and every woman Eve'. Hudson
believes with Rousseau that we have fallen from the state of
nature. Science will not return us to Eden, conjure back the state
of the prelapsarian Adam and Eve. The protagonist of the novel
is accordingly called Abel. His journey into the rainforest represents the attempt of a man who comes after the fall to return to
Eden by means of a willed primitivism.

In the prologue to the novel, Abel is met by the narrator in
Georgetown; he lives in a shadowy room, harbouring a dark
secret and an urn filled with mysterious ashes. He is Frankenstein
as met by Walton, or the Mariner viewed through the eyes of
the wedding-guest: he has gone outside society, penetrated to the
heart of nature and come back with some terrible knowledge.
There is a structural resemblance to *Heart of Darkness*, published
four years earlier, though with the difference that, unlike Kurtz,
Abel survives to narrate his own story.

Abel's dream has been to visit the 'primitive wilderness' of the
tropical rainforest and to encounter 'its savage inhabitants, with
their ancient customs and character, unadulterated by contact
with Europeans'. In order to get travel papers, he masquerades as
an adventurer in search of knowledge that will be of benefit to
the process of colonization, but in his heart he has no sympathy
for the white man's ambitions. Among the 'degenerate' Indians in
the trading outposts on the edge of the jungle he sees enacted
'the last act in the great American tragedy' – the tragedy, that is,
of domination through alcoholic intoxication.

As Abel penetrates deeper into the forest, he progressively
abandons his European outlook. He gives up first on the idea of
writing a book about his journey (mastery through geographic
narrative), then on the quest for gold which had led Sir Walter
Raleigh on the first English-speaking expedition into the interior

of Guiana. To propitiate a native, he hands over his tinderbox, sign of Promethean fire. Eventually he finds himself alone and without instruments of calculation or domination in the 'wild paradise' of the rainforest itself. Sheltering beneath its leafy canopy, he is enchanted by the grace of monkeys: 'With that luxuriant tropical nature, its green clouds and illusive aerial spaces, full of mystery, they harmonised well in language, appearance, and motions; – mountebank angels, living their fantastic lives far above earth in a half-way heaven of their own.' 'Mountebank angels' and 'half-way heaven' suggest that the path to life reaches backwards to our Darwinian cousins, not upwards in quest of a supposedly transcendent divinity which really resides only in the human breast.

On further acquaintance with a part of the forest which the native inhabitants are afraid to enter, Abel catches a glimpse of a being who seems half-bird and half-girl, who sings a natural language that he cannot understand. He then undergoes his Fall. He speaks of the forest as 'my beloved green mansions'. His claim of ownership, his appropriation of the place as a house (a mansion at that – not merely a humble hut such as that in which Thoreau dwelt for a year in Walden woods), is analogous to the moment of fall into property at the beginning of part two of Rousseau's discourse. Abel then tries to grasp, to possess, the bird-girl who embodies the spirit of the place, with the result that he is instantly bitten by a snake. He runs to get help back at the village, but loses his way and physically falls down a precipice at another edge of the forest. We can hardly miss the lapsarian symbolism. But there is an important variant on the traditional fall narrative. Abel has already tried to kill the snake, and the bird-girl has prevented him; now the snake is protecting the girl. The fall is brought about by the man who comes from the city. The serpent is victim, not perpetrator – D. H. Lawrence, a keen reader of Hudson, undertook a similar revision of tradition in his poem 'Snake'.

Coming round after his Fall, Abel finds himself being tended by an old man who lives on the fringes of the special forest place with his adopted granddaughter, Rima. She is the bird-girl, though beyond the forest she is pale and meek, whereas within its confines she is animated, vibrant, alive and shimmering. Rima is a literal embodiment of the influence of environment on both physique and temperament.

> Have you ever observed a humming-bird moving about in an aërial dance among the flowers – a living prismatic gem that changes its colour with every change of position – how in turning it catches the sunshine on its burnished neck and gorget plumes – green and gold and flame-coloured, the beams changing to visible flakes as they fall, dissolving into nothing, to be succeeded by others and yet others? ... And have you seen this same fairy-like creature suddenly perch itself on a twig, in the shade, its misty wings and fanlike tail folded, the iridescent glory vanished, looking like some common dull-plumaged little bird sitting in a cage? Just so great was the difference in the girl, as I had seen her in the forest and as she now appeared under the smoky roof in the firelight.

Hudson is at his best in this passage, as he plays off live motion against death-like stillness, outdoors against in, natural light against artificial, simultaneously writing with ornithological accuracy about the hummingbird and evoking the symbolic spirit of being-in-the-state-of-nature which is represented by Rima.

Rima is bird and butterfly and leaf and flower and monkey all in one; her voice is the voice not only of bird, but also of insect, of wind and of water. Abel's falling in love with Rima is an allegorical narrative of fallen man's yearning for a reunion with nature. There is an irony here: since nature is represented as female, desire for her is inevitably accompanied by the possibility of sexual possession. In *The Purple Land*, Hudson had written against the urge 'to conquer Nature, find out her secrets', yet here in the very act of returning to nature, in rejection of the Baconian–Cartesian urge, Abel finds himself wishing to penetrate Rima's secrets and in this sense to conquer her. Hudson registers the irony through the effect on Rima of her reciprocal love for Abel: because she has previously lived in oneness with all living things, the act of falling in love with an individual, who is moreover a man unable to speak her natural language, alienates her from herself. She cannot understand her own feelings. We might say: it is all very well for us to love nature, but the idea of nature loving us is incomprehensible. To try to comprehend the idea will be to anthropomorphize nature, and to anthropomorphize nature may be to begin to destroy it (her?). *Green Mansions* turns on a double bind: once Abel has fallen in love with Rima he will always be cut off from his fellow humans in society; meanwhile, when Rima falls in love with Abel she exposes her vulnerability to man.

The encounter with Abel makes Rima conscious of her difference from him: 'She had begun to realise, after knowing me, her isolation and unlikeness to others, and at the same time to dream that all human beings might not be unlike her and unable to understand her mysterious speech and to enter into her thoughts and feelings.' The effect of this fall into a knowledge of difference is that Rima contracts a desire to discover her own kind, to seek the lost tribe of humans-in-the-state-of-nature from which she has sprung. Having dwelt immanently in nature, she has not previously been concerned with history and geography. Now, because of Abel, she undergoes her own fall from natural into historical and geographical identity. Abel takes her to the top of a mountain, where he marks out boundary lines and piles up stones, converting the land into a giant map with which he teaches her the names of places across the continent where she has never been. To tell her about other worlds is to begin to alienate her from her own dwelling.

Among the names, she hears one which brings back dim memories of her childhood. Thus she falls into history. Her quest for origins takes her on a journey away from the sacred forest where she dwells to the place where the old man who brought her up first encountered her injured pregnant mother. On arrival, Rima discovers that the tribe is indeed lost, that her mother was the last survivor. A terrible price is paid for this knowledge: by going on the journey in pursuit of origins, Rima vacates the forest and allows the natives to enter it. Once they have established themselves there, they are in a position to kill her on her return. They do so by burning down a great tree in which, birdlike, she has hidden. Abel returns, his spirit broken; he undergoes purgation and penance in the forest, 'a period of moral insanity' which leads to orgiastic meat-eating and eventually to the destruction of both the environment and the native tribe. Finally, Abel picks out Rima's ashes from the charred remnant of the tree and returns to civilization bearing them in an urn.

The allegorical possibilities are striking. Abel's desire to return to nature has destroyed the very nature he desired. Penetration of the virgin place perforce deprives it of its virginity: in this, Abel's story may be read as a prophetic admonition to ecotourists. All that remains of Rima is a name and a heap of ash in a well-wrought urn marked with a textual inscription. In Spanish, the language of Hudson's lost childhood, Rima is 'rhyme' or 'poetry'. Allegorically, then: poetry, or more specifically the kind of narrative represented by *Green Mansions: A Romance of the Tropical Forest*, is all that remains of the spirit of nature. The language in which Rima communicates with birds cannot be communicated to the reader; instead, Rima is caged into language. The language of art is a sign of our distance from nature, even as it is a seeking after lost nature: poets want to sing like nightingales or skylarks because they know that they do not have the freedom of flight and the pure expressive capacity of real birds. *Green Mansions* is an elegy for the lost forest inscribed on the pulped cellulose fibres of fallen trees.

*

Where else will you find Rima now? Not on a tour to the diminished and still diminishing rainforest of South America. No, you will find her sculpted in inorganic material – Portland stone – by Jacob Epstein on a memorial to the life of W. H. Hudson (plate 1).

Of all the arts, sculpture is the one in which the artist works over his raw material most physically. Epstein conquers his slab of stone, transforms nature into art. The 'Rima' bas-relief is a great but deeply alienated work. To adapt Marshal Bosquet's remark about the charge of the Light Brigade, '*C'est magnifique, mais ce n'est pas la nature.*' Epstein's *Rima* is alienated not least in her environment. The monument stands far away from the Patagonia where HMS *Beagle* took Darwin and where Hudson spent the idle days of his youth. It is in a highly artificial green mansion, a space intensively managed so as to function as the lung of the metropolis: you will find Rima by an ornamental pond in London's Hyde Park.

Whereas 'primitive' communities in the state of nature made sense of their place in the world by means of animistic stories concerning gods and nature-spirits, we have only *representations* of nature. To Western man, the virgin rainforest is a powerful *idea*. The reality is that the moment we go there – in a jet plane, say, or with a television camera – it it is no longer virgin. As will be shown in my analysis of the 'picturesque' in chapter five, when we go out from the city to the country our response to what we see is shaped by cultural conditions.

Hudson's fiction of Rima and Epstein's image of her fill the gap left by what Adorno and Horkheimer, in an essay I will discuss in the next chapter, call 'the extirpation of animism'. The city park is a place of recreation because it is an artificial re-creation of the state of nature. Hyde Park was laid out in the seventeenth century for the recreational benefit of well-to-do Londoners. The continuous expansion of London over the centuries has been the surest sign of the development of Britain from a predominantly agricultural to a mercantile, then an industrial and now a post-industrial economy. Social and economic change have meant that to an increasingly high proportion of the population, the green world has become Other. The state of nature is the repressed which returns in the form of such fantasies as nostalgia for 'merrie England' and the desire to retire to a cottage with roses round the door. The city park and the garden suburb are the best that politicians and town planners can do towards realizing the fantasy.

In the nineteenth century, Frederick Law Olmsted began his 'Conception of the Plan' for the design of New York's Central Park with the proposition that 'The Park throughout is a single work of art, and as such subject to the primary law of every work of art, namely, that it shall be framed upon a single, noble motive'. Olmsted's noble motive was the preservation of a green space in the centre of what was becoming one of the most densely populated cities in the world. Every New Yorker must thank him for it. The park answers to a psychological need in all of us. Because Central Park is a 'work of art', it is a *representation* of the state of nature. *But that does not make it unreal*: it is a representation which we may experience, a re-creational space in which we can walk and breathe and play. In the remainder of this book, I want to consider the possibility that other works of art, mostly poems, may create for the mind the same kind of re-creational space that a park creates for the body.

According to Starobinski, Rousseau argued that civilization veils the transparency of nature; I want to ask if poetry can unveil that transparency. I think of the book as an 'experiment in ecopoetics'. The experiment is this: to see what happens when we regard poems as imaginary parks in which we may breathe an air that is not toxic and accommodate ourselves to a mode of dwelling that is not alienated.

At the same time, it is necessary to recognize that experiments tend to be conducted in artificial conditions. The imagination is a perfect laboratory, cleansed of the contaminations of history. The true poet has to be simultaneously a geographer of the imagination and a historian of the alienations and desecrations that follow the march of 'civilization'. *Green Mansions* was written when the British empire was at its zenith. Even as it laments the death of Rima, it partakes of the myth of superiority which licenses the genocide of the native tribe. A century on, we cannot escape the melancholy knowledge that ecocide and genocide go hand in hand.

If in our imagination we are to follow W. H. Hudson back into the tropical forest, we should perhaps also take with us the ironic self-awareness of a more modern poet, Elizabeth Bishop (1911–79). Like Hudson, she knew South America. From 1951 to 1974 she spent much of her time in Brazil.

Bishop begins her poem 'Brazil, January 1, 1502' with the timeless beauty of the rainforest. Each new year for five hundred years, the forest is the same. The precise botanic eye of the poet picks out each part, both the exquisite small things and the startling large ones, whilst simultaneously framing the whole as if Nature were an embroiderer:

> Januaries, Nature greets our eyes
> exactly as she must have greeted theirs:

every square inch filling in with foliage—
big leaves, little leaves, and giant leaves,
blue, blue-green, and olive,
with occasional lighter veins and edges,
on a satin underleaf turned over;
monster ferns
in silver-gray relief,
and flowers, too, like giant water lilies
up in the air—up, rather, in the leaves—
purple, yellow, two yellows, pink,
rust red and greenish white;
solid but airy; fresh as if just finished
and taken off the frame.

As if Nature were an embroiderer. Bishop usually prefers simile to metaphor because the words 'like' and 'as' carry with them the knowledge of 'unlike', of difference. Typically, Bishop will compare something in nature with something man-made. In her poem 'Florida', for instance, green hummocks sprouting grass are like 'ancient cannon-balls' and long thin wading birds are 'S-shaped'. Bishop's imagery always respects nature as it is and for itself, while at the same time recognizing that we can only understand nature by way of those distinctively human categories, history (the cannonball) and language (the shape of the letter 'S'). Thus although the biological life of the rainforest endures on a timescale far beyond the human, once the poet addresses herself to the place, the environment can no longer be 'virgin' or unaffected by the human. In order to write about a place, we have to find a name for it. On 1 January 1502, the Portuguese sailed into a bay on the eastern coast of South America, thought it was a river and named it from the date: River of January, Río de Janeiro. From that moment on, Brazil was sucked into European history.

Furthermore, the Westerner's perception of the place cannot but be influenced by Western aesthetics. Bishop's poem carries as epigraph some lines from Kenneth Clark's book *Landscape into Art*, a study of how the artistic representation of nature is always just that – a representation, part of the meaning of which is prior representations and symbolic formations. 'Embroidered nature

... tapestried landscape' runs the epigraph, alluding to a section in Clark's book concerning stylized representations of the 'hortus conclusus', the paradisal enclosed garden of medieval iconography.

'Brazil, January 1, 1502' ends with the 'fall' into empire. The European male introduces 'a brand-new pleasure' to the rainforest: the desire to possess. Brazil becomes the 'hortus conclusus' with sexual pleasure added on:

> Just so the Christians, hard as nails,
> tiny as nails, and glinting,
> in creaking armor, came and found it all,
> not unfamiliar:
> no lovers' walks, no bowers,
> no cherries to be picked, no lute music,
> but corresponding, nevertheless,
> to an old dream of wealth and luxury
> already out of style when they left home—
> wealth, plus a brand-new pleasure.
> Directly after Mass, humming perhaps
> *L'Homme armé* or some such tune,
> they ripped away into the hanging fabric,
> each out to catch an Indian for himself—
> those maddening little women who kept calling,
> calling to each other (or had the birds waked up?)
> and retreating, always retreating, behind it.

In the stanza's final image, the rape of the native women and the rape of the virgin forest are brought together by means of a direct allusion to Rima. At the age of seventeen, Bishop wrote of Hudson's *Green Mansions*:

> I wished that the book had been twice as long when I put it down, and I was filled with longing to leave for South America immediately and search for those forgotten bird-people. It seemed still unfinished, even more than that delightful region in my mind I told about, and I felt sure that if I could only find the right spot, the right sun-lighted arches of the trees, and wait patiently, I would see a bright-haired figure slipping

away among the moving shadows, and hear the sweet, light
music of Rima's voice.

Lorrie Goldensohn quotes this passage in her marvellous study of
Bishop, and then reports that on sailing to Brazil on the SS
Bowplate the poet and a Miss Breen 'confess that the same
romantic images have drawn them to the tropics, an early and
unforgettable part of which for each woman has been her early
reading of W. H. Hudson'. (Miss Breen, 'a retired police lieuten-
ant, six feet tall', puts in an appearance in 'Arrival at Santos', a
poem of disembarkation which precedes 'Brazil, January 1, 1502'
at the beginning of Bishop's collection, *Questions of Travel*.)

'Just so the Christians': Bishop knows that as a visitor to
Brazil, not a native inhabitant of the forest, she is in the position
of the colonizer, not of Rima. Elizabeth Bishop shared Friedrich
Schiller's knowledge that Nature is calling to us in a voice like
that of our primal mother. But together with that Romantic
knowledge she carried a wry, ironic, modern recognition that in
the very act of answering the call we penetrate the veil of Nature's
purity. In so doing, we force Rima to retreat, always to retreat
further and further into an ever-diminishing unknown. When
there is no more unknown, when the last of the tropical rainforest
has been cleared, it may then be only in art – in poetry – that we
will be able to hear the cry of Rima.

3

A Voice for Ariel

Meanwhile, man, precisely as the one so threatened, exalts himself and postures as lord of the earth. In this way the illusion comes to prevail that everything man encounters exists only insofar as it is his construct. This illusion gives rise in turn to one final illusion: it seems as though man everywhere and always encounters only himself.

> (Martin Heidegger,
> 'The Question concerning Technology')

THE FINELY PRINTED text of *The Tempest* holds prime position in the first Folio edition of William Shakespeare's plays. Whether by chance or choice, Shakespeare's friends and fellow-actors who prepared the Folio for the press gave pride of place to the dramatist's final solo-authored work. It is fitting: *The Tempest* does seem to be a summation of Shakespeare's art and his thinking about art.

He sets a plot in motion, even making it conform to the classical unity of time. He conjures up a storm. He uses Ariel and company as agents in a drama over which he watches. He stages a masque. At the end of the play, he renounces his art and goes into retirement. These are all things which may be said of both Prospero and the author of *The Tempest*. So it is that there is a long tradition in which Prospero is read as an allegorical representation of his own creator. Prospero: 'the very Shakspeare himself, as it were, of the tempest', remarked Samuel Taylor Coleridge in one of his lectures.

When we speak of a 'Romantic', such as Coleridge, we often mean someone who regards the creative artist as a person of peculiar – quasi-magical, quasi-divine – power. The Romantic poet conjures something out of nothing through the sheer force of his imagination. Thus Kubla Khan is to Coleridge as Prospero is to Shakespeare.

Shakespeare's *The Tempest* and Coleridge's 'Kubla Khan' confront us with one of the central questions of aesthetics: do we admire the play or the poem for its familiarity or its strangeness, for its truth to nature or its autonomy as a kind of 'other world'? A work of art may be admired because it answers to a prior sense of how the world is. Prospero, Kubla: yes, their behaviour conforms to our expectation of how a powerful man will show off his power. Alternatively, the work of art may be admired because it is beautiful, exotic, unknown: how lovely to imagine a sunny pleasure-dome with caves of ice or an isle that is full of noises, sounds and sweet airs that give delight and hurt not.

For most readers and spectators, the admiration of a play or poem is compounded of both responses. The first, with its emphasis on truth to nature and experience, may be described as the mimetic approach. The second, with its emphasis on difference from nature and experience, may be described as the imaginative. The mimetic approach has a way of sliding into a didactic one. In place of the criterion of truthfulness to *the world as it is* comes that of truthfulness to *the world as it ought to be*. People of a didactic disposition will praise or blame a work according to some value-system: does it conform to what we believe about the desirability of, say, divine justice or sexual equality? Those for whom art is more playground than classroom will not be interested in such questions. Revelling in the imaginative approach, they will say, 'I am not interested in the religious position or the implicit gender and race politics of Shakespeare and Coleridge; I like these works because of their strangeness, *The Tempest* because personally I have never heard a spirit in the air and "Kubla Khan" because my experience of ice is that it melts when exposed to sunlight.'

Since the time of Coleridge, works of imagination have, for good or ill, elicited the attentions of a class of professional readers – call them critics, call them academics. Among these professionals, the relative sway of the mimetic, the didactic and the imaginative has fluctuated. In the Victorian period, Matthew Arnold spoke for an elevated notion of the mimetic: 'to see the object as in itself it really is'. The imaginative probably reached its zenith at the end of the nineteenth century, with the cry 'art for art's sake' and Oscar Wilde's desire 'to see the object as in itself it really is not'. At the end of the twentieth, for all the playfulness of 'deconstructionist' modes of reading, the didactic held the ascendancy. A kind of millennial puritanism took grip, and what were once known as 'works of literature' became 'texts' which had to be 'interrogated' with regard to their allegiances of gender, race and class.

The New Didacticism, as it might be called, reversed an older moralism. Where previous generations had found a humanistic ideal in what was regarded as the wisdom of Prospero, the New Didacticism began from a critique of humanism and all its works. Traditional 'liberal humanist' criticism read from the point of view of Prospero, who uses his magical power in order to control the forces of nature (the spirits of the isle) so that they may assist him in a series of acts of moral education. Postmodern criticism, perhaps beginning from Walter Benjamin's dictum that there is no document of civilization which is not also a document of barbarism, drew attention to the acts of oppression involved along the way. The New Didacticism read *The Tempest* from a different point of view: that of Caliban. The play came to be regarded as either an embodiment of, or a meditation upon, the poetics of imperialism. Meanwhile, an alternative strand of the New Didacticism read from the point of view of Caliban's mother, Sycorax: it was the patriarchy which called Prospero a sage and his magic white, Sycorax a witch and her powers black.

The origins of the New Didacticism may be traced back to the social and cultural upheaval of the 1960s. After the collapse of Communism in eastern Europe at the end of the 1980s, it became apparent that the enduring influence of the earlier decade of ferment was to be found not in high politics, but in cultural attitudes. The radicalism of the 1960s failed in so far as there were not many Marxist or Maoist revolutions in sight as the twentieth century came to its end, but succeeded in so far as racism and sexism became unacceptable in the more advanced quarters of Western society. The New Didacticism, otherwise known as post-colonialism and feminism, was the intellectual arm of this revolution of social values.

Early in his book *We Have Never Been Modern*, the historian of science Bruno Latour reflects on the fact that 1989 was marked not only by the fall of the Berlin Wall, but also by the first international conferences (in Paris, Amsterdam and London) on the global state of the planet. The West began to crow that 'we have won the Cold War'. But it also had to admit that 'we have invented ecocides as well as large-scale famine':

> The perfect symmetry between the dismantling of the Wall of shame and the end of limitless Nature is invisible only to the rich Western democracies. The various manifestations of socialism destroyed both their peoples and their ecosystems, whereas the powers of the North and the West have been able to save their peoples and some of their countrysides by destroying the rest of the world and reducing its peoples to abject poverty. Hence a double tragedy: the former socialist societies think they can solve both their problems by imitating the West; the West thinks it is the sole possessor of the clever trick that will allow it to keep on winning indefinitely, whereas it has perhaps already lost everything.

Ecocide: the systematic destruction of dwelling places in the name of progress, of the globalization of capital. If there is such a thing as a historical rupture, a moment of what Michel Foucault calls 'epistemic change', then surely one occurred in 1989. Suppose that Latour is correct about the hidden symmetry of the rupture: should we not then be rereading the literature of the past in the light of this bringing together of politics and ecocide, as feminists and post-colonialists have reread and revised the literary canon in the light of their concerns?

After all, besides feminism and anti-racism, a third form of 1960s radicalism also survived in the wider culture: environmentalism. Indeed, by the end of the century more people in the West were involved in environmental action and protest of various kinds, from local planning disputes to the international issues raised by such pressure groups as Greenpeace, than in any other form of political activism. As feminist literary theory is to women's rights and post-colonial reading to anti-racism, so one would have expected there to be a flourishing literary ecocriticism to go with the environmental movement. But, so far as I am aware, only a single book of explicitly ecological literary criticism was published during the 1980s, the growth decade of feminist and post-colonial criticism. And even through the nineties there were dozens of works of feminism and studies of the representation of ethnicity for any one book which addressed literature in relation to questions of ecology and environment.

Modern environmental consciousness is traditionally dated from the publication in 1962 of Rachel Carson's indictment of the pesticide DDT, *Silent Spring*. The title of that book is a reminder of political ecology's dependence on literary imagery: it is an allusion to the absence of birdsong imagined in John Keats's poem 'La belle dame sans merci'. So why is it that ecological literary criticism has developed so much more slowly than other ways of reading forged in the smithy of sixties radicalism?

Much of the work in feminist and post-colonial theory has been done by people who are beneficiaries of the cultural revolutions of which that work is a part: women and people of colour. There is even a certain suspicion of those who take it upon themselves to 'speak on behalf of the Other', as the jargon puts it, namely male feminists and white analysts of race. The potential beneficiaries of an acknowledgement of the rights of nature – the land, the ocean, the polluted air, the endangered species – cannot, however, speak for themselves. The ecocritic has no choice but to speak on behalf of the Other. The ecocritical project always involves *speaking for* its subject rather than *speaking as* its subject: a critic may speak as a woman or as a person of colour, but cannot speak as a tree. Readers of colour find it easy to project themselves into Caliban, women readers into Sycorax or Miranda. But it is not easy for any of us to project ourselves into a character who is specifically non-human and is only gendered in a shadowy way. Perhaps that is why postmodern criticism has been almost silent about Ariel.

But the problem goes deeper than this. Literary discourse takes place in the realm of culture, which, as we have seen, is by definition in opposition to the realm of nature. A central question in environmental ethics is whether to regard humankind as part of nature or apart from nature. It is the task of literary ecocriticism to address a local version of that question: what is the place of creative imagining and writing in the complex set of relationships between humankind and environment, between mind and world, between thinking, being and dwelling?

A very central place, the Romantic tradition tells us. In his essay 'On Naïve and Sentimental Poetry' Friedrich Schiller suggested that as soon as we experience the pressure of civilization, we yearn nostalgically for the nature we have lost. Where may 'she' be rediscovered? *'Im fernen Auslande der Kunst'*, says Schiller, in the distant foreign land of art, we hear the tender voice of our lost mother nature. Art is the place of exile where we grieve for our lost home upon the earth.

For Schiller, the modern poem is perforce either an elegy for a lost unity with nature or a satire on 'the contradiction between actuality and the ideal'. Ultimately, elegy and satire are but two modes of expressing the same 'alienation from nature'. 'The poets are everywhere, by their very definition, the *guardians* of nature,' Schiller wrote in 1795. 'They will either *be* nature, or they will *seek* lost nature.'

The essay 'On Naïve and Sentimental Poetry' reinflects Rousseau's story of our fall away from nature. It argues that the ancient poet and the child are 'naive' in the positive sense that they don't think about their relationship with their environment: they are part of nature. But the moderns have fallen into self-consciousness. That we have feelings (sentiments) about nature demonstrates that we are separated from it (her?). Our self-consciousness is a product of our striving to transcend the constraints of nature (instinct, biology, mortality) and, as such, it is a sign of 'progress'. But at the same time, our longing for nature is like an invalid's longing for health.

According to Schiller, neither an ancient poet nor a modern child would understand the questions 'What do you feel about this landscape? Do you find it beautiful?' Categories such as 'feeling about' and 'beautiful', even the framing of environment into 'landscape', are themselves symptoms of the loss of integration with nature. What is vulgarly called 'nature poetry' is usually consumed in a spirit of nostalgia. It evokes a lost pre-urban world, a lost childhood, a lost Eden. The mode of pastoral has always been closely linked to the mood of elegy. The idealized pastoral realm of 'Arcadia' was invented two thousand years ago by Virgil, the supreme poet of urbanity, of the city, of Roman imperialism. You only need Arcadia when your reality is Rome.

For Schiller, the exemplary poetic genre was the *idyll*, where there is no restless division between internal and external worlds, between self and environment:

> The poetic representation of innocent and contented mankind is the universal concept of this type of poetic composition. Since this innocence and this contentedness appear incompatible with the artificial conditions of society at large and with a certain degree of education and refinement, the poets have removed the location of idyll from the tumult of everyday life into the simple pastoral state and assigned its period before the *beginnings of civilisation* in the childlike age of man.

The myth of the lost idyll is powerful because it seems to work both historically and psychologically. We look at shepherds or Native Americans or Australian Aboriginals and idealize them, *idyllize* them, into a 'state of nature' which we have lost. We lament our own alienation and tell ourselves that once there was a time when all of humankind lived in their happy state. Historically, we assign that state to a 'period before the beginnings of civilization'. We find support for this primitivism when we remember that the root of the word 'civilization' is Latin *civilis*, 'of the city'.

Schiller calls the pre-civilizational idyll the 'childlike' age of man. Psychologically, we associate the 'state of nature' with infancy. According to William Wordsworth's theory of child development in *The Prelude*, the baby first gains security from the mother's breast and 'gather[s] passion from his mother's eye'. Then, gradually,

> Along his infant veins are interfused
> The gravitation and the filial bond
> Of Nature that connect him with the world.

'Nature' here is a second mother, with whom we have a 'filial bond'. So it is that when Wordsworth writes a few lines later 'I held mute dialogues with my mother's heart', the mother is both

'Nature' and the woman who bore him. 'Ecofeminism' is that discourse which addresses the causes and effects, the strengths and the dangers, of the traditional personification of Nature as mother.

The adult Wordsworth invested his strongest poetic energy in those moments of reverie when he held 'mute dialogue' with nature. Quintessential Wordsworthian *poiesis* occurs in the moment of silence when the owls do not respond to the boy's mimic hooting. In the mute dialogue, the poet imagines himself at one with nature again. That which was lost has been found. The poet *is* nature. But a mute dialogue is an oxymoron. Once the *logos*, language, is introduced, the gap is opened again. The attempt to reanimate the moment linguistically is, in Schiller's term, a seeking after lost nature. The writer's image of nature is always refracted through language: Ariel only speaks when brought into the service of Prospero. 'What is the pastoral convention, then, if not the eternal separation between the mind that distinguishes, negates, legislates, and the originary simplicity of the natural?' asked one of the pre-eminent literary theorists of the late twentieth century, Paul de Man: 'There is no doubt that the pastoral theme is, in fact, the only poetic theme, that it is poetry itself.'

If de Man is correct, essential ecocriticism may not be a form of political criticism in the manner of feminism and post-colonialism. No one could say that the question concerning gender or the question concerning race *is poetry itself*. Ecocriticism does have a contribution to make to green politics, as post-colonial and feminist reading contribute to race and gender politics, but its true importance may be more phenomenological than political. If that is the case, 'ecopoetics' will be a more helpful denomination than 'ecocriticism'. Ecopoetics asks in what respects a poem may be a making (Greek *poiesis*) of the dwelling-place – the prefix eco- is derived from Greek *oikos*, 'the home or place of dwelling'. According to this definition, poetry will not necessarily be synonymous with verse: the poeming of the dwelling is not inherently dependent on metrical form. However, the rhythmic, syntactic and linguistic intensifications that are characteristic of verse-writing frequently give a peculiar force to the *poiesis*: it could be that *poiesis* in the sense of verse-making is language's most direct path of return to the *oikos*, the place of dwelling, because metre itself – a quiet but persistent music, a recurring cycle, a heartbeat – is an answering to nature's own rhythms, an echoing of the song of the earth itself.

In Greek tragedy, the demands of the *oikos*, the household, the domestic space which is conventionally seen as woman's domain, frequently clash with the necessities of the *polis*, the public place of governance and social relations. When Aristotle said that man is a political animal, he meant that we have a tendency to gather into groups and eventually to build cities. Our word 'political' derives from *polis*, the Greek word for the city-state. Once we have built our cities, once we have fallen into the political, nature perforce becomes the object of our politics. For this reason, ecopoetics finds itself pulled from the phenomenological to the political, drawn towards questions concerning gender, race and power. Why is Nature gendered as female? Is it a coincidence that imperialism has always led to environmental degradation? What is the relationship between political 'progress' and attitudes to nature?

'The Concept of Enlightenment' is instructive here. In a celebrated essay with this title, Theodor Adorno and Max Hork-heimer made a number of suggestive connections. Enlightenment means progressive thought. Its ambition has been to free human beings from superstition and fear. By disabusing mankind of the superstitious illusion that kings sit on the throne by divine right, Enlightenment prepares the way for democratic revolution and the transfer of sovereignty to the people. 'The program of the Enlightenment was the disenchantment of the world; the disso-lution of myths and the substitution of knowledge for fancy.' The key formula for the successful running of the programme was that of Francis Bacon, whom Voltaire (high priest of Enlightenment) called 'the father of experimental philosophy'. Bacon's formula was 'knowledge is power':

> Despite his lack of mathematics, Bacon's view was appropriate
> to the scientific attitude that prevailed after him. The concor-
> dance between the mind of man and the nature of things that

he had in mind is patriarchal: the human mind, which over-
comes superstition, is to hold sway over a disenchanted
nature. Knowledge, which is power, knows no obstacles:
neither in the enslavement of men nor in compliance with the
world's rulers. As with all the ends of bourgeois economy in
the factory and on the battlefield, origin is no bar to the
dictates of the entrepreneurs: kings, no less directly than
businessmen, control technology; it is as democratic as the
economic system with which it is bound up. Technology is
the essence of this knowledge. It does not work by concepts
and images, by the fortunate insight, but refers to method,
the exploitation of others' work, and capital.

This, for Adorno and Horkheimer, is the 'dialectic' of Enlightenment: its programme is liberation, its effect is enslavement.
Technology is the instrument which enslaves nature and exploits
the masses. *Dialectic of Enlightenment* was written during the
Second World War: on battlefields around the world and in the
concentration camps of eastern Europe, technology knew no
obstacles. And it was written in the place that is most 'artificial',
most alienated from nature: Los Angeles, the city that was once a
desert, the city of the automobile. For Adorno and Horkheimer,
writes the cultural geographer Mike Davis, Los Angeles was 'the
crystal ball of capitalism's future' – 'confronted with this future,
they experienced all the more painfully the death agony of
Enlightenment Europe.'

In a groundbreaking study of the dialectical play of technology
and the pastoral ideal in the cultural values of the United States,
the critic Leo Marx read Shakespeare's *Tempest* as 'a prologue to
American literature' – its topography 'anticipates the moral geography of the American imagination'. But there is a larger sense in
which *The Tempest* is a prologue to the whole thrust of technological modernity. Though exiled from city to island, Shakespeare's
Prospero is the prototype of Enlightenment Man.

In his *Magnalia Naturæ*, Bacon proposed that the new philosophy would give man the power to raise storms, control the
seasons and hasten the harvest; by studying nature, one could
come to understand it and take control of its forces. Shakespeare's
play may be read as an allegorical anticipation of the project of

mastery which came to be called Baconian method and then Enlightenment. Prospero's magic is a form of technology, used to harness the powers of nature, which are dramatized in the figures of Ariel and fellow-spirits. Prospero's explicit programme is enlightened and humanistic: he wishes to free his antagonists into self-knowledge. But his method is the exploitation of the work of others, Ariel and Caliban. 'Men pay for the increase of their power with alienation from that over which they exercise their power,' write Adorno and Horkheimer. 'Enlightenment behaves towards things as a dictator toward men. He knows them in so far as he can manipulate them.' Caliban initially welcomes Prospero to the island, but Prospero's assumption of power over him leads to alienation between them. Prospero buys Ariel's gratitude by freeing the spirit from the old enchantment of Sycorax, but the freedom quickly proves itself a new form of servitude, bringing its own alienation. Prospero can only acknowledge his *love* for Ariel and company after he has finished using their energetic labour and natural capital. Ariel will only become truly free after all the humans have left the island.

The ecological form of the dialectic of Enlightenment is this: Enlightenment's instrumentalization of nature frees mankind from the tyranny of nature (disease, famine), but its disenchantment of nature licenses the destruction of nature and hence of mankind. 'Men have always had to choose between their subjection to nature or the subjection of nature to the Self.' But: the further technology advances, the closer this choice comes to a crisis.

That crisis is as likely to be spiritual as material. 'The disenchantment of the world is the extirpation of animism. . . . Animism spiritualized the object, whereas industrialism objectifies the spirits of men.' Enlightenment's antagonist in this respect is Romanticism, which is a protest against the objectification of the spirit. For Adorno and Horkheimer, poetry is the only means of re-enchanting the world: 'With the progress of enlightenment, only authentic works of art were able to avoid the mere imitation of that which already is. . . . The work of art still has something in common with enchantment: it posits its own, self-enclosed area, which is withdrawn from the context of profane existence, and in which special laws apply.' That self-enclosed area might be called Ariel's Island or Kubla's Garden. To go there in imagination is to rediscover enchantment without having to pay the price of destroying the ecosystems of real islands, as one would by, say, colonizing the Caribbean – whether as an eighteenth-century plantation owner or a twentieth-century package tour operator.

*

In his *Discours sur le colonialisme* of 1955, Aimé Césaire, the Caribbean theorist of *négritude*, warned against the ecological consequences of the First World's destruction of the Third: 'I am talking . . . about food crops destroyed, malnutrition permanently introduced, agricultural development oriented solely toward the benefit of the metropolitan countries, about the looting of products, the looting of raw materials'. The Senegalese writer Léopold Senghor defined *négritude* as 'the sum total of the values of the civilization of the African world'. *Négritude* reclaims and celebrates that 'Otherness' which whites have for centuries projected onto blacks. For Senghor, whilst European values divide and sterilize, African ones unify and make fertile through 'communal warmth, the image-symbol and the cosmic rhythm'. The critic Lawrence Buell understands *négritude* as a form of modern pastoral or, to use Schiller's term, *idyll*: 'It evokes a traditional, holistic, nonmetropolitan, nature-attuned myth of Africanity in reaction to and critique of a more urbanized, "artificial" European order – and evokes it, furthermore, from the standpoint of one who has experienced exile and wishes to return.' The language of *négritude*, then, presents us with one possible modern form of ecopoetics.

An ecopoetic reading of *The Tempest* might therefore take the form of a rewriting of the play for the theatre of *négritude*. In 1968, Césaire undertook such a rewriting and called it *Une tempête*. Not *the* tempest of Shakespeare, but *a* tempest for our time. For Césaire, 'Caliban is the man who is still close to his beginnings, whose link with the natural world has not yet been broken'. In *Une tempête*, Prospero is 'l'anti-Nature', whilst Caliban is at one with nature through his hearing of the voices of the isle.

In Césaire's reimagining of Shakespeare, Prospero stays put on the island in a desperate desire to ensure that it remains 'civilized'. But once he has let go of his power over Ariel, he cannot succeed in his endeavour. He finds the island being overrun with 'unclean nature', with peccaries, wild boars and – his particular bugbear – grinning opossums. Caliban, meanwhile, is released: the final words of the play are his cries of freedom, 'heard from afar among the noise of the surf and the twittering of birds'. *Une tempête* is more than an assimilation of Shakespeare into the discourse of *négritude*: it is also a starting-point for an imagining of the voice not of a nation or a race, but of the ravaged earth itself.

Contemporaneously with Césaire's *Une tempête*, the English-speaking Caribbean writer Edward Kamau Brathwaite published a poem called 'Caliban'. An analysis of it will reveal the rich potential, but also the pitfalls, of an ecopoetics that grows out of post-colonial consciousness.

Brathwaite, who was born in Barbados in 1930, went to university at Cambridge and was published by Oxford. His work is written in a distinctively Caribbean voice, but it reconfigures rather than entirely rejects the 'high' English cultural tradition that is epitomized by Oxbridge. Unlike certain younger black anglophone poets of Caribbean origin, such as Michael Smith and Linton Kwesi Johnson, whose work relies entirely on the oral and vernacular traditions of reggae and rap, Brathwaite moves between jazz or folk rhythms on the one hand and 'traditional' allusion and diction on the other. His work thus enacts a passage between the old world and the new; his own passage into the literary tradition is a sometimes liberated, sometimes uneasy, reversal of the middle passage of his forebears into slavery.

The three volumes of Brathwaite's 'New World Trilogy' are called *Rights of Passage* (1967), *Masks* (1968) and *Islands* (1969). They are triangulated upon the Atlantic slave trade: in both style and reference they move between England, Africa and the Caribbean. The overall structure of the trilogy proposes that after the passage to slavery in the plantations, it becomes essential for the black to wear masks. To begin with, he or she will inherit alienated Western man's mask-making, inauthentic and associated with social roles (the black personae such as Uncle Tom being subservient). But by following the path of *négritude* and making the passage in reverse, returning to Africa and recovering its traditions – the animism, the rituals and the rhythms of the Ashanti nation – a more creative, spiritual use of masks can emerge. The mask becomes that of the god. It is then possible to re-enchant the islands of the Antilles, to make them a place of grace and beauty, not of oppression.

The classic literary-dramatic role for Brathwaite, as for Césaire, is Caliban. His poem of this title occupies a pivotal position in the collection *Islands*, which itself works through a development similar to that of the trilogy as a whole – its five sections are entitled New World, Limbo, Rebellion, Possession and Beginning. 'Caliban' is in the middle of Limbo, but within the poem 'limbo' brings a glimpse of freedom.

This description of *Islands* is misleading, insofar as it implies a sequential, historical narrative. Part of Brathwaite's project is to collapse different historical moments, to read the present by making the past simultaneous with it:

> It was December second, nineteen fifty-six.
> It was the first of August eighteen thirty-eight.
> It was the twelfth October fourteen ninety-two.
>
> How many bangs how many revolutions?

The poem begins in Castro's Havana, but it views modern Caribbean history through the longer perspective that reaches back via the beginnings of the Cuban revolution and the nineteenth-century abolition of slavery to Columbus's first sighting of land on his voyage in 1492. The opening stanza of 'Caliban' holds together prophets past and present. It is written in the historian's knowledge that everything is already known, but is always having to be learned again:

> Ninety-five per cent of my people poor
> ninety-five per cent of my people black
> ninety-five per cent of my people dead
> you have heard it all before O Leviticus O Jeremiah
>   O Jean-Paul Sartre

Sartre is there because he wrote the preface to Frantz Fanon's *Wretched of the Earth*, one of the foundation texts of the racial liberation movement, but the voice who is speaking these lines is not that of the European prophet. The latter's empathetic voicing with the wretched could not but itself be a form of colonialism, of Prospering – I, Jean-Paul Sartre, great white French intellectual, speak with and hence for the Other. But when Brathwaite replies, the white man is not the subject: he is addressed with an 'O', he becomes the Other. This change from object to subject is crucial to the creative renewal of the once oppressed which has occurred in post-colonial literatures.

When it is Caliban who 'writes back', as in this poem, the voice is multiple. 'Caliban', after all, is the creation of another great white European. The Cuban revolutionary writer Roberto Fernández Retamar argued that the position of Caliban is the only available one for the 'new world' writer: he has no choice but to use the tool – the language – bequeathed to him by Prospero. At school in Barbados, Brathwaite had to read Shakespeare, Jane Austen and George Eliot: 'British literature and literary forms, the models which had very little to do, really, with the environment and the reality of non-Europe'. He seized on Caliban because Caliban *could* be read as having a great deal to do with his own environment and reality, because he found in Caliban a prophecy of his own historical situation. It is a usable prophecy exactly because – unlike Sartre's – it is not directly couched as such. There is a certain scepticism in the attitude to Jean-Paul Sartre since he comes, as Retamar puts it, from the 'elsewhere' of the European metropolis, 'the colonizing centers, whose "right wings" have exploited us and whose supposed "left wings" have pretended and continue to pretend to guide us with pious solicitude'. It is different with Shakespeare. Because of what John Keats called his negative capability, because he was not trying to guide Retamar's and Brathwaite's 'us' with pious solicitude, they have no compunction about adopting one of his voices.

The process of writing back necessitates the creation of a new style, and here too Caliban can help. Brathwaite says of the English poetic mainstream: 'the pentameter remained, and it carries with it a certain kind of experience, which is not the experience of a hurricane. The hurricane does not roar in pentameters. And that's the problem: how do you get a rhythm which approximates the *natural* experience, the *environmental* experience?' The answer is in *'nation language*, which is the kind of English spoken by the people who were brought to the Caribbean, not the official English now, but the language of slaves and labourers'. The language, that is to say, which binds, indeed works to create, the black nation. This language and this nation initially cannot help but be parasitic upon the colonizing language and nation, as Caliban is upon Prospero, yet as they develop they take on their own identity, their own freedom.

How does nation language sound? It is 'the *submerged* area of that dialect which is much more closely allied to the African aspect of experience in the Caribbean. It may be in English: but often it is an English which is like a howl, or a shout or a machine-gun or the wind or a wave.' Many of Brathwaite's poems move between the voices of the English tradition and of nation. In his lecture *History of the Voice*, from which I have been quoting this account of nation language, Brathwaite cites John Figueroa's 'Portrait of a Woman' as an example of double-voiced West Indian poetry: 'the "classical", even *Prosperian* element – the *most* part of the poem – is in English. The marginal bit, that of the voice and status of the domestic helper, Caliban's sister, is in a nation but a nation still sticky and wet with the interposition of dialect.' Section one of 'Caliban' is in traditional English: 'Ninety-five per cent of my people poor' is a pentameter, albeit one in which the stress patterns are already straining for release from the constraints of the iamb. But in sections two and three Caliban speaks in the rhythms of nation:

> Ban
> Ban
> Cal-
> iban
> like to play
> pan
> at the Car-
> nival;

> pran-
> cing up to the lim-
> bo silence
> down
> down
> down
> so the god won't drown
> him
> down
> down
> down
> to the is-
> land town

The allusion here is to 'Ban, Ban, Ca-Caliban' in *The Tempest*'s song of rebellion, 'No more dams I'll make for fish'. Caliban expresses his freedom by deconstructing the name that Prospero has given him; the vigorous rhythm of his song is an affront to Prospero's rod-like pentameter world. It may be imagined as a rudimentary form of nation language. For Shakespeare's Caliban, 'Freedom, high-day!' is an illusion: he has merely exchanged one master, one god, for another. Brathwaite revises the situation by combining Caliban's anthem of freedom with Ariel's song of watery metamorphosis, 'Full fathom five'. When the Caribbean Caliban bends his back and passes beneath the limbo stick, the music and dance transform him: because he has gone

> down
> down
> down

he can rise

> up
> up
> up

A note in Brathwaite's glossary reminds us that 'limbo' is not only a state of spiritual darkness and exclusion, it is also

> a dance in which the participants have to move, with their bodies thrown backwards and without any aid whatsoever

under a stick which is lowered at every successfully completed passage under it, until the stick is practically touching the ground. It is said to have originated – a necessary therapy – after the experience of the cramped conditions between the slave-ship decks of the Middle Passage.

The limbo is first performed with

> eyes
> shut tight
> and the whip light
> crawl-
> ing round the ship
> where his free-
> dom drown

But it becomes a means to freedom and celebration:

> sun coming up
> and the drummers are praising me
>
> out of the dark
> and the dumb gods are raising me
>
> up
> up
> up
>
> and the music is saving me

In Ariel's song in the original play, Alonso has gone down, down, down, but as the action unfolds we watch his soul rise up, up, up. From recognition of sin in act three,

> Methought the billows spoke and told me of it,
> The winds did sing it to me, and the thunder,
> That deep and dreadful organ-pipe, pronounced
> The name of Prosper. It did bass my trespass,

he passes to penitence in act five: 'Thy dukedom I resign, and do entreat / Thou pardon me my wrongs'. In Brathwaite's poem, Caliban follows a similar course – down, then up – by means of the limbo dance.

The key difference is in the kind of god. Alonso's is a high Renaissance Christian God, reached through the linguistic formality of confession. The Caribbean Caliban is raised by gods who are dumb save in the music. As Brathwaite puts it in 'The Making of the Drum', a poem of great importance in *Masks*,

> God is dumb
> until the drum
> speaks

In each case, human art – Prospero's magic, the drummer and the dancer – brings about a perception of something named as divine. But where the hurricane of Alonso's god roars in pentameters, Brathwaite's Caliban finds a god of his own environment and culture. It is a defining characteristic of Shakespeare's Caliban that he hears the music of the isle, and that Prospero's failure to understand this must vitiate any monovocal Prosperian reading of the play. The music of the isle is the key to Brathwaite's poetry, too. But he makes a different music, that of his own isles, of Afro-Caribbean culture.

That culture is seen to be close to nature in a way that has been renounced by Western man. The 'modernization' – Westernization, Americanization – of Havana described in the first part of 'Caliban' is decadent ('the police toured the gambling houses / wearing their dark glasses / and collected tribute'). That modernization is also an assault on nature. Where Ariel's song imagines a creative transformation from dead bone to living coral, economic progress is conceived here as the destructive transformation of living coral into dead concrete:

> out of the living stone, out of the living bone
> of coral, these dead
> towers; out of the coney
> islands of our mind-
>
> less architects, this death
> of sons, of songs, of sunshine;
> out of this dearth of coo ru coos, home-
> less pigeons, this perturbation that does not signal health.

When Caliban finds the god in the dance, what he is really achieving is a reunification with nature. The movement is the same as that in Césaire's *Une tempête*, where Prospero is anti-nature and Caliban's freedom means a unification of his voice with those of the birds and the surf. For Brathwaite, the legacy of European and American empire in the Antilles is the death not only of sons of Africa, but also of songs, of sunshine, of birds, of coral. As I write, the reefs around such islands as Barbados are dying, as raw sewage is pumped from the beachside hotels, and locals earn a living by breaking off chunks of coral and selling them to tourists.

The hyphen across Brathwaite's stanza-break passes judgement on Western man. Economic development, high-rise apartments resembling rabbit hutches, come 'out of the coney / islands of our mind-' – but the 'mind' is transformed into 'our mindless architects'. Brathwaite's turn of 'mind' to 'mindless' is a rebuke to the *res cogitans* for its quest to master nature.

As Robert Pogue Harrison has demonstrated in his remarkable book, *Forests: The Shadow of Civilization*, imperialism has always brought with it deforestation and the consuming of natural resources. Since the Enlightenment privileging of 'mind', Western man has mapped his own place in the world so as to justify this:

> In his *Discourse on Method* Descartes compares the authority of tradition to a forest of error, beyond which lies the promised land of reason. Once he arrives in that promised land, Descartes redefines his relation not only to tradition but also to nature in its totality. The new Cartesian distinction between the *res cogitans*, or thinking self, and the *res extensa*, or embodied substance, sets up the terms for the objectivity of science and the abstraction from historicity, location, nature, and culture. What interests us about Descartes in this context is the fact that he sought to empower the subject of knowledge in such a way that, through its application of mathematical method, humanity could achieve what he called 'mastery and possession of nature.'

We only know ourselves when we confront our Other. Fanon and Simone de Beauvoir taught us that the defining Others of

Western man are the black and woman, but in the beginning man's shadow was the forest which he cleared in order to make a space for himself. 'A sylvan fringe of darkness defined the limits' of Western civilization's cultivation, writes Harrison, 'the margins of its cities, the boundaries of its institutional domain; but also the extravagance of its imagination.'

What does a civilization do when it has chopped down its own forests? It launches expeditions across that other boundary, the sea, and finds new lands to devastate. Thus the island becomes as the forest. Harrison's argument begins with the passage from *The New Science* of Giambattista Vico which I quoted apropos of Frankenstein in my previous chapter: 'This was the order of human institutions: first the forests, after that the huts, then the villages, next the cities, and finally the academies'. The 'progress' of civilization is a progression away from the forest and destructive of the forest. Man dislodges the trees in order to see the sky. His sky-gods – Jupiter, Jehovah, the quest to conquer space – displace the tree-gods, the nature spirits which connect 'primitive' communities to their environment. But Vico leaves one step out of his sorry progression: he should have written 'next the cities, soon the colonies, and finally the academies'. The greatest enemy of the forest is empire. Early in the *Metamorphoses*, Ovid reminds us that in the Golden Age (Schiller's infancy of mankind) man was content to remain in his own land, but with the Iron Age (the era of technology) came the felling of trees, the building of ships, the building of empire. One of the many respects in which the *Metamorphoses* is a rebuke to that great apologia for empire, Virgil's *Aeneid*, is its anthropomorphic sympathy for trees. Give a tree a human past and it can no longer merely be raw material for ship-building. Harrison's *Forests* keeps returning, threnodially, to the symbiosis between imperialism and deforestation: before the Athenian empire, the hills of Attica were canopied; before the Roman empire, the length of North Africa was wooded and fertile; before the Venetian empire, forest stretched from the lagoon to the Alps; before the American empire, the rainforest spread across Brazil.

The poem 'Caliban', then, is not only about culture against culture, white against black, European against African ways of seeing. It is also about culture against nature. This raises doubts about the New Didacticism's assumption that *The Tempest* must be read only in terms of cultural confrontation. White readers of the play in relation to the 'discourse of colonialism' focus on Prospero and Caliban because the troubled relationship between master and slave encourages talk of hostile exchange between culture and culture. Such readers have political reasons for denying the possibility of exchange between culture and nature. Nature, they say, is just someone else's culture. The cultural critic Eric Cheyfitz is typical when he suggests in a book called *The Poetics of Imperialism* that 'In *The Tempest* nature is not nature but culture'. Césaire's and Brathwaite's linking of Caliban with nature proposes something very different: that racial oppression and the exploitation of nature go hand in hand.

*

There are, however, problems with a model which praises black culture for being in touch with nature in a way that white culture isn't, for if imported into 'white' ways of thinking it runs the risk of forgetting the history of the West's despoliation of indigent cultures, and retaining the image of black traditions as Other – only this time a desirably primal, earth-true Other. When a sophisticated European reader allegorizes the character of Caliban, there is always the risk of condescending primitivism: for Robert Browning, Caliban meditating upon his god Setebos was the embodiment of Darwin's 'missing link' between ape and man. Having acknowledged the ecopoetic force of *négritude*, the white reader must be wary of appropriating a language that is not his own, of doubly speaking on behalf of the Other. The male practitioner of ecofeminist reading faces the same problem. So in thinking about a rereading of *The Tempest* in terms of culture and nature, it may be wise for the reader who is perforce a troubled Prosperian to follow an alternative track and consider an improvisation on the voice of Ariel – that voice which was silenced by late twentieth-century criticism's special interest in Caliban.

In 1822, the last year of his life, Percy Bysshe Shelley wrote a group of lyric poems to his friend Jane Williams. One of them is called 'With a Guitar. To Jane'. It begins

> Ariel to Miranda; – Take
> This slave of music for the sake
> Of him who is the slave of thee.

Composed in the same tetrameter as Prospero's epilogue, it is a kind of second epilogue to *The Tempest*, written from Ariel's point of view. Jane is Miranda, her husband Edward Williams is Ferdinand and Shelley himself, Ariel. The poem is a 'token / Of more than ever can be spoken'; it lightly and touchingly mediates Shelley's admiration for Jane through the fantasy of Ariel being silently and unrequitedly in love with Miranda. Shelley's ideal or intellectual love finds its analogy in Ariel's nature as a disembodied spirit of fire and air. The impossibility of that love's realization in the material world is expressed in an image suggestive of Ariel's fate at the hands of Sycorax: 'And now, alas! the poor sprite is / Imprisoned for some fault of his / In a body like a grave'. The elegant conceit which allows the poet-lover out of his bind is that the spirit of his art will be held in the guitar which he gives Jane together with the poem, and that when she plays it he will be able to continue serving her as she makes music out of him. But where does the guitar come from?

> The artist who this idol wrought
> To echo all harmonious thought
> Felled a tree, while on the steep
> The woods were in their winter sleep
> Rocked in that repose divine
> On the wind-swept Apennine.

To make a guitar, you must fell a tree; to harness the power of Ariel, you must split open a pine. Shelley's poem claims that because it was felled while sleeping in winter, the tree 'felt no pain' and that now it is a guitar it is living 'in happier form again'. In the light of Shelley's Neoplatonism, the latter phrase may be presumed to imply that in its guitar-form the tree transcends its original particular Apennine hillside and makes a music which holds together

> all harmonies
> Of the plains and of the skies,

> Of the forests and the mountains,
> And the many-voiced fountains,
> The clearest echoes of the hills,
> The softest notes of falling rills,
> The melodies of birds and bees,
> The murmuring of summer seas,
> And pattering rain and breathing dew
> And airs of evening.

In this account, art – the music of the guitar which is metonymic of the poem itself – offers the ideal or intellectual form of nature. In *The Tempest*, it is in response to Stephano and Trinculo's hearing of Ariel's music that Caliban speaks of how he has sometimes heard something which a Renaissance audience would have thought of as approximating to the music of the spheres. So here, the Ariel music of the guitar knows

> That seldom heard mysterious sound,
> Which, driven on its diurnal round
> As it floats through boundless day
> Our world enkindles on its way.

In another sense, however, this music does not constitute nature perfected. Early in each of the poem's two verse-paragraphs there is a noun which questions the status of the guitar. In the first, it is a 'slave': Prospero uses that word of Ariel, but does so more frequently of Caliban. In the first chapter of *A Philosophical View of Reform*, Shelley had described the struggle for liberty in terms of the abolition of slavery and the enfranchisement of poetry. The presence of the word 'slave' here, with its Calibanesque undertow, suggests that poetry may nevertheless be dependent on certain enslavements of its own. And in the second verse-paragraph there is a suggestion of Bacon's term for false mental images: 'The artist who this *idol* wrought'. The apparently ideal may in fact be an idol. The premise of Ariel's unrequited love for Miranda and the positioning of the poem as a second epilogue to *The Tempest* establish a sense of loss, an elegiac tone, that cannot be unwritten by the gift of the guitar. 'Slave', 'idol' and 'felled' break up the harmonious movement of the couplets; 'wrought', twice used of the making of the guitar, suggests a beating into shape, the hard working of iron as well as wood. If something has to be wrought, resistance is implied.

> – and so this tree –
> O that such our death may be –
> Died in sleep, and felt no pain.

That the tree died in sleep and felt no pain implies that a tree might be killed whilst awake and in that case feel pain. An optative like the parenthetic 'may' in these lines is always provoked by fear of its forceful opposite.

The price of art is the destruction of a living tree. You can't have music without dead wood. You can sing a poem to a local audience, but you cannot disseminate it more widely – or hope that it will endure beyond your death or the death of your most committed listeners who have learnt your words – without paper, papyrus, electronic reproduction device or some other medium which has required the working-over of raw materials. You create culture by enslaving nature. Prospero makes gape a pine and threatens to rend an oak in order to display his power. In this, he is anti-nature. His technology is an image of that 'mastery and possession of nature' which Descartes believed was within the grasp of *res cogitans*, the mind of man. Shelley was an inheritor of Cartesian dualism – his Neoplatonism was an attempt to get round it – and it does seem to me that at a profound level his poem registers the irony of the post-Cartesian condition. What are the highest things that the guitar tells of? They are *res extensa*: plains, skies, forests, mountains, birds, bees, seas, rain and dew. Art is an attempt to recover the very thing which has been destroyed so that art can be made.

Nevertheless, the end of *The Tempest* is still there as an image of the possibility of renunciation of the claim to mastery and possession of nature. We don't know where Caliban goes at the end of the play, but we do know that Ariel is free and that the island will be his again. In a general sense, *The Tempest* continues to function as an exemplary humanist text because it is a vehicle through which later cultures reflect on pressing contemporary concerns. Formally speaking, it achieves its exemplarity through its multivocality. It does not offer the sole voice of Prospero. The presence of Caliban is an enabling voice for poets like Brathwaite and Césaire, while Shelley thinks as Ariel and even as the tree in which Ariel was confined. In a particular sense, *The Tempest* was and remains an exemplary humanist text because it is set on an island that is its own place. In the sixteenth century, the imaginary island was a place in which one could reflect upon the ideal society in the manner of Sir Thomas More's *Utopia*. In our twenty-first century, we need to treasure the memory or the myth of an island which Prospero has left, an ecosystem which man is content to leave alone. Post-colonialism has restored a voice to Caliban. Ecopoetics asks us to imagine that Ariel can be set free.

The freedom of birds – Keats's nightingale, Shelley's skylark – is a necessary imagining. I stand in the field behind my house, watching and listening as the skylark rises. My heart leaps up. But my mind has fallen into knowledge: a biologist will be able to explain to me why the lark rises. Freedom has nothing to do with it. The freedom of the lark is only in my imagination, just as the state of nature – Arcadia, Ariel's island – is but a necessary dream. Maybe the true poets are those who hold fast to the dream even as they recognize it as a dream. We have spent much of this chapter thinking back to the island of the Shakespearean imagination which forces the European mind to re-examine itself. To end the chapter, let us hear a voice from a real island where Western man has again and again been forced to confront the strangeness, the beauty and the violence of a nature that is Other. The voice is that of Les Murray, Australia's truest poet, meditating on a bird's flight, then coming down to earth with knowledge of the food chain:

> ### ARIEL
> Upward, cheeping, on huddling wings,
> these small brown mynas have gained
> a keener height than their kind ever sustained
> but whichever of them fails first
> falls to the hawk circling under
> who drove them up.
> Nothing's free when it is explained.

Not free when explained. But that does not stop us gaining the keen height each time we read the poem.

4

Major Weather

Well! if the Bard was weather-wise . . .

(Coleridge, 'Dejection')

Ours is a Government that now seems to depend very
much upon the *weather*.

(William Cobbett, *Rural Rides*)

I had a dream, which was not all a dream.
The bright sun was extinguish'd, and the stars
Did wander darkling in the eternal space,
Rayless, and pathless, and the icy earth
Swung blind and blackening in the moonless air;
Morn came and went – and came, and brought no day,
And men forgot their passions in the dread
Of this their desolation; and all hearts
Were chill'd into a selfish prayer for light:
And they did live by watchfires – and the thrones,
The palaces of crowned kings – the huts,
The habitations of all things which dwell,
Were burnt for beacons; cities were consumed,
And men were gathered round their blazing homes
To look once more into each other's face;
Happy were those who dwelt within the eye
Of the volcanos, and their mountain-torch:
A fearful hope was all the world contain'd;
Forests were set on fire – but hour by hour
They fell and faded – and the crackling trunks
Extinguish'd with a crash – and all was black.

(Lord Byron, 'Darkness')

IT WAS IN THE EARLY 1980s that I first encountered Byron's poem 'Darkness', of which these are the opening lines. I heard it quoted by the then leader of the British Labour Party, Michael Foot. The party was avowedly in favour of unilateral nuclear disarmament; membership of the Campaign for Nuclear Disarmament was at its highest ever; the women's peace camp at Greenham Common, Fortress UK's principal base for American cruise missiles, was yoking gender politics and defence policy as never before; E. P. Thompson had just written *Protest and Survive*; and scientists were telling us about something called 'nuclear winter' – the dust blasted into the stratosphere by the explosion of the ICBMs would blot out the sun for three years, destroying all but the most resilient forms of life upon the planet. Michael Foot quoted from the close of the poem, hailing Byron as a prophet who foreknew that war would ultimately lead to global winter:

> The world was void,
> The populous and the powerful was a lump,
> Seasonless, herbless, treeless, manless, lifeless –
> A lump of death – a chaos of hard clay.
> The rivers, lakes, and ocean all stood still,
> And nothing stirr'd within their silent depths.

The Romantic in me was uplifted by Foot's futuristic reading. The literary critics was more sceptical: the poem could not really be about nuclear winter, so what was it about?

In 1986, there arose with the publication of volume four of the Oxford edition of Byron's *Complete Poetical Works* the possibility of 'Darkness' being elucidated. That edition's headnote to the poem consists principally of a catalogue of possible literary sources: *The Last Man*, which was an anonymous translation (published in 1806) of a French novel by Cousin de Grainville; 'various apocalyptic passages in the bible'; Burnet's *Sacred Theory of the Earth*; 'various commonplaces of Enlightenment science', to be found in Buffon and Fontenelle; the conclusion to the *De rerum natura* of Lucretius; and 'M. G. (Monk) Lewis, who came to Diodati on 14 August 1816 and who helped to shift the conversations with the Shelleys, Polidori, and B[yron] on to grim subjects'. This is a rich list, but does it not evade the poem every bit as much as Foot did? The politician's rhetorical appropriation propels the poem into its future; the scholar's elucidation of sources fossilizes it in its past. Its present, its significance in 1816, is in neither case addressed. Neither the politician nor the scholar has an answer to the obvious questions: what led Byron to write a poem about the extinction of sunlight in the summer of 1816 and what would have come to the minds of his readers when the poem was published with *The Prisoner of Chillon* later that year?

The Oxford edition pins the poem's date of composition down to the five weeks between 21 July and 25 August 1816. The key which unlocks the impulse behind the poem is, I believe, found in an apparently flippant remark in a letter of Byron to Samuel Rogers, dated 29 July 1816: 'we have had lately such stupid mists – fogs – rains – and perpetual density – that one would think Castlereagh had the foreign affairs of the kingdom of Heaven also – upon his hands.' The summer weather around Lake Geneva is always variable, but in 1816 Byron found it particularly irksome. A month earlier, he had complained in a letter to John Murray of the 'stress of weather'.

Could this be where 'Darkness' begins: with the stress of weather? The poem opens, 'I had a dream, which was not all a dream. / The bright sun was extinguish'd'. Does it stretch credulity too far to suppose that the first clause of the second sentence follows from the second clause of the first sentence? That the extinguished sun was not all a dream? Might the origin of the poem not be the absence of sunshine in June, July and August 1816?

It rained in Switzerland on 130 out of the 183 days from April to September 1816. The average temperature that July was an astonishing 4.9° Fahrenheit below the mean for that month in the years 1807–24. As Byron shivered in Geneva, so did his readers back home. In London it rained on eighteen days in July 1816 and on only one day did the temperature reach 70°; during the same month the previous year, the temperature was over 70° on nineteen days and it only rained three times. 70° was recorded on only two days in August, whereas the figure for the previous year was thirteen. At noon on 1 September 1816, the temperature in

London was 47°; the average noon temperature in the first half of the previous September had been 63°.

The pattern was the same across Europe and the United States. Consult the meteorological reports and you will find that 1816 was the worst summer ever recorded; indeed, it became popularly known as 'the year without a summer'. The bad weather led to failed harvests. To continue with the example of Switzerland: annual harvests for that country have been graded by economic historians on a scale of one to six, according to yield. 1816 achieved a minimal one. As a result of the poor harvests, there was a hemispheric subsistence crisis, marked by violent price fluctuation, basic food shortage and concordant public disorder.

What caused the bad weather? In the popular imagination it was frequently associated with the unusual visibility of sun spots. The darkening of the sun led to fears of apocalypse – the exact situation of Byron's poem. More precise observers noted a consistently dense haze permanently on the horizon – 'It had nothing of the nature of a humid fog. It was like that smoking vapour which overspread Europe about thirty years ago,' wrote Dr Thomas D. Mitchell in the *New York Medical Repository*.

'Smoking vapour' is a good intuition. Benjamin Franklin had observed similar atmospheric conditions back in 1784 and suggested that the cause might have been volcanic vapour. There is an unintentional irony in the lines in which Byron says that those who live close to volcanoes are lucky because they are accorded at least some light and warmth in the darkened world, for as it happens the eruption of Tambora volcano in Indonesia in 1815 killed some 80,000 people on the islands of Sumbawa and Lombok. It was the greatest eruption since 1500. The dust blasted into the stratosphere reduced the transparency of the atmosphere, filtered out the sun and consequently lowered surface temperatures. The effect lasted for three years, straining the growth-capacity of life across the planet. Beginning in 1816, crop failure led to food riots in nearly every country in Europe. Only in 1819 were there good harvests again. The index for the Swiss harvest that year shot up to a maximal six.

Editors have a tendency to explain literary works with reference to other literary works. The Oxford headnote to 'Darkness', with its network of sources, treats the poem as a purely textual weave. Because a poetic composition is a cultural phenomenon, it is related to other phenomena in the culture. It is not explained in terms of nature.

But Byron does not set culture apart from nature. What is striking about both the remark in the letter to Rogers and the poem itself is Byron's easy yoking of politics and nature. The letter jokingly blames the ministry of Castlereagh for the bad weather; 'perpetual density' is taken to be simultaneously a meteorological and a socio-political condition. The poem darkly narrates a history in which war temporarily ceases as humankind pulls together in the face of inclement weather but is then renewed on a global scale as a result of the famine consequent upon the absence of sunlight. The global struggle for subsistence leads ultimately to the extinction of mankind. In 1815, Byron and his public witnessed the cessation of a European, indeed worldwide, war which had lasted for more than twenty years; in 1816, they endured the year without a summer. The poem is as contemporary as it is apocalyptic. The first referent for any reader of the poem in 1816 would surely have been not Lucretius or de Grainville's novel *The Last Man*, but the sunless summer they had just undergone and the fear of famine brought with it.

But contemporary as it was, the poem remains powerfully prophetic: how far away the nuclear forebodings of the Cold War seem now, how near the vision of a world seasonless, herbless, treeless, the rivers, lakes and oceans silent. When Michael Foot read 'Darkness' he had in his mind the Mutually Assured Destruction of the Cold War. When we read 'Darkness' now, Byron may be reclaimed as a prophet of – to adopt Bruno Latour's word, cited in my previous chapter – ecocide.

*

According to Latour, the modern critical stance has sought to 'establish a partition between a natural world that has always been there, a society with predictable and stable interests and stakes, and a discourse that is independent of both reference and society'. Late twentieth-century literary criticism and theory participated in what Latour calls 'the work of purification' which 'creates two entirely distinct ontological zones: that of human beings on the one hand; that of nonhumans on the other'. For Latour and his intellectual master Michel Serres, ecocide sounds the death knell of the 'modern Constitution', inaugurated by Bacon and Descartes, which effects these separations. Serres asks in his *Le contrat naturel*:

> who, then, is inflicting on the world, which is henceforth a common objective enemy, this harm that we hope is still reversible, this oil spilled at sea, this carbon monoxide spread in the air by the millions of tons, these acidic and toxic chemicals that come back down with the rain? Whence comes this filth that is choking our little children with asthma and covering our skin with blotches? Who, beyond private and public persons? What, beyond enormous metropolises, considered either as aggregations of individuals or as networks of relations? Our tools, our arms, our efficacy, in the end our reason, about which we're so legitimately vain: our mastery and our possessions.
>
> Mastery and possession: these are the master words launched by Descartes at the dawn of the scientific and technological age, when our Western reason went off to conquer the universe. We dominate and appropriate it: such is the shared philosophy underlying industrial enterprise as well as so-called disinterested science, which are indistinguishable in this respect. Cartesian mastery brings science's objective violence into line, making it a well-controlled strategy. Our fundamental relationship with objects comes down to war and property.

Mastery and possession are the driving forces not only of science but also of capitalism. Karl Marx added his signature to the modern Constitution when he claimed that man was superior to the animals by virtue of his 'working-over of inorganic nature'. So too did the literary criticism of the Cold War era, locked as it was into a model of inter-cultural conflict.

The Lisbon earthquake of 1755 gave the direst affront to post-Cartesian aspiration precisely because it was a reminder that man was not master of nature. Bad weather was a scandal to the modern Constitution. As Serres has remarked, the Enlightenment was one long attempt to repress the weather, to dispel the clouds of unknowing: 'the eighteenth century can be defined quite simply, in both its epistemology and its history, as the erasure of "meteors".' But, as the Lisbon earthquake shows, we cannot master nature, erase the meteors. The earth has its way of striking back, most drastically with earthquakes and volcanic eruptions, but more often with plain old bad weather. This is the insight of the age of ecocide. Knowledge in this age does not confine itself to local politics, to Corn Laws and the moral economy of the rioting crowd. It asks for the cause of flooding in Bangladesh and finds the answer in the deforestation of the Himalayan foothills; it looks at starvation in Africa and discovers that imperialism has always been accompanied by ecological exploitation.

The modern Constitution presupposed a Newtonian concept of order in nature. It is not a coincidence that James Thomson's poem in praise of Newton was published with *The Seasons* in 1730. Thomson celebrated the variety of the seasons, but the thrust of his argument was that the weather itself had a fundamental order, a concord in its discord; disorder resided in the morality of the observer and was accordingly a matter of human agency. The constancy of nature was something against which to measure the vicissitudes of culture.

But nature is not stable. Weather is the primary sign of its mutability. The Chaos theory of the 1990s put disorder back into nature. It can be demonstrated mathematically that a small intervention upon the environment in one part of the world can have a massive effect on the other side of the world. Chaos theory has been able to explain the unpredictability of the weather as Newtonian theory could not.

The modern Constitution was above all premised on a strict separation between culture and nature. Yet in 1748, Charles-Louis de Secondat, Baron de Montesquieu published an analysis of *The Spirit of the Laws* of different societies in relation to their respective climates, and in 1807 Alexander von Humboldt produced an *Essay on the Geography of Plants* which arged that history was a function of environment, that humans are products of their climate, that the imaginative and aesthetic sense of different peoples is shaped by the landscapes, the very rock-formations, which surround them. The varying configurations of the human species may be mapped by climate and soil, just as the distribution of plants may be so mapped. We who claim to be modern have taken the Cartesian Constitution for granted and ignored the insistence of Montesquieu and Humboldt that ideology may be influenced by the weather. Because they work indoors in their air-conditioned libraries, the modern analysts of ideology – like Frankensteins enclosed in their laboratories – have forgotten about the weather.

Perhaps, however, to insist that the weather, considered as a synecdoche for the environment, is the prime influence which causes the differentiation of human communities is to be both premodern and postmodern. The idea is an ancient one, going back at least to Hippocrates' treatise *On Airs, Waters and Places*. And it is a dangerous one, when inflected racially: historically, it has been used to bolster assumptions about the superiority of Europeans over Asians and Africans. But at the same time it is an idea which may be given a strikingly anti-racial inflection, and in this it is proleptic of post-colonial values. Luc Ferry cites the argument of Immanuel Kant, which was developed from that of Montesquieu: 'it was the people on the peripheries, to the North and to the South, who avoided the influence of the civilization developed, in the center, by Europe', but 'in these two regions, *it was nature, not race, that constrained men to a marginal status*'. The cold north is too harsh, the hot Caribbean too luxurious and sloth-inducing, for culture to cut itself off from nature and advance itself down the road to capital and empire. According to this argument, difference is created by environment and not by racial essence. There is, indeed, no such thing as racial essence. Move people to a different environment and they will behave according to the conditions of that environment; they will not be bound by their racial origin.

We who have signed the social contract but refused to draw up a natural contract have been blind to the weather. In the post-colonial, postmodern, post-1989 world, we have to come out of the hermetically sealed laboratory: the experiment of planned socialism has failed, the confidence of science has been shaken. We have to learn to attend once more to the weather: to read the signs of the times in the signs of the skies, as our ancestors did. For my local purpose here as a reader of English poetry written in the second decade of the nineteenth century: in the age of ecocide we need to attend to things which were invisible to the cultural criticism of the Cold War era, to such questions as why there was bad weather in the years 1816 to 1818. The answer to that specific question is a simple one: the eruption of Tambora.

The weather is the primary sign of the inextricability of culture and nature. Serres points out in *Le contrat naturel* that peasants and sailors know the power of the weather in ways that scientists and politicians do not. Romanticism listens to the wisdom of sailors and peasants – of Coleridge's Mariner and Wordsworth's Michael. It challenges the moderns' separation of culture from nature. Romanticism knows that, in Latour's phrase, 'a delicate shuttle' has woven together 'the heavens, industry, texts, souls and moral law'.

With this in mind, I want to reflect further in this chapter upon some of the things that Romantic and post-Romantic poetry can say to us in an age of global climatic change. I have begun with Byron's 'Darkness' because of all Romantic poems it is the one that seems to me most directly responsive to the global climatic change of the Romantics' own time. I now want to turn to Keats's 'To Autumn'. I propose that in order to read it livingly in the age of ecocide we must begin with the knowledge that we have no choice but to live with the weather.

As the meteorological reports for July 1816 are the key context for Byron's 'Darkness', so our understanding of 'To Autumn' should begin with the knowledge that the weather was clear and sunny on thirty-eight out of the forty-seven days from 7 August to 22 September 1819, and that in the week of 15–22 September temperatures were in the mid-60s, whereas in the corresponding week in each of the three previous years they had been in the mid-50s. Remember the meteorological and consequent agricultural pattern: the terrible summer and failed harvest of 1816, bad weather and poor harvests continuing in 1817 and 1818, then at last in 1819 a good summer, a full harvest, a beautiful autumn.

To Autumn

Season of mists and mellow fruitfulness,
    Close bosom-friend of the maturing sun:
Conspiring with him how to load and bless
    With fruit the vines that round the thatch-eves run;
To bend with apples the moss'd cottage-trees,
    And fill all fruit with ripeness to the core;
        To swell the gourd, and plump the hazel shells
    With a sweet kernel; to set budding more,
And still more, later flowers for the bees,
Until they think warm days will never cease,
        For summer has o'er-brimm'd their clammy cells.

Who hath not seen thee oft amid thy store?
    Sometimes whoever seeks abroad may find
Thee sitting careless on a granary floor,
    Thy hair soft-lifted by the winnowing wind;
Or on a half-reap'd furrow sound asleep,
    Drows'd with the fume of poppies, while thy hook
        Spares the next swath and all its twined flowers:
And sometimes like a gleaner thou dost keep
    Steady thy laden head across a brook:
    Or by a cyder-press, with patient look,
        Thou watchest the last oozings hours by hours.

Where are the songs of spring? Ay, where are they?
    Think not of them, thou hast thy music too,–
While barred clouds bloom the soft-dying day,
    And touch the stubble-plains with rosy hue;
Then in a wailful choir the small gnats mourn
    Among the river sallows, borne aloft
        Or sinking as the light wind lives or dies;
And full-grown lambs loud bleat from hilly bourn;
    Hedge-crickets sing; and now with treble soft
    The red-breast whistles from a garden-croft;
        And gathering swallows twitter in the skies.

This is not an escapist fantasy which turns its back on the ruptures of Regency culture, as late twentieth-century criticism
tended to suggest. No: it is a meditation on how human culture

can only function through links and reciprocal relations with nature.

For Keats, there is a direct correlation between the self's bond with its environment and the bonds between people which make up society. The link is clear in the letters he wrote around the time of the composition of 'Autumn'. At the end of August 1819, he writes to Fanny Keats:

> The delightful Weather we have had for two Months is the highest gratification I could receive – no chill'd red noses – no shivering – but fair Atmosphere to think in – a clean towel mark'd with the mangle and a basin of clear Water to drench one's face with ten times a day: no need of much exercise – a Mile a day being quite sufficient – My greatest regret is that I have not been well enough to bathe though I have been two Months by the sea side and live now close to delicious bathing – Still I enjoy the Weather I adore fine Weather as the greatest blessing I can have.

The measure of human happiness, Keats suggests, is not a matter of government decree, is not determined by the high politics of Fat Louis and Fat Regent, to whom he refers dismissively later in the same letter. There are more basic necessities: good weather, clean water to wash and bathe in, unpolluted air in which to exercise. Aware of his poor lungs, Keats took up residence in Margate where Dr A. P. Buchan practised medicine and wrote his seminal book on the healthy atmosphere of the Thanet peninsula, *Practical Observations concerning Sea-Bathing* (1804). The emergence in the early nineteenth century of discourses of sea-bathing and ozone are crucial here.

In his journal-letter of 21 September 1819 to the George Keatses, Keats moves easily from human bonds ('Men who live together have a silent moulding and influencing power over each other – They interassimilate') to the bond between self and environment ('Now the time is beautiful. I take a walk every day for an hour before dinner and this is generally my walk'). The walk is described: it traces a path from culture to nature, from cathedral and college to meadow and river. Between theorizing about interassimilation and describing his walk in the fresh autumn air, Keats writes 'I am not certain how I should endure loneliness and bad weather together'. Life depends on sociability and warmth: in order to survive, our species needs both social and environmental networks, both human bonds and good weather.

'To Autumn' is a poem about these networks. That it is a weather poem is manifest from the passage describing its genesis in the other famous letter which Keats wrote on Tuesday 21 September 1819, to J. H. Reynolds:

> How beautiful the season is now – How fine the air. A temperate sharpness about it. Really, without joking, chaste weather – Dian skies – I never lik'd stubble fields so much as now – Aye better than the chilly green of the spring. Somehow a stubble plain looks warm – in the same way that some pictures look warm – this struck me so much in my sunday's walk that I composed upon it. I hope you are better employed than in gaping after weather. I have been at different times so happy as not to know what weather it was.

The consumptive has no choice but to gape after weather. The key context for this passage could well be the poor air quality of the years 1816–18 – Byron's 'perpetual density', the effect of Tambora. Health, wrote Keats in his late letters, is the greatest of blessings, the cornerstone of all pleasures. When his body was finally opened by Dr Clark, Dr Luby and an Italian surgeon, 'they thought it the worst possible Consumption – the lungs were intirely destroyed – the cells were quite gone'. Air quality is of the highest importance for those whose lungs have been invaded by *Mycobacterium tuberculosis*. Keats was hurried to his death less by the reviewers, as Byron supposed, than by the weather. Perhaps when he refers to the 'different times' at which he was 'so happy as not to know what weather it was', he is thinking nostalgically of the time before the bad weather of the immediate post-Tambora years which tragically coincided with the first taking hold of his pulmonary tuberculosis. The good summer and clear autumn of 1819 very literally gave him a new lease of life.

'To Autumn' itself is a poem of networks, links, bonds and correspondences. Linguistically, it achieves its most characteristic effects by making metaphors seem like metonymies. Mist and fruitfulness, bosom-friend and sun, load and bless, are not 'naturally' linked pairs in the manner of bird and wings. One would expect the yoking of them to have the element of surprise, even violence, associated with metaphor. But Keats makes the links seem natural: the progression of one thing to another through the poem is anything but violent or surprising. The effect of this naturalization within the poem is to create contiguity between all its elements.

The world of the poem thus comes to resemble a well-regulated ecosystem. Keats has an intuitive understanding of the underlying law of community ecology, namely that biodiversity is the key to the survival and adaptation of ecosystems. Biodiversity depends on a principle which we might call *illusory excess*. In order to withstand the onslaught of weather an ecosystem needs a sufficient diversity of species to regenerate itself; species which serve no obvious purpose in one homeostasis may play a vital role in changed environmental circumstances. Their superfluousness is an illusion; they are in fact necessary. The wild flowers in the second stanza of 'To Autumn' are an excellent example: in terms of the agricultural economy, the flowers which seed themselves in the cornfield are a waste, an unnecessary excess, but under different environmental conditions they could be more valuable than the corn. The wild-flower which Keats names is the poppy. The flower may be chosen not only for aesthetic effect – the red dots contrasting with the golden corn, as in Monet's *Wild Poppies* – and because of its traditional associations with mortality, but also as a reminder of medicinal value. 'The fume of poppies' makes us think of opiates against pain and care. Spare the next swath with your reaping-hook, says Keats, and you might just gain medical benefit; spare the remaining rainforests, say ecologists, and you might just find a cure for some present or future disease among the billions of still unstudied plant species you would otherwise annihilate.

The ecosystem of 'To Autumn' is something larger than an image of agribusiness. Agribusiness sprays the cornfields with pesticides, impatient of poppies and gnats. Agribusiness removes hedgerows, regarding them as wasteful; 'To Autumn', in contrast, listens to hedge-crickets. The poem is concerned with a larger economy than the human one: its bees are there to pollinate flowers, not to produce honey for humans to consume ('later flowers for the bees', not bees for human bee-keepers).

But the imaginary ecosystem of the text is also something larger than a piece of descriptive biology. There are not only links within the biota – flower and bee, the food chain that associates gnat and swallow – but also links between the discourses which the modern Constitution sought to separate out. The poem not only yokes external and internal marks of biological process (the bending of the apple tree, the swelling of the gourd), it also yokes community and chemistry (bosom-friend and sun), physics and theology (load and bless), biology and aesthetics (a link which we may express through the two halves of the word which describes the closing images of the poem: bird-song). And crucially, it refuses to sign the Cartesian constitution which splits apart thinking mind and embodied substance. In contrast to Keats's earlier odes, there is no 'I' listening to a nightingale or looking at an urn: the self is dissolved into the ecosystem. In his journal-letter, Keats wrote of his ideal of interassimilation between men; in the poem he is interassimilated with the environment. Indeed, environment is probably the wrong word, because it presupposes an image of man at the centre, *surrounded* by things; ecosystem is the better word exactly because an ecosystem does not have a centre, it is a network of relations.

Insofar as the poem does have a centre and does anthropomorphize, it is given a 'patient look' which seems distinctively female. The human figures in the central stanza – winnower, reaper, gleaner and cider-presser – are not in process of 'working over inorganic nature' in the manner of Marxian man. They are suspended, immobile. The winnower's hair is balanced in the wind, the gleaner balances herself in equilibrium with the eddies of the brook, the reaper is asleep under the influence of the poppy, the cider-presser is winding down in entropic rhythm with the oozings.

In contrast to those feminists who seek to denaturalize traditional images of masculinity and femininity, ecofeminists reappropriate and celebrate the idea of woman's closeness to the rhythms of mother earth. A line of work beginning with Sherry

Ortner's essay 'Is Female to Male as Nature is to Culture?', and best exemplified by Carolyn Merchant's book *The Death of Nature*, posits direct links between Enlightenment science, masculinity and technology on the one hand, the exploitation of women and the exploitation of the earth on the other. Keats's images of wise female passivity and responsiveness to nature are prototypically ecofeminist.

If we return to the letter to Reynolds with this in mind, we will notice that it offers more than a weather report. It mediates between meteorology and mythology. The unblemished sky is compared to Diana, mythical goddess of chastity. This allusion fits with the poem's feminized relationship with nature. Keats would have read in Lemprière's *Classical Dictionary* that the poppy was sacred to Diana. Several of the goddess's traditional functions and associations suggest that she may be regarded as a spirit of ecological wholeness: she was supposed to promote the union of communities; she was especially worshipped by women; she seems originally to have been a spirit of the woods and of wild nature who was subsequently brought into friendly accord with early Roman farmers. But this latter shift also reveals the illusion upon which the poem is based. Diana, with her associations of woodland, chase and pool, is pre-eminently the presider over a pre-agrarian world. The meadows in which she runs are never harvested. Chastity is an ancient image of untouched – virgin – land. It might be said that a more appropriate presider for the poem would be one of Diana's opposites, the fertile Cleopatra: 'he ploughed her and she cropped', says Enobarbus of Caesar and Cleopatra. The male farmer ploughs, the female land is cropped.

In both letter and poem, Keats celebrates the stubble, that which remains after the cropping and the gathering. This land is worked-over, not virgin. The aestheticized still-point of the poem occurs at the moment when humankind has possessed and emptied the land. But where in the 'Ode on a Grecian Urn' the objective correlative was a human artwork which was celebrated precisely because it transcends time, 'To Autumn' offers only a momentary suspension upon the completion of harvest. At the close of the poem, the gathering swallows and the full-grown lamb are already reminding us of the next spring. Famously,

Keats renounces that quest for aesthetic transcendence which is to be heard yearning through his earlier odes. Instead, he embraces the immanence of nature's time, the cycle of the seasons.

'By chance or wisdom,' writes Serres, 'the French language uses a single word, *temps*, for the time that passes and for the weather outside, a product of climate and of what our ancestors called meteors.' 'To Autumn' is a poem of both time and the weather. In this respect, it mediates between exterior and interior ecologies. Ecosystems evolve in time through the operation of weather; the ecology of the human mind is equally dependent on the two senses of *temps*. Our moods are affected by the weather. Our identities are constituted in both time and place, are always shaped by both memory and environment. Romantic poetry is especially concerned with these two constitutions. It is both a mnemonic and an ecologic. Weather is a prime means of linking spatiality and temporality – this could be why so many major Romantic poems are weather poems. A Romantic poem may be regarded as a model of a certain kind of being and of dwelling; whilst always at several removes from the actual moment of being and place of dwelling in which it is thought and written, the poem itself is an image of ecological wholeness which may grant to the attentive and receptive reader a sense of being-at-home-in-the-world.

Let us read 'To Autumn' backwards. The poem ends with an at-homeness-with-all-living-things (swallow, robin, cricket, lamb, willow, gnat). The final stanza's river and distant hill are not virgin ecosystems, but they are less touched by humankind than is the intermediate farmed environment of the middle stanza. Where the poem has begun is with an intensively managed but highly fertile domestic economy in a cottage-garden. The movement *of* the poem is thus like that of the inspirational walk out of Winchester: from culture to nature. But the movement through the poem, with its intricate syntactical, metrical and aural inter-linkings, is not one which divides the culture from the nature. There is no sense of river, hill and sky as the opposite of house and garden. Rather, what Keats seems to be saying is that to achieve being-at-homeness-in-the-world you have to begin from your own dwelling-place. Think globally, the poem might be saying – act locally.

*

With its thatch-eves, mossed cottage-trees and morning mistiness, Keats's imaginary dwelling-place is built upon the Nether Stowey cottage-home described by Coleridge in his blank-verse meditation of 1798, 'Frost at Midnight'. The verbal echoes sound from the closing section of 'Frost':

> Therefore all seasons shall be sweet to thee,
> Whether the summer clothe the general earth
> With greenness, or the redbreast sit and sing
> Betwixt the tufts of snow on the bare branch
> Or mossy apple-tree, while the nigh thatch
> Smokes in the sun-thaw; whether the eave-drops fall
> Heard only in the trances of the blast,
> Or if the secret ministry of frost
> Shall hang them up in silent icicles,
> Quietly shining to the quiet Moon.

At the micro-political level of ideology, the celebration in 'Frost at Midnight' of snug – though surely not smug – domestic virtue may be related to a Burkean defence of 'home' against French revolutionary innovation during the invasion fear of 1798. At the macro-political level of ecosophy (Greek *sophos*, 'wisdom', concerning the *oikos*), it is a meditation on the relationship between being and dwelling, achieved through a subtle inter-play of what Serres calls *les deux temps*.

The secret ministry of the frost (weather) is the exterior analogue for the equally secret interior ministry of the memory (time). As the frost writes upon the window pane, so memory writes the poet's identity. By the end of the night both the environment of the cottage and the ecology of the poet's mind will have subtly evolved. The poet has learnt to dwell more securely with himself, his home and his environment. But the structure of the evolution is that of a topological network, not a Newtonian sequence of action and reaction. The distinction is one made by Serres in his *Éclaircissements*. If you take a handkerchief and lay it flat to iron it, you can define fixed distances between points on it: this is the geometry of the classical age. But if you crumple up the handkerchief to put it in your pocket, two points that were far apart can be near together or even superimposed on one another: this is the topology of networks. For Serres, both time and the weather are structured according to this kind of topology.

Chaos theory has the means to understand these relationships: fractal geometry. As Keats seems to have had an intuitive knowledge of the importance of illusory excess as a principle of community ecology, so may Coleridge have had an intuitive knowledge of the fractal structure of time and weather. How may we measure the motions of 'Frost at Midnight'? The pattern of the frost; the flickering of the flame and the flapping of the film on the grate; the flowings of breeze, wave, cloud, thaw-steam, eve-drop and icicle? They describe shapes which are fractal, not classically geometric. The poet's abstruser musings have dim sympathy with these motions because they have a similar structure, in that the poem's temporal structure is not classically sequential, but crumpled like Serres' handkerchief in such a way that it makes manifest neighbourings ('*voisinages*') which are invisible to the modern Constitution.

The temporal structure may be simplified as present-past-future-present. In its imagining of the baby Hartley's future, the poem proposes an ideal mode of dwelling in which the human subject is set into a new relationship with the objects of nature:

> But *thou*, my babe! shalt wander like a breeze
> By lakes and sandy shores, beneath the crags
> Of ancient mountain, and beneath the clouds,
> Which image in their bulk both lakes and shores
> And mountain crags.

The child is imagined as becoming like the weather, the breeze which plays across both land and water. But, more than this, the Enlightenment form of spatial perception is shattered: the parallelism of 'beneath the crags' and 'beneath the clouds' breaks down the rigid distinction between solid and vaporous matter, while the image of the clouds imaging the lakes and crags reverses the classical structure of substance and shadow (real mountain above, illusory image reflected in water below). The dislocation – the *pliage* – is such that it no longer seems appropriate to talk about human subject and natural object. The Cartesian subject/object distinction is made to vanish.

The imagined relationship between Hartley and nature is like the articulated relationship between Samuel and Hartley. The italicized *thou* strives to replace the dialectic of subject and object with an intercourse of I and thou. Where the subject/object relationship is one of power, the I/thou is one of love. Bond and tie replace mastery and possession. An ecofeminist language of nurture and care, as against male technological exploitation, is again apposite. What is truly radical about 'Frost at Midnight' is Coleridge's self-representation as a father in the traditional maternal posture of watching over a sleeping baby. In ecofeminist terms, this realignment of gender roles clears the way for a caring as opposed to an exploitative relationship with the earth.

Michel Serres asks: 'In politics or economics, by means of the sciences, we know how to define power; but how can we *think fragility*?' I ask myself: what might be the legacy of Romantic poetry in the twenty-first century? And on reflection I think that the answer to one question is the answer to the other: Romantic poetry can enable us to think fragility. Byron's 'Darkness' proposes that when ecosystems collapse, human bonds do so too. Keats's 'To Autumn' and Coleridge's 'Frost at Midnight' are thinkings of our bonds with each other and the earth, thinkings of fragile, beautiful, necessary ecological wholeness. To quote Serres once more:

> Modernity neglects, speaking in absolute terms. It cannot and will not think or act toward the global, whether temporal or spatial.
>
> Through exclusively social contracts, we have abandoned the bond that connects us to the world, the one that binds the time passing and flowing to the weather outside, the bond that relates the social sciences to the sciences of the universe, history to geography, law to nature, politics to physics, the bond that allows our language to communicate with mute,

passive, obscure things – things that, because of our excesses, are recovering voice, presence, activity, light. We can no longer neglect this bond.

While we uneasily await a second Flood, can we practise a diligent religion of the world?

Some organisms, it is said, disappeared from the face of the Earth as a result of their enormous size. This still astonishes us, that the biggest things should be the weakest, like the whole Earth, Man as megalopolis or Being-every-where, even God. Having long enjoyed the death of these grand and fragile entities, philosophy today is taking refuge in small details, which give it a sense of security.

Whose diligent shoulders can henceforth sustain this immense and fissured sky, which we fear, for the second time in a long history, will fall on our heads?

*

'To Autumn' and 'Frost at Midnight' are among English poetry's greatest contemplations of time and the weather. I want to close this chapter by collapsing time and following 'To Autumn' forward to what Yvor Winters calls 'probably the greatest American poem of the twentieth century and certainly one of the greatest contemplative poems in English': Wallace Stevens's 'Sunday Morning', written in New York in 1915, and published in the poet's first volume, *Harmonium*, in 1923.

Stevens's most sensitive reader, Helen Vendler, has demon-strated that the close of 'Sunday Morning' is an imitation of 'To Autumn'. Stevens replaces Keats's gathering swallows with more urban birds, namely undulating pigeons, but Vendler notes that at the same time his introduction of 'wilderness forms' in place of Keats's 'domestic ones' gives the rewriting a distinctively American inflection. Stevens is rewriting not only Keats but also the New England Puritan tradition in which an errand into the wilderness becomes the road to God. The woman in the poem is not spending her 'Sunday Morning' in church; instead, she is taking 'late / Coffee and oranges in a sunny chair'. In place of the dove, traditional representation of the Holy Spirit, there is an image of a bright green cockatoo woven into a rug.

The second stanza asks:

Why should she give her bounty to the dead?
What is divinity if it can come
Only in silent shadows and in dreams?
Shall she not find in comforts of the sun,
In pungent fruit and bright, green wings, or else
In any balm or beauty of the earth,
Things to be cherished like the thought of heaven?
Divinity must live within herself:
Passions of rain, or moods in falling snow;
Grievings in loneliness, or unsubdued
Elations when the forest blooms; gusty
Emotions on wet roads on autumn nights;
All pleasures and all pains, remembering
The bough of summer and the winter branch.
These are the measures destined for her soul.

In stanza one, a green cockatoo instead of the holy spirit. In stanza two, a denial of transcendence. For Stevens, spiritual fulfilment is to be found neither in formal religious observance nor in contemplation of the hereafter, but in the 'comforts of the sun' and the 'beauty of the earth'. To understand him fully, we must accept the real presence of the sun whilst simultaneously granting that a poem can only ever offer a woven image of a cockatoo, not a cockatoo itself.

The barometer of our spiritual moods is our emotional reaction to weather. We feel as we feel because of the rain, the snow, the wind, 'The bough of summer and the winter branch'. In place of Keats's autumn day, Stevens has 'gusty / Emotions on wet roads on autumn nights'. Whenever I read the poem, I misread 'gusty' as 'gutsy'. I chastise myself for so doing, but then decide that the misreading is felicitous: the weather, like great poetry, works within our guts. Throughout our lives we respond to place, to changes in our surroundings; we measure ourselves through our dwellings, recalling our histories through time and the weather. Each of us remembers that drive, that autumn night, those wet leaves.

As Keats in 'To Autumn' gives up on the quest for transcendence that ached through his previous odes, so Stevens in 'Sunday Morning' refuses to translate the forms of nature into divinities.

His sky is not Jove's domain; it is a 'dividing and indifferent blue'. The blue of the sky is indifferent to us. There is nothing above this sky. Keats's swallow flies again in Stevens's fourth stanza, its passage a sign of the returning cycle of the seasons rather than a journey towards a paradise beyond the biological world. The swallow's wings arc in a 'consummation' of the seasons, the noun serving to evoke death – the 'consummatum est' of Christ, Hamlet's 'consummation devoutly to be wished'. 'Death is the mother of beauty', Stevens writes in the fifth stanza and reiterates in the sixth. His poem is a celebration of things that are valuable because they are mortal, because they are fragile. 'Sunday Morning' is about learning to put aside the immortal longings of the old religion and the equally transcendent urges of that technological frame of mind the ultimate end of which is to conquer space and time, to master the weather, to stop the clock which counts us to our death.

The poem ends with images of contented dwelling upon our island-earth, with acceptance of biology, of contingency, of chaos. To respect time and the weather may be the means of living and dying gracefully:

> We live in an old chaos of the sun,
> Or old dependency of day and night,
> Or island solitude, unsponsored, free,
> Of that wide water, inescapable.
> Deer walk upon our mountains, and the quail
> Whistle about us their spontaneous cries;
> Sweet berries ripen in the wilderness;
> And, in the isolation of the sky,
> At evening, casual flocks of pigeons make
> Ambiguous undulations as they sink,
> Downward to darkness, on extended wings.

'The mood of autumn,' wrote Stevens in a letter, is 'the mood in which one sums up and meditates on the actualities of the actual year'. Stevens's poetry always attaches great importance to actuality, but it is also acutely aware of mortality. Perhaps that awareness was bound up with his daily work for the Hartford Accident and Indemnity Company. To think poetically about 'life insurance' is a strange thing. Stevens lived among actuaries, experts in statistics who calculate life expectancies, insurance risks and premiums. 'Actuality' is derived from medieval Latin *actualitas*, an entity; 'actuary' from *actuarius*, a bookkeeper. Stevens's writing life was a testing of the difficult, necessary relationship between bookkeeping and entities. The poem belongs to the book and not the world; it is the 'supreme fiction'. But the poet longs to ground his being in the actualities of the world. The strivings of the imagination must be reconciled with connection to the earth.

Perhaps this reconciliation may be achieved through an acceptance of time and the weather. Consider two extraordinary late poems, in which Stevens returns to some of the themes of 'Sunday Morning', though stripping his language of its former Keatsian excess and lushness. 'World without Peculiarity', written in 1948 and published in the collection *The Auroras of Autumn*, begins with dissonance between human mortality and the biotic cycle, disconnection between the memory of dead parents and 'The red ripeness of round leaves'. Dislocation initially prompts a troubled questioning, a sense that we should be something more than mere earth which returns to earth:

> What good is it that the earth is justified,
> That it is complete, that it is an end,
> That in itself it is enough?

But then the poem moves to an acceptance. It is perhaps enough that we are part of the earth and the earth is part of us: 'It is the earth itself that is humanity'. Sometimes there are moments when 'difference' disappears and the earth seems not 'the meaningless place' but a home where all things 'Become a single being, sure and true'. Human beings have the unique capacity to imagine infinity; that capacity is one of the forces which drives the technological quest. But we also have a necessary capacity to imagine finitude. Stevens in his late poems seems to be saying something similar to the later Heidegger, who argued that the authenticity of *Dasein* is finally lodged in its being towards death.

The closing poem of Stevens's last collection, *The Rock*, written in 1954, is called 'Not Ideas about the Thing but the Thing Itself':

> At the earliest ending of winter,
> In March, a scrawny cry from outside
> Seemed like a sound in his mind.
>
> He knew that he heard it,
> A bird's cry, at daylight or before,
> In the early March wind.
>
> The sun was rising at six,
> No longer a battered panache above snow . . .
> It would have been outside.
>
> It was not from the vast ventriloquism
> Of sleep's faded papier-mâché . . .
> The sun was coming from outside.
>
> That scrawny cry – it was
> A chorister whose c preceded the choir.
> It was part of the colossal sun,
>
> Surrounded by its choral rings,
> Still far away. It was like
> A new knowledge of reality.

As always with Stevens, the moment of vision – or, more exactly, of aural insight – is hedged around with ironies and uncertainties. The cry from the world outside *seems like* a cry in the mind; an owl is not a chorister and a 'c' is a mark in the text, not the world. 'It was *like* a new knowledge of reality', it was not reality itself. But the poet knows that sometimes the discipline he needs is one which renounces the work of metaphor and simile, of striving to connect and thus perforce to confront the disconnections. Only through what Stevens in 'An Ordinary Evening in New Haven' called an 'intricate evasion of *as if*' can he give up on ideas about the thing and hear the thing itself. Only then can he let the owl be an owl. Is that possible? Towards the end of his manifesto poem, 'Notes toward a Supreme Fiction', Stevens quietly insists that it may be. If we do not impose, we may discover:

To discover an order as of
A season, to discover summer and know it,

To discover winter and know it well, to find,
Not to impose, not to have reasoned at all,
Out of nothing to have come on major weather,

It is possible, possible, possible.

5

The Picturesque Environment

Am I,
To see in the Lake District, then,
Another bourgeois invention like the piano?

(W. H. Auden, 'Bucolics III: Mountains')

Should we have stayed at home,
wherever that may be?

(Elizabeth Bishop, 'Questions of Travel')

LET US RETURN for a moment to Keats's account of the walk which was the occasion for the composition of 'To Autumn': 'Now the time is beautiful. I take a walk every day for an hour before dinner and this is generally my walk.' The time is beautiful: it is beautiful at this time of day, this time of year. It is beautiful because the weather is beautiful. Again, time is weather. But what makes the time beautiful?

T. W. Adorno opens his discussion of 'The beauty of nature' as follows:

Beginning with Schelling, who titled his major work on aesthetics *Philosophy of Art*, aesthetics has shown an almost exclusive concern with works of art, discontinuing any systematic investigation of 'the beautiful in nature', which had occasioned some of the most perspicuous analyses in Kant's *Critique of Judgment*. Why was natural beauty dropped from the agenda of aesthetics? The reason was not that it was truly sublated in a higher realm, as Hegel would have us believe. Rather, the concept of natural beauty was simply repressed. Its continued presence would have touched a sore spot, conjuring up associations of acts of violence perpetrated by every work of art, as a pure artefact, against the natural. Wholly man-made, the work of art is radically opposed to nature, which appears not to be so made.

For Hegel, works of art were purely human. They were indeed regarded as the purest, the highest creations of the human, the embodiment of freedom and dignity, those qualities which, according to the Enlightenment, make us more than mere animals. Hegelianism proposes that the great work of art reconciles us symbolically to the world. Aesthetics must therefore be silent about the fact that art can only be achieved by perpetrating violence against the world in the manner described by Shelley in his poem on the felling of a tree for the manufacture of a musical instrument. Adorno accuses idealist aesthetics of laying waste to 'all that is not under the sway of the subject', of failing to respect the difference of nature's entities.

The opposition between art and nature, between Prospero and Ariel/Caliban, is the very core of 'aesthetics' as it was constituted as a discipline of thought during the Enlightenment. When eighteenth-century aesthetics becomes nineteenth-century aestheticism, Oscar Wilde writes that

> What Art really reveals to us is Nature's lack of design, her curious crudities, her extraordinary monotony, her absolutely unfinished condition. Nature has good intentions, of course, but, as Aristotle once said, she cannot carry them out. When I look at a landscape I cannot help seeing all its defects. It is fortunate for us, however, that Nature is so imperfect, as otherwise we should have no art at all. Art is our spirited protest, our gallant attempt to teach Nature her proper place ... Nature is so uncomfortable. Grass is hard and lumpy and damp, and full of dreadful black insects. Why, even [William] Morris's poorest workman could make you a more comfortable seat than the whole of Nature can.

Human beings have comfortable chairs and houses designed in proper proportions – not to mention beautiful artworks and elegant, paradoxical, epigrammatic Wildean conversations. These are things which 'Nature' lacks and so we should be eternally grateful for their invention.

But Adorno, in his very different way as much a master of the paradox as Wilde, suggests that the case is not so simple:

> in their antithetical opposition man and nature are dependent on each other: nature on the experience of a mediated and objectified world, art on nature which is the mediated plenipotentiary of immediacy. Reflections on natural beauty, therefore, are an integral and inalienable part of any theory of art.

Nature only *appears* to be not man-made, for in order to imagine a totality of entities the world must be 'mediated and objectified'. Air, trees, rocks, grass, water and so forth exist, but they only become 'Nature' when they are mediated by human consciousness, when a subject makes them its objects of attention. Then again, according to Adorno, man depends on nature every bit as much as nature depends on man. This is because nature functions for man as 'the mediated plenipotentiary of immediacy'. Adorno explains what he means by this a little later in his analysis:

> Delight in nature is tied up with the notion of the subject as being-for-itself and potentially infinite. The subject projects itself on to nature, gaining a sense of nearness to nature by virtue of its isolation. The subject's helplessness in a society petrified into second nature prompts it to seek refuge in first nature.

With that phrase 'second nature' Adorno is alluding to Marx's notion of false consciousness, the idea that ideology has the power to make us assume in our day to day lives that the conditions in which we live – wage-slavery, economic inequality – are inherent in the nature of the world, whereas they are in fact the result of a particular, and changeable, social system such as capitalism. Adorno proposes that one of the functions of 'first nature' for modernity is as a place of refuge for the individual consciousness. To be myself alone on a mountainside is to be-for-myself, rather than to be petrified into my social self as a worker. So it is that to be alone on a mountainside is to feel within oneself the potential for infinitude.

For Adorno, there is a historical core to our delight in nature, a core which 'both legitimates and detracts from natural beauty'. He argues that 'As long as nature had not yet been repressed, its seeming indomitability was a source of fear'. It is well known that in the seventeenth century, mountains tended to elicit only disgust (a symptom of fear), whereas in the eighteenth century they tended to elicit delight. Adorno would say that the increasing technological domination of nature which marked the eighteenth century led to the repression of nature's wildness. The repressed returns, but as a shiver of delight rather than a shudder of true impotence, in the frisson which eighteenth-century aestheticians called 'the sublime'. The aesthetic appreciation of wild landscape thus emerges as the counter-tide of technological modernity: 'Over long periods of time, the appreciation of natural beauty amalgamated itself with the suffering of the lone subject in an instrumentalized and mutilated world'. Natural beauty 'represents the recollection of a non-repressive condition that may never have existed'. That is both its necessity and its limitation, its strength and its weakness.

Adorno reconciles the opposition between nature and art by means of an ingenious dialectic. Hegel had argued in his *Aesthetics* that art is an attempt to overcome the deficiency of natural beauty. The clever remarks of Vivian in Wilde's 'Decay of Lying', quoted above, are in this respect Hegelian. Adorno replies that out of the opposition comes a potential redemption:

> art is influenced by the fact that nature is not yet what it
> appears to be; and this condition will last as long as nature is
> exclusively defined in terms of its opposition to society. Art
> accomplishes what nature strives for in vain: it opens its eyes.
> Nature in its appearance – that is, nature in so far as it is not
> an object to be worked upon – in turn provides the expression
> of melancholia, peace or what have you. Art stands in for
> nature by abolishing the latter in effigy.

Nature is not just an image of beauty, it is also an object that is worked over and commodified, but the beauty of nature neverthe-less offers us a promise of freedom, peace and belonging. By withdrawing into its own realm and thus obliterating the scars of commodification, art has the capacity to redeem that promise. When we contract ourselves to respond sympathetically to an artwork, we are following the same logic as when we let ourselves go and inhale the fresh air of the park or the country. Even as it is a cry against the commodification and instrumentalization that characterize modernity, contemplation of the beauty of art and nature is a strong and necessary deed:

> Like every promise, the beautiful in nature is feeble in that it is just a promise and strong in that it cannot be blotted out once it has been received. Words tend to bounce off nature as they try to deliver nature's language into the hands of another language foreign to it. But this is not to say that there cannot be sunny days in southern countries which seem to be waiting to be taken notice of, never mind the teleological fantasy that seems to be implied in such a statement. When a day like this draws to a close, radiating the same peaceful brilliance it did when it began, a message seems to be inscribed in it. It says not all is lost yet, or perhaps it says, more affirmatively, that everything will be all right.

This could serve equally well as a description of Keats's feelings on the autumn day when he says 'Now the time is beautiful' and our feelings when we respond sympathetically to his ode 'To Autumn'.

'Just how inextricably natural and artistic beauty are interlocked', writes Adorno a little earlier, 'can be seen by looking more closely at the essence of what appreciation of natural beauty is':

> First of all, it focuses exclusively on nature as appearance, never on nature as the stuff of work and material reproduction of life, let alone as a substratum of science. Like the aesthetic appreciation of art, that of nature centres on images. Nature is perceived as appearance of the beautiful and not as an object to be acted upon. This abnegation of the purpose of self-preservation, then, is just as crucial to the aesthetic perception of nature as it is to that of art. In this respect they hardly differ.

If you are a peasant or a sailor, your relationship with nature will be bound up with self-preservation; if you live in the luxury of technological modernity, your relationship with nature will be aesthetic. It will be bound up with the image and the gaze. So let us think about some *images* of natural beauty.

The prolific Anthony Trollope rose to an unusual pitch of emotional intensity in his late novel *He Knew He Was Right* (1869). It is a tale of sexual jealousy of almost Othello-like proportions. The central character, Louis Trevelyan, is driven to melancholy and eventual madness by his utterly unfounded conviction of his wife's adultery. In the depths of his despair, he holes up alone in a secluded house called Casalunga in the hills above Siena. In a classic example of what Trollope's contemporary John Ruskin called the 'pathetic fallacy', the arid hilly landscape is made to mirror the bleakness of the character's mood. Trollope's illustrator, Marcus Stone, catches the moment in stark monochromatic tones (plate 2).

The unkempt hair, the pose of contemplation and the black clothing are traditional attributes of the melancholy man. But, try as we might, we cannot imagine this figure to be Hamlet or a despairing lover from older times. Why not? Because of the intimate link between his emotions and the environment in which he is placed. His body seems to grow from the black rock, the landscape beyond to be an emanation of his interior life. This kind of self-conscious identification between mood and environment is not characteristic of older representations of melancholy. Ruskin showed that the pathetic fallacy is distinctly a mark of the modern – we would say the Romantic – artist.

In defence of the idea of natural beauty, Adorno wryly notes that 'However true it may be that anything in nature can be considered beautiful, empirical propositions to the contrary are also true, e.g. a statement to the effect that the landscape of Tuscany is more beautiful than the surroundings of Birmingham or Pittsburgh'. From the poetry of Byron and Shelley to late twentieth-century tourist brochures aimed at well-to-do Americans and northern Europeans, the Tuscan hills have been associated with picture-postcard beauty. So in order to make those hills echo Trevelyan's black mood in the novel, Trollope had to write explicitly against the grain of convention:

Olives and vines have pretty names, and call up associations of landscape beauty. But here they were in no way beautiful. The ground beneath them was turned up, and brown, and arid ... The occupants of Casalunga had thought more of the produce of their land than of picturesque or attractive appearance.

Illustrator Marcus Stone had to work equally hard to avoid calling up associations of landscape beauty, to produce a picture that was not picturesque. He did not entirely succeed. Various characters visit Trevelyan at Casalunga and express amazement that any human being could live in such an uninviting place, but if there is any Romantic blood in us, when we look at the illustration we will feel the urge to change places with Trevelyan, to be among those hills instead of in our library. An image of an impassioned man among the mountains inevitably suffuses us with the thrill of the sublime, with the recollection of, say, John Martin's representation (plate 3) of the following rhapsodic lines from Thomas Gray's poem, 'The Bard' (from *Odes*, 1757):

> On a rock, whose haughty brow
> Frowns o'er old Conway's foaming flood,
> Robed in the sable garb of woe,
> With haggard eyes the poet stood;
> (Loose his beard and hoary hair
> Streamed, like a meteor, to the troubled air).

The two associations which I have here brought to bear upon Stone's illustration of Trevelyan at Casalunga are strikingly divergent. The suggestion that we feel the urge to changes places with Trevelyan implies a projection of the reader's self into a real mountainous landscape – which could be Tuscany, but might as well be the English Lake District or the American Adirondacks. To make such a suggestion is to conceive a book illustration as an evocation of nature as well as a visualization of a piece of fictive text. Yet to speak of that same illustration as working within the tradition of the painterly sublime is to relate it not to nature, but to a previous work of art.

Gray was doing something similar when he composed his

lines about the poet on the rock. On the one hand, he was among the first English men of letters to be inspired by mountain scenery, to which he was initially exposed when he visited the Grand Charteuse alone as a young man. On the other hand, his notion of a Bard was derived from a body of ancient Celtic poetry in which he took a deep antiquarian interest. Equally, he admitted in a letter to a friend that the figure of the Bard, beard and hair streaming in the wind, was inspired by a previous work of art: 'the thought . . . is borrow'd from painting. Rafael in his Vision of Ezekiel (in the Duke of Orleans' Collection) has given the air of head, which I tried to express, to God the Father.'

At one level, what we are addressing here is the perennial problem of artistic representation in any form, whether painting, poetry or fiction: artists try to tell you something about the world, about life – they hold up a mirror to nature – but they can only do so via a repertoire of techniques and conventions that are inherited from previous art. At another level, though, the problem is peculiarly acute in the case of representations of a return to the wild. Stone's Trevelyan and Martin's Bard are intended to be gathered into their secluded environment, to have an unmediated oneness with untrammelled nature. The intrusion of artistic tradition is necessary to both the compositional process and the affective response, but it contaminates the purity of the relationship with nature itself. An artistic representation of a figure in a landscape cannot but be *mediated*. Is it possible, though, for a figure to stand in a natural landscape and relate to it in a manner that is *unmediated*? In this chapter, I want to reflect upon this question in relation to that aesthetic tradition which Trollope invokes only in order to dismiss: I want to 'call up associations of landscape beauty' and explore some of the paradoxes of the 'picturesque'.

*

In the autumn of 1769, Thomas Gray visited the English Lake District and wrote a series of letters, soon to be published in the form of a continuous journal, in praise of the mountains, lakes and vales he found there. A few years later, Thomas West published *A Guide to the Lakes*. That massive branch of the modern tourism industry, the journey back to nature, has its origins here. The early tourists went armed with guidebook, sketchpad, Claude glass and sometimes camera obscura. We still take the guidebook, but our key piece of equipment is the modern descendant of the camera obscura. When we see an especially fine view, we take a photograph of it. If we stop to think about the procedure, this is a rather strange thing to do.

'There is,' writes Malcolm Andrews in an excellent book on the origins of picturesque tourism, 'a peculiar circularity in the tourist's experience. He values the kind of scenery which has been aesthetically validated in paintings, postcards and advertisements; he appraises it with the word "picturesque"; and then he takes a photograph of it to confirm its pictorial value.' In participating in such a process, we turn the places we visit into commodities, implicitly or explicitly encouraging others to follow our footsteps there, and thus to make them ever less pristine, less 'natural' and uncontaminated by the signs and relics of mass humanity. Poets and painters are worse culprits than humbler individuals such as ourselves: where we only show our snapshots to family and friends, they disseminate their picturesque images to a huge, undiscriminating public of potential fellow-pilgrims. Consider two of the most popular volumes of Regency poetry: Lord Byron's *Childe Harold's Pilgrimage* sent thousands trekking to the Falls of Terni, while Samuel Rogers' *Italy* provided a pocket compendium of picturesque destinations from the Alps to Naples, functioning for nineteenth-century travellers as a kind of versified Fodor or Blue Guide.

Let us look at James Baker Pyne's lithograph of Windermere, the first port-of-call on the Lake Tour (plate 4). To the right, one can just make out a group of well-to-do figures who have ascended to an elevated station from which they may gain an excellent view of the lake and the hills beyond. But the figure in the foreground, his rustic dress indicating that he is a local rather than a tourist, is pointing to something else: the train that is moving across the valley to the left. Instead of the tourist regarding the native labourer as part of the picturesque scene, the local is looking at the trainload of visitors, regarding them as anthropological curiosities. Pyne's irony is now somewhat lost, since steam trains have themselves joined the repertory of picturesque tourism; for the picture to regain its impact, we would have to drive a six-lane highway through the centre of it.

From our point of view, the irony inevitably rebounds on William Wordsworth. He did more than anyone to popularize his native Lakeland landscapes, and in so doing bring in the trainloads of day trippers whom he then said would destroy the place. In the final section of this chapter, it will be suggested that Wordsworth was a subtle critic of the picturesque, but he was at the same time an active participant in the movement and an economic beneficiary of it. His best-selling publication was not a volume of poetry but a *Guide to the Lakes*. The text of Wordsworth's guide first appeared in print as the accompanying commentary to a series of archetypally picturesque landscape engravings by the Reverend Joseph Wilkinson, entitled *Select Views in Cumberland, Westmoreland* [sic], *and Lancashire*. Typical of Wilkinson's work is a view of Windermere, pre-railway, with human figures placed harmoniously in the landscape. Equally characteristic is his rendition of a pair of picturesque – because dilapidated – cottages in the village of Applethwaite (plate 5).

A little pleasing peasant poverty is a necessary prerequisite for the picturesque. If your scene is to be peopled, it should be with beggars or, better still, colourful gypsies. They are the human equivalent of run-down buildings. Neither prosperous yeomen nor well-maintained tenements will do. Buildings only answer to the prescription if they are in a state of decay. Your generic picturesque prospect will usually include a carefully placed ruin. In Thomas Love Peacock's comic novel *Headlong Hall* (1816), a pleasant walk by the lake in the landscaped grounds of the hall is rudely interrupted by a tremendous explosion: Squire Headlong's ruined tower being insufficiently tumbledown for a refined taste, he has taken it upon himself to speed the process of decay with the assistance of some well-laid gunpowder.

Thus Sir Uvedale Price in a treatise which distinguishes between the classically beautiful and the romantically picturesque:

A temple or palace of Grecian architecture in its perfect entire state, and with its surface and colour smooth and even, either in painting or reality is beautiful; in ruin it is picturesque. Observe the process by which time, the great author of such changes, converts a beautiful object into a picturesque one. First, by means of weather stains, partial incrustations, mosses, etc., it at the same time takes off from the uniformity of the surface, and of the colour; that is gives a degree of roughness and variety of tint. Next, the various accidents of weather loosen the stones themselves; they tumble in irregular masses ... Sedums, wall-flowers, and other vegetables that bear drought find nourishment in the decayed cement from which the stones have been detached: birds convey their food into the chinks, and yew, elder, and other berried plants project from the sides; while the ivy mantles over other parts and crowns the top.

The influence of time, for which another word is weather, transforms what was once a human imposition into a part of the landscape itself.

The paradox of the picturesque is clearly visible in Price's description of a ruin. The scene is composed on aesthetic principles, the emphasis being on pleasing variety gathered into unity by a crowning feature such as ivy. Viewed thus, it is like a picture, hence picturesque. It is like a picture because many influential landscape paintings of the previous century, notably those of Claude Lorrain, were dotted with ruined temples and palaces which served as moral reminders of the decay of human endeavour and the inevitability of mortality. But at the same time, Price has an eye that is as committed to the particularities and energies of nature as it is to the harmonies and traditions of art. He regards the processes of time as less a memento mori than a manifestation of nature's wonderful powers of regeneration, organic life's capacity to infiltrate the most seemingly desolate places. The observation of sedum, wall-flower and bird-shelter is more Gilbert White than Claude Lorrain.

Because of their obsession with the rules of taste, it is hard to recover the freshness of vision that animates the handbooks of the picturesque. A movement that began with a desire to return to the simplicity of natural forms had become trapped by its own prescriptive jargon.

> 'You must not inquire too far, Marianne – remember I have no knowledge in the picturesque, and I shall offend you by my ignorance and want of taste if we come to particulars. I shall call hills steep, which ought to be bold; surfaces strange and uncouth, which ought to be irregular and rugged; and distant objects out of sight, which ought only to be indistinct through the soft medium of a hazy atmosphere. . . .'
>
> 'It is very true,' said Marianne, 'that admiration of landscape scenery is become a mere jargon. Every body pretends to feel and tries to describe with the taste and elegance of him who first defined what picturesque beauty was. I detest jargon of every kind, and sometimes I have kept my feelings to myself, because I could find no language to describe them in but what was worn and hackneyed out of all sense and meaning.'

Jane Austen was working on the first draft of *Sense and Sensibility* in the 1790s, when the fashion for the picturesque was at its height. The theory that the ideal landscape was characterized by 'that peculiar type of beauty, which is agreeable in a picture' was associated so closely with the name of the Reverend William Gilpin that Marianne does not need to mention his name. She refers only to 'him who first described what picturesque beauty was'. Jane Austen can assume that her readers would have been familiar with the 'jargon' that characterized Gilpin's descriptions of scenery. For instance:

> On the spot, no doubt, and even in the first distances, the marks of the spade, and the plough; the hedge, and the ditch; together with all the formalities of hedge-row trees, and square divisions of property, are disgusting in a high degree. But when all these regular forms are softened by distance – when hedge-row trees begin to unite, and lengthen into streaks along the horizon – when farm-houses, and ordinary buildings lose all their vulgarity of shape, and are scattered about, in formless spots, through the several parts of a

distance – it is inconceivable what richness, and beauty, this mass of deformity, when melted together, adds to landscape.

Edward Ferrars in *Sense and Sensibility* does not regard farmhouses and the marks of agricultural labour as vulgar or disgusting. He takes a pragmatic view of landscape. His 'idea of a fine country' is one which 'unites beauty with utility'. He is more interested in productive agriculture – 'rich meadows and neat farm houses', 'tidy, happy villagers' – than the stock properties of the picturesque ('crooked, twisted, blasted trees' and 'ruined, tattered cottages'). He is an embodiment of Enlightenment man, who regards nature as something that must be tamed, ordered and made serviceable to the community. He has no time for waste, for the surplus of heathland that cannot be farmed. 'I am not fond of nettles, or thistles, or heath blossoms'. Effectively he says to Marianne: to stand around waxing lyrical on the subject of well-composed prospects, rugged hills, hazy horizons, twisted trees and Gothic banditti is a luxury affordable only to the wealthy and healthy; the important thing – especially in a time of bad harvests – is to feed the people.

Marianne accepts Edward's critique of the jargon of the picturesque, the notion that precise Gilpinesque terms must be attached to each individual feature of the landscape. Yet she holds fast to her insistence that anyone capable of feeling strongly – anyone of sensibility – will respond passionately to a wild landscape. She looks with 'compassion' on her sister Elinor, who is destined to marry a man incapable of thrilling to the sight of rocks and promontories.

Is Marianne any less of an exploiter of nature than Edward? The superficial answer is 'yes': no utilitarian, she would disapprove of intensive land-management in the name of agricultural productivity (i.e., enclosure); she would want a space to be left for that which has no utilitarian value – rocks, twisted trees, thistles, heath blossoms. In later times, she would have been an advocate for the idea of the National Park. Her ideal holiday would be spent visiting the Peak District, the Lake District or the Highlands of Scotland. A latter-day Marianne would perhaps even have signed a petition objecting to the extension of the railway from

Kendal to Windermere or the ploughing of a motorway through Twyford Down.

The origins of the conservation movement may be traced back to the principles of picturesque tourism. Together with his fellow authors of guides to places of natural beauty, Gilpin created a taste for travel to such areas as the English Lakes and the Scottish mountains. By the end of the nineteenth century, the number of people with the leisure and income to indulge that taste had increased to such an extent that tourism itself began to change those places, with the result that organizations such as the National Trust were formed for the purpose of protecting the most celebrated picturesque spots.

But what is the rationale of conservation? Proponents of the establishment of a system of English and Welsh National Parks did not base their arguments on a theory of nature's rights. Rather, they argued from human needs. To look at a lake or walk on a mountain makes us feel relaxed; the encounter with nature is a form of recreation, all the more necessary because of the stress and alienation of urban modernity. So the argument went. In its way, this position is as utilitarian as that of Edward Ferrars. The admirer of picturesque scenery pretends to be submitting to the power of nature, but in fact she is taking something for herself from it, using it as a source of nourishment for the spirit, just as the man who encloses land does so in order to increase its yield of nourishment for the body. Marianne loves wild landscape not for itself, but because it is a testing-ground for her own romantic sensibility.

The encounter with nature is a form of recreation: it is also an act of re-creation. The very word 'landscape' makes the point. A land-scape means land as shaped, as arranged, by a viewer. The point of view is that of the human observer, not the land itself. The classic picturesque view is seen from a 'station', a raised promontory in which the spectator stands above the earth, looking down over it in an attitude of Enlightenment mastery. Land-scape was originally a technical term in painting; it denoted an artistic genre, not something in nature. Hence the term 'pictur-esque': a stretch of land that resembles a painting. We are in danger of going through Alice's looking-glass here. The ultimate gesture of the picturesque is that in which the genteel viewer stands on her promontory, turns her back on the view itself and takes out a Claude glass. The glass re-creates the landscape in the style of the paintings of Claude Lorrain: nature is framed and then made to change its hues as filters of different tints are put in place across the glass. Gilpin's images tend to reproduce both the oval shapes and the sepia hues of Claude.

Oscar Wilde remarked that there was no fog in London before the Impressionists started painting. His point was that our perception of nature is pre-determined by aesthetic categories. The admirer of picturesque landscape standing with her back to the landscape is the ancestor of the idealist aesthete – of Hegel, of Wilde, even of the band of post-structuralists who loftily dismiss the notion of referentiality from text to world. There are, however, dangers in concentrating solely on your act of representation, in supposing that there is nothing outside the frame of the Claude glass: turn your back on the unpredictability and contingency of nature, confine yourself to the realm of the aesthetic and the theoretical, and you will fall into many a scrape. So discovers that parody of Gilpin's tourist, Dr Syntax (plate 7).

The brilliance of Thomas Rowlandson's Dr Syntax caricatures is that they parody the contradictions of the picturesque not only in their substance but in their very form. Consider the title-page of Syntax's first tour, *In search of the Picturesque* (plate 6). Ostensibly, the picturesque tourist is going in search of nature, but what he is actually looking for are beauties pre-determined by art. His ideal would therefore be to find a text inscribed upon the land: a ruin which picks out the letters P I C. How do you find a picturesque prospect? Do you look around at the landscapes through which you are travelling? No, you look down at a text, at your copy of Gilpin or West's or Wordsworth's *Guide to the Lakes*. Since you're not actually looking where you're going, you may get lost (plate 8). Oh well, why not paint a picturesque landscape of the signpost itself:

> 'Tis all in vain
> To find my way across the plain;
> So here my fortune I will try,

And wait till some one passes by:
Upon that bank awhile I'll sit,
And let poor Grizzle graze a bit;
But as my time shall not be lost,
I'll make a drawing of the post;
And, tho' your flimsy tastes may flout it,
There's something *picturesque* about it:
'Tis rude and rough, without a gloss,
And is well covered o'er with moss;
And I've a right (who dares deny it?)
To place yon group of asses by it.
Aye! that will do: and now I'm thinking,
That self-same pond where Grizzle's drinking,
If hither brought 'twould better seem,
And, faith, I'll turn it to a stream;
I'll make this flat a shaggy ridge,
And o'er the water throw a bridge;
I'll do as other sketchers do –
Put any thing into the view;
And any object recollect,
To add a grace, and give effect.
Thus, tho' from truth I haply err,
The scene preserves its character.
What man of taste my right will doubt,
To put things in, or leave them out?
'Tis more than right, it is a duty,
If we consider landscape beauty:–
He ne'er will as an artist shine,
Who copies nature line by line;
Whoe'er from nature takes a view,
Must copy and improve it too:
To heighten ev'ry work of art,
Fancy should take an active part:
Thus I (which few, I think, can boast)
Have made a Landscape of a Post.

Syntax feels free to alter what he actually sees in order to make
it conform to picturesque principles. To anyone who actually
inhabits the country, the whole procedure will seem very bizarre
(plate 9). The bemused fisherman in 'Dr Syntax sketching on the

Lake' is anticipating Pyne's device of turning the gaze of the native back reflectively on the tourist.

It is easy enough to recompose a landscape, but credulity is stretched by the attempt to redispose living forms. Gilpin devoted many pages to the proper arrangement of cattle (plate 10). Rowlandson forces us to imagine what it would be like to make cattle submit to proper arrangement (plate 11). The caricature is called 'Dr Syntax drawing after nature', but you cannot imagine nature to be so conformable. Formally, the elegant line and sepia wash of Gilpin's cows bestow an aura of timeless peace analogous to that of the winding herd crossing the lea in Thomas Gray's 'Elegy Written in a Country Churchyard', whereas Rowlandson's use of caricature's sharpenings, elongations and bright colours snaps all illusions of 'naturalness'. This is why the very form of Dr Syntax is a critique of the picturesque: caricature is by definition 'unrealistic', for implicit mocking allusion to the art of accurate portraiture always intrudes between its images and their 'originals' in the world.

One of the oddities of Gilpin's picturesque tours is that, though they concern visits to actual regions of Britain, they rarely illustrate actual scenes. Nearly all his drawings are of imaginary, ideally picturesque landscapes. In order to focus exclusively on what picturesque scenes should be like, Gilpin avoided the distractions of reality. He proposes that there is nothing so good as a ruined abbey (plate 12) for completing a picturesque landscape, yet the illustration of one which he inserted into his Wye tour is not an accurate representation of Tintern, the tailor-made abbey which stood crumbling by the Wye. The clear implication is that even along a river as delightful as the Wye, picturesque perfection can never be achieved. That is only possible in the mind of the artist. The task of Gilpin's reader is to go the Wye, the Lakes or Scotland and make the imaginative attempt to transform fine, but necessarily blemished, prospects into the true picturesque. In other words, nature must be re-envisioned as art.

I have called this a Through the Looking-Glass procedure: appropriately enough, the Dr Syntax project had its origins in analogous topsy-turvydom. The norm of book illustration is for the text to come first, the illustrations second. In the case of the tours of Dr Syntax, it is the other way round: the poems illustrate the illustrations, not vice-versa. William Combe, the writer, was not acquainted with Rowlandson: he was sent a new picture each month, and he composed his verse-narrative around it.

Although my argument has been advanced by way of caricature, the point is deadly serious. The picturesque was among the first artistic movements in history to throw out the Classical premiss that art should imitate nature and to propose instead that nature should imitate art. It sought to treat entire landscapes in the manner in which earlier cultures designed gardens: formal Renaissance gardens, and in different ways the classic gardens of China and Japan, enclosed and remade natural spaces according to aesthetic principles. But the whole point of the formal garden was that it was a controlled space, an 'inside' that was different from untamed nature 'outside'. The eighteenth-century reaction against formality in garden design, the vogue for landscape gardening, was sister to the picturesque because the landscaper sought to break down the distinction between the garden itself and the nature beyond – such devices as the ha-ha meant that the eye could not distinguish between what was within and what was without the domain of the gardener. Like a picturesque view, a landscaped park is seemingly natural, but in fact highly artful.

Adorno's argument that the aestheticization of nature was the inevitable consequence of the advent of technological modernity offers a historical explanation of why the picturesque emerged when it did. And there is an inevitable historical irony about its emergence: in valuing art above nature whilst pretending to value nature above art, the picturesque took to an extreme a tendency of Enlightenment thought which has had catastrophic ecological consequences.

In the fourth section of his *Discourse on Method*, René Descartes considered the possibility that everything which entered his mind was as false as his dreams. It followed from the thought that everything might be false that *the mind which had this thought* must be something substantial and true. Descartes thus formulated the first principle of his philosophy: 'I think therefore I am'. With this move, the mind and its processes became the starting-point of philosophy; the rest of nature becomes separate and secondary. The Cartesian system is dualistic, framed so as to distinguish between subject and object, mind and world. Descartes was no Pyrrhonist: he firmly believed in the existence of the external world, and indeed in God's management of the laws of nature, but by proposing that the mind is its own place he opened the way for a denigration of material nature and an exaltation of human consciousness. The forces of nature could be seen to be there only to be harnessed by the might of man's inventive mind.

From his first principle, Descartes moved inexorably towards the final section of the *Discourse*, in which he wrote of a practical philosophy which would enable us to know 'the power and effects of fire, water, air, the stars, the heavens and all the other bodies which surround us' – we may then put them 'to all the uses for which they are appropriate, and thereby make ourselves, as it were, masters and possessors of nature'. We will invent 'an infinity of devices by which we might enjoy, without any effort, the fruits of the earth and all its commodities'. The ground is laid for the triumph of technology.

The industrial revolution of the late eighteenth and early nineteenth centuries is conventionally seen as the period in which technology first wrought a large-scale transformation of social conditions through the harnessing – the consumption – of natural resources, such as coal and iron. The positive effects of this transformation have been manifold (without them, you would not have the health, warmth, prosperity, leisure and prospect of longevity to be reading this book). The negative ones will become apparent the moment we note that this was the period in which the word 'pollution' took on its modern sense.

Whilst industrialization and urbanization were the visible practical consequences of the technological advances of the seventeenth and eighteenth centuries, the key theoretical consequence of Cartesian dualism was the development of a philosophy of mind which reached its apogee with the Kantian revolution of the late eighteenth century. For Immanuel Kant and his followers, we cannot know things-in-themselves (*noumena*), we can only know our idea of things in our own mind (*phenomena*). Our ways of knowing are pre-determined by the forms and categories of consciousness.

Let us think in Cartesian terms about the exchange regarding the picturesque in *Sense and Sensibility*. Though Edward is the technological Cartesian, Marianne is an epistemological one. 'I think therefore I am'; 'I am pleased by this landscape, therefore this landscape is worth preserving'. People who participate in conservation movements are now called 'environmentalists'. Again, the word is revealing. 'Environ' means 'around'. Environmentalists are people who care about the world around us. The world *around us*: anthropocentrism, the valuation of nature only in so far as it radiates out from humankind, remains a given. It is not a paradox that environmentalism was begotten by the picturesque, an aesthetic theory. Any environmental campaigner will tell you that it is easy to raise money for the defence of natural phenomena that are regarded as beautiful (a clear lake in the mountains, an old-growth forest) or that have anthropomorphic appeal (a cuddly giant panda, a seemingly smiling and linguistically well-endowed dolphin). It is much harder to gain interest in un-picturesque but ecologically crucial phenomena such as peat-bogs and earthworm communities.

Stopping a few motorways and saving a few spotted owls will not solve the world's ecological crisis. There is indeed a case for the argument that Western environmentalism – keeping *our* countryside picturesque – exacerbates world-wide ecological degradation by shipping the production processes that cause the worst pollution out to the Third World where *we* won't notice them and in so doing shipping them out to where *they* can't afford to regulate them. The name Bhopal is eloquent shorthand for this sad story. The argument in question is one of the causes of the division within the Green movement between 'environmentalists', children of the picturesque who are interested in particular conservation causes, and 'deep ecologists', who argue that the only means of saving the earth is nothing less than a complete transformation of Western value systems. At the centre of the deep ecological project is a critique of Cartesian dualism and mastery, of what is sometimes termed 'the arrogance of the Enlightenment'.

William Wordsworth has often been held up as one of the begetters of environmentalism. This is justifiable in view of his love of the Lake District and, in particular, such interventions as his 'Sonnet on the projected Kendal and Windermere Railway', with its castigation of 'false utilitarian lure' and its rousing appeal for the very winds and torrents to join in 'protest against the wrong'. But his deeper importance may, it seems to me, be as an ecological critic of the Enlightenment. The closing section of this chapter will try to demonstrate that his most famous 'landscape' poem stands in the same relation of critique towards the picturesque as deep ecology stands towards environmentalism.

*

The eleventh book of Wordsworth's long autobiographical meditation, *The Prelude*, is entitled 'Imagination, how impaired and restored'. In that book, Wordsworth suggests that there comes a time in our intellectual growth when we trust ourselves to Reason above all other faculties. We could call such a time the moment of Enlightenment. Of course there are 'obvious benefits' to be drawn from it. But for Wordsworth there is also danger. The moment of Enlightenment is very good at being the 'enemy of falshood' – say at resisting the tyranny of arbitrary monarchical power and the superstition of priesthoods. But it is less good at being 'the friend / Of truth'. The reason for this is that Enlightenment prefers 'to sit in judgement than to feel'.

Imagine a way of imagining the world that begins in feeling and not in judgement. What consequences might there then be for political economy? In a note published in the *Morning Post* on 16 October 1844, together with the sonnet on the projected railway extension to Windermere, Wordsworth wrote:

> The degree and kind of attachment which many of the yeomanry feel to their small inheritances can scarcely be over-rated. Near the house of one of them stands a magnificent tree, which a neighbour of the owner advised him to fell for profit's sake. 'Fell it,' exclaimed the yeoman, 'I had rather fall on my knees and worship it.' It happens, I believe, that the intended railway would pass through this little property, and

I hope that an apology for an answer will not be thought necessary by one who enters into the strength of the feeling.

'Fell it,' says the utilitarian judgement, the profit motive, the man of Enlightenment. 'Worship it,' says the believer in the rights of nature, the man endowed with strength of feeling.

The passage in book eleven of *The Prelude* goes on to give a specific example of what Wordsworth calls the 'presumption' of the judgement. There was a time, he writes, when he took a kind of pleasure in nature which 'pleased / Unworthily'. The unworthiness was the result of a spirit of judgement and comparison:

> disliking here, and there
> Liking, by rules of mimic art transferr'd
> To things above art.

In the next line, Wordsworth calls this tendency 'a strong infection of the age'. There can be no doubt that he is referring to the picturesque and its attempt to judge nature by the rules of art (which should rather itself mimic nature). Wordsworth claims that he was never guilty of passing reductive judgements on particular landscapes in the jargon of the picturesque. The claim is slightly disingenuous, given the extent to which such early works of his as 'An Evening Walk' and 'Descriptive Sketches' were couched in conventional picturesque language. But this may pass, since Wordsworth goes on to blame himself for falling into the same trap – of judging, of comparing, of presuming – as Gilpin and his disciples:

> giving way
> To a comparison of scene with scene,
> Bent overmuch on superficial things,
> Pampering myself with meagre novelties
> Of colour or proportion, to the moods
> Of time or season, to the moral power,
> The affections and the spirit of the place
> Less sensible.

The tourist's restless quest for novelty and the aesthete's taste for pleasing combinations of colour and satisfying proportions are here contrasted to less tangible things – time, morality, feeling and spirit. That the former overrode the latter was, Wordsworth then suggests, not merely the result of the force of the faculty of judgement and the vogue for the picturesque. There was

> another cause,
> More subtle and less easily explain'd
> That almost seems inherent to the Creature,
> Sensuous and intellectual as he is,
> A two-fold Frame of body and of mind.

It is, in other words, Cartesian dualism that makes us err in our dealings with nature.

Wordsworth sees that the posturing of the picturesque is but a manifestation of a presumption that is inherent in the Enlightenment account of mankind which sets the mind apart from the body, the *res cogitans* above the *res extensa*. He proposes that the error is inherent in the Cartesian account of *Homo sapiens*, but only 'almost seems inherent to the Creature' itself. Wordsworth's 'almost' leaves space for an alternative account, which, he implies, will be offered by his own work – by what may be called his 'ecopoetic'.

The Cartesian error is one 'In which the eye was master of the heart'. As the eye is master of the heart and the judgement master of the feelings, so mankind is master of nature. 'Despotic', 'absolute dominion', 'This tyranny': these are the terms in which Wordsworth describes the condition. Enlightenment may have been a path to social liberation, but it was also a programme for ecological imperialism. The older Wordsworth implies that the young Wordsworth's eye-driven relationship to nature was as rapacious as that of an eighteenth-century empire-builder's to his colonies:

> Yet was I often greedy in the chace,
> And roam'd from hill to hill, from rock to rock,
> Still craving new combinations of new forms,
> New pleasure, wider empire for the sight,
> Proud of its own endowments, and rejoiced
> To lay the inner faculties asleep.

The language here is extremely close to that in which Wordsworth described his first visit to the Wye valley in August 1793.
As in this passage he roams from hill to hill and rock to rock,
hungry to expand the empire of his gaze, so when he revisits the
Wye in 1798 he looks back on the time five years earlier when he
'bounded o'er the mountains' like a roe, consuming the colours
and forms of rock, mountain and wood with an insatiable
'appetite'

> That had no interest of a remoter charm
> By thought supplied, or any interest
> Unborrowed from the eye.

The similarity suggests that the twin critique of the picturesque
and of Cartesianism in book eleven of *The Prelude* is a gloss or
commentary upon the poem that concludes the first volume of
Lyrical Ballads, the lines that have become known as 'Tintern
Abbey'.

Before or during his walk through the Wye valley in July 1798
Wordsworth read Gilpin's *Observations on the River Wye ...
Relative Chiefly to Picturesque Beauty: Made in the Summer of the
Year 1770*. Gilpin begins the narrative of his Wye tour as follows:

> We travel for various purposes – to explore the culture of
> soils – to view the curiosities of art – to survey the beauties of
> nature – and to learn the manners of men; their different
> polities, and modes of life.
>   The following little work proposes a new object of pursuit;
> that of examining the face of a country *by the rules of picturesque
> beauty*.

The language of this exordium is locked within Cartesian dualism:
the traveller is the *subject*, the environment he visits the *object*.
The Wye valley is a face to be examined, not a home in which to
dwell.

Gilpin regarded the 'mazy course' and 'lofty banks' of the
River Wye as the key to its beauty, but the spot he singled out as
being the most picturesque was a product of human history, not
geological time. In his northern tour, having described a range of

picturesque natural features, he added another, of an 'artificial kind', namely 'the ruins of abbeys; which, being naturalized to the soil, might indeed, without much impropriety, be classed among its natural beauties'. Ruined abbeys, he claimed, are among the most picturesque beauties of the English landscape. So it was that the high point on the Wye tour, picturesquely secluded in a harmonious vale, was Tintern Abbey:

> A more pleasing retreat could not easily be found. The woods, and glades intermixed; the winding of the river; the variety of the ground; the splendid ruin, contrasted with the objects of nature; and the elegant line formed by the summits of the hills, which include the whole; make all together a very inchanting piece of scenery. Every thing around breathes an air so calm, and tranquil; so sequestered from the commerce of life; that it is easy to conceive, a man of warm imagination, in monkish times, might have been allured by such a scene to become an inhabitant of it.

Gilpin noted with surprise and delight that within half a mile of the site of the abbey there were great ironworks – and yet that one would not know this whilst walking and meditating amongst the ruins. He was writing, of course, without any awareness of the environmental effects of mining and industry. When he continued his journey downstream, he remarked that

> one great disadvantage began here to invade us. Hitherto the river had been clear, and splendid; reflecting the several objects on it's banks. But it's waters now became ouzy, and discoloured. Sludgy shores too appeared, on each side; and other symptoms, which discovered the influence of a tide.

To our jaundiced eyes, such symptoms as sludge and discoloration discover the influence less of a tide than of the ironworks. For picturesque tourists, on the other hand, impressive new industrial sites were objects of admiration just as much as ancient ruins and imposing cliffs. Visitors on the Wye tour saw no contradiction in praising the valley's seclusion from the bustle of commerce, but also the wonders of the great ironworks at New Weir. For a painter such as Thomas Wright of Derby, the industrial sublime elicited the same feelings as the natural.

The ruined abbey at Tintern was always regarded as the high point of the Wye tour. Samuel Ireland comes to it at the climax of his *Picturesque Views on the River Wye*, published in 1797, the year before Wordsworth's poem (plate 13 is from this book). Ireland wrote of how contemplation of Tintern encouraged awe and religious sentiment, inspired meditation on time and tyranny. Given this conventional response, the title of Wordsworth's poem would have come as a surprise to readers educated in the picturesque: 'Lines written a few miles above Tintern Abbey, On revisiting the banks of the Wye during a tour, July 13, 1798.' Where previous visitors stood amidst the abbey ruins and reflected on mortality, Wordsworth pointedly locates his poem at an unspecified spot several miles upstream and makes his subject not death but 'the life of things'. A footnote at the bottom of the page on which the poem begins in the 1798 edition of *Lyrical Ballads* informs the reader that 'The river is not affected by the tides a few miles above Tintern', thus further emphasizing that this is definitely not a poem located at the site of the abbey. (Plate 14: This painting by P. J. de Loutherbourg displaces the ruin to the background; to imagine the poem properly, we need to go further and blank it out altogether.)

The absence of the abbey from the poem has two main effects. First, it critiques the picturesque assumption that 'artificial' features such as ruins (and, for that matter, iron-furnaces) may be classed as part of nature. The question of England's national religion is a distraction from the poet's purpose. Wordsworth has anticipated Adorno's recognition that a taste for picturesque ruins is likely to be imbued with reactionary politics:

> While it is true that nowadays an aesthetic relationship to the past is liable to be poisoned by an alliance with reactionary tendencies, the opposite standpoint of an ahistorical aesthetic consciousness that brushes the dimension of the past into the gutter as so much rubbish is even worse. There is no beauty without historical remembrance. In a state of freedom – particularly freedom from nationalism – mankind would be

able innocently to appropriate culturescapes along with the historical past as a whole.

By erasing the abbey, Wordsworth ensures that the 'culturescape' of the poem is free from nationalism. He writes of local, not national affections, a matter to which I return in chapter eight.

The second effect of the absence is the transfer of religious sentiment from Christianity to nature:

> Once again
> Do I behold these steep and lofty cliffs,
> Which on a wild secluded scene impress
> Thoughts of more deep seclusion, and connect
> The landscape with the quiet of the sky.

'Lofty cliffs' is the conventional language of the picturesque, but where in Gilpin the traveller is the subject and the landscape the object, Wordsworth effects a grammatical and phenomenological shift: the sentence begins with the perceiving eye as the subject ('I behold'), but in the subordinate clause the cliffs become the subject. The reader's first impression is that 'thoughts of more deep seclusion' are being pressed on Wordsworth's mind – and that is of course the process by which the poem comes to be written – but what Wordsworth in fact states is that the thoughts are impressed on the scene itself. Nature is made capable of feeling. The 'I' is written out, or rather absorbed into the scene. Religious retreat meant seclusion from worldliness and submission of the self to the divine will; Wordsworthian 'deep seclusion' means dissolution of the self from perceiving eye into ecologically connected organism.

The vocabulary is not confined to the language of the eye, the stock in trade of the picturesque gazer. Wordsworth also makes us hear sound – or more precisely, the sound of silence. To begin with, there is a 'scene' and a 'landscape', but by the end of the sentence the impress of the cliffs has made a connection with 'the quiet of the sky'. The key word – emphasized through Wordsworth's favourite metrical trick of suspension at the line-ending – is 'connect'. Where the picturesque looks, the ecopoetic connects.

A successful ecosystem is one which is held in balance. There will be predator species, but their predations remain sustainable. Less than a few miles below Tintern Abbey, ironwork was destroying the bioregional balance and polluting the Wye. A few miles above, Wordsworth finds a cottage-economy which does not 'disturb' the ecosystem:

> These plots of cottage-ground, these orchard-tufts
> Which at this season, with their unripe fruits,
> Among the woods and copses lose themselves,
> Nor with their green and simple hue disturb
> The wild green landscape.

As the poet's self is lost by means of the impress of the cliffs, so here the predatory aspect of agricultural production is imagined to be lost within the larger landscape. The colour green is attached to both orchard and uncultivated land. This is an image of sustainable productivity, in contradistinction to the Cartesian ambition of developing an 'infinity of devices by which we might enjoy, without any effort, the fruits of the earth and all its commodities'. When Wordsworth looks at the 'wreathes of smoke' on the horizon, his feeling of connectedness leads him to suppose that it might come not from the Cartesian ironwork observed by Gilpin but from the fires of 'vagrant dwellers in the houseless woods', in other words gypsies who know the moment when they have taken enough from a particular spot of earth and must therefore move on.

In the central section of the poem, Wordsworth turns to the psychological work which nature can do for alienated urban man. The crucial move here is the idea of quieting the eye, giving up on the picturesque quest for mastery over a landscape, and submitting instead to an inner vision which enables one to 'see into the life of things'. The memory of the Wye valley teaches the poet that all 'things', even apparently dead matter such as earth and rock, have a life, an animating spirit. We may call this pantheism: 'I, so long / A worshipper of Nature'. Or we may call it a recognition of what in our time the ecologist James Lovelock has called the Gaia hypothesis, the idea that the whole earth is a single vast, living, breathing ecosystem:

> And I have felt
> A presence that disturbs me with the joy
> Of elevated thoughts; a sense sublime
> Of something far more deeply interfused,
> Whose dwelling is the light of setting suns,
> And the round ocean, and the living air,
> And the blue sky, and in the mind of man,
> A motion and a spirit, that impels
> All thinking things, all objects of all thought,
> And rolls through all things.

Wordsworth's distinctive version of the Gaia principle refuses to carve the world into object and subject; the same force animates both consciousness ('the mind of man') and 'all things'. Is a river or a plant the object of thought or is it itself a thinking thing? Wordsworth says that it is both and that the distinction between subject and object is a murderous dissection.

The principles of the picturesque involved the carving-up of the perceiver's environment. According to Gilpin's *Observations on the River Wye*, every view has four parts. In the case of a river valley, there is the area (the river itself), then there are two side-screens (the banks, which mark the perspective) and the front-screen (the angle which points out the winding). The views along the Wye were regarded as pleasurably variable because of the contrast of the screens (different elevations on opposite banks) and the folding of the side-screens over each other with the winding of the river. Wordsworth refuses to look at his environment in this painterly way. By turning from sight to sound and feeling, and thence to the temporal dimension of memory, he connects his consciousness to the ecosystem. For Gilpin, ground, wood, rocks and buildings were 'ornaments' of an aesthetically arranged construction, whereas Wordsworth builds up instead of breaks down. His metaphysic of 'presence' unites air, water and mind.

Adorno attacks the modern equivalent of picturesque travel on the following grounds:

> Integrated in the commercial world (as 'tourist industry', for example) and devoid of its critical sting, the immediate

apprehension of nature has become neutralized. As nature becomes synonymous with national parks and wildlife preserves, its beauty is purely tokenistic. Natural beauty is an ideological notion because it offers mediatedness in the guise of immediacy.

Wordsworth anticipates this line of argument in his critique of the picturesque. Though he is himself on a tour through the Wye valley, he attempts to overcome the mediatedness that is the consequence of the tourist's status as gazer. Instead, his poem seeks to replicate 'the immediate apprehension of nature'.

Is human consciousness part of nature? For the picturesque theorist, it is not: the perceiving, dividing eye stands above and apart from its 'prospect'. That strand of environmentalism which emphasizes the conservation of landscapes of 'natural beauty' adopts the same stance. The converse position is that of Wordsworth's ecopoetic: 'the mind of man' can be part of nature. 'Lines written a few miles above Tintern Abbey' offers not a *view* in the manner of the picturesque, but an exploration of the inter-relatedness of perception and creation, a meditation on the *networks* which link mental and environmental space.

The difference between the ecopoetic approach and that of the picturesque spectator is made clear by something Wordsworth said to Aubrey de Vere late in his life. The two men were discussing how modern poets wrote about nature; Wordsworth took down various volumes from his shelves and found a descriptive passage by an unnamed poet; he said that it was clever but it was not nature: 'it is the writing of a person who vainly endeavours to blend together as much as he sees, whether congruous or incongruous, into a single picture'. Wordsworth continued,

This is the way in which he did his work. He used to go out with a pencil and a tablet, and note what struck him, thus: 'an old tower,' 'a dashing stream,' 'a green slope,' and make a picture out of it ... But Nature does not allow an inventory to be made of her charms! He should have left his pencil behind, and gone forth in a meditative spirit; and, on a later day, he should have embodied in verse not all that he had noted but what he best remembered of the scene; and he would have then presented us with *its soul*, and not with the mere visual aspect of it.

Where the picturesque was under the tyranny of the eye, leading to the reductive enumeration into parts mocked by Edward Ferrars, Wordsworth went in quest of the spirit of the whole. The quest was well served by his compositional method. He did not take out his notebook like Gilpin or the unnamed poet cited here: according to his own account, he felt the poem a few miles upstream from the abbey, began composing it in his head after leaving Tintern, and concluded it on entering Bristol at the end of the day; not one line was written down until he reached Bristol.

Once the poem is written down, once the feeling is reconstituted in language, the vision of ecological integration is perforce disrupted. Ecosystems stay in one place; they are not circulated in the manner of published poems. Language is itself a symptom of humankind's apartness from other species and our consequent power to destabilize ecosystems. The poet is often more vagrant than dweller, for he finds his home in the *logos* and not the *oikos*. As Adorno put it in a passage I quoted earlier, 'Words tend to bounce off nature as they try to deliver nature's language into the hands of another language foreign to it'. 'We see into the life of things' writes Wordsworth. Ecopoesis knows that things have a life, but it also has to recognize that it can only communicate that knowledge in the form of propositions by using the divided Cartesian language of subject ('we see') and object ('the life of things').

How does Wordsworth deal with this problem? In book eleven of *The Prelude*, he describes how his imagination was 'corrected' after its fall into the Cartesian trap:

> Amid the turns and counter-turns, the strife
> And various trials of our complex being,
> As we grow up such thraldom of that sense
> Seems hard to shun: and yet I knew a Maid,
> Who, young as I was then, conversed with things
> In higher style: from appetites like these
> She, gentle Visitant! as well she might

Was wholly free, far less did critic rules
Or barren intermeddling subtleties
Perplex her mind; but wise as Women are
When genial circumstance hath favor'd them,
She welcom'd what was given and craved no more.
Whatever scene was present to her eyes,
That was the best, to that she was attuned
Through her humility and lowliness,
And through a perfect happiness of soul
Whose variegated feelings were in this
Sisters, that they were each some new delight:
For she was Nature's inmate.

Not mastery, then, but sisterhood; not the arrogance of enlightenment, but the humility of dwelling. Wordsworth proposes that it is women who are wise in matters ecological. Picturesque *feeling for* nature can only occur when one stands in the position of the spectator looking out or down upon an environment. Tourism thus shares industry's instrumental attitude towards nature. Whereas the tourist is a traveller, an outsider, the attuned and nurturing woman, Wordsworth suggests, is a dweller, an 'inmate' who *feels with* nature.

The same move is made towards the end of 'Lines written a few miles above Tintern Abbey'. Woman – in *The Prelude* his wife Mary, in 'Lines' his sister Dorothy – is the power which draws man back to integration with nature. In the closing verse-paragraph of 'Lines', in which Dorothy Wordsworth is introduced, the key word is 'healing'. Orthodox feminists would say that to praise woman thus is to condescend to her, to strip her of reason and speech, to entrap her. Does not 'inmate' suggest a prison cell? Ecofeminists would reply that the supposedly higher faculties which woman is here denied are precisely those Cartesian presumptions with which we must do away if we are to save the earth. They would appreciate the move by which Wordsworth expels from his vision the patriarchal God once worshipped by the monks of Tintern Abbey and worships instead a maternal Nature. Could it be that Mary's intuitive conversation with nature is actually the higher style? We need to consider the possibility that to be an inmate of nature might be a condition of freedom, not imprisonment, that the earth may only be healed if the human mind becomes a mansion for all lovely forms instead of an engine-house for the invention of an 'infinity of devices by which we might enjoy, without any effort, the fruits of the earth and all its commodities'.

Beauty is a quality ascribed to entities by humans. Adorno recognized that even to talk about the beauty of nature is to violate what he called the 'non-identity' of nature as the epitome of the non-human. But he also recognized that the experience of natural beauty may be a means of transcending the tyranny of subjectivity and social oppression, an allegory of a *beyond* for which we must strive. 'If you exclaim "what a sight!" in some natural setting, you detract from its beauty by violating the silence of its language'. That, as Wordsworth knew, is the trouble with picturesque tourism. Dorothy's silence in the poem is a sign not of condescending objectification, but of William's respect for her attunement to the place. The impossible task of the ecopoet is to speak the silence of the place. 'Lines written a few miles above Tintern Abbey', with its language of tentative striving and its honest profusion of negative prefixes ('some *un*certain notice', 'this *un*intelligible world'), is as a close as any poem has ever reached to such a speaking.

Wordsworth's 'Lines' go beyond the enumeration of picturesque beauties to a wholly felt, but perforce not fully describable, sense of 'the indeterminable quality of things'. This last phrase is Paul Valéry's, as quoted by Adorno in his *Aesthetic Theory*:

As an indeterminate something, natural beauty is hostile to all definition. It is undefinable, much like music, which in Schubert drew considerable inspiration from this abstract similarity with nature. As in music, the beautiful in nature is like a spark flashing momentarily and disappearing as soon as one tries to get hold of it. Art imitates neither nature nor individual natural beauty. What is does imitate is natural beauty as such. This puts the finger on the paradox of aesthetics as a whole, which is intimately tied up with the paradox of natural beauty. The subject matter of aesthetics, too, is defined negatively as its undefinability. That is why art needs philosophy to interpret it. Philosophy says what art cannot say: by not saying it. The paradoxes of aesthetics are those of its subject matter. As Valéry remarked, 'the beautiful may require the slavish imitation of the indeterminable quality of things.'

6

Nests, Shells, Landmarks

Nothing exists for its own sake, but for a harmony greater
than itself, which includes it. A work of art, which accepts
this condition, and exists upon its terms, honors the
Creation, and so becomes a part of it.

(Wendell Berry – poet, farmer, ecologist – in his
'Notes: Unspecializing Poetry')

JOHN CLARE WAS an agricultural worker who witnessed the
changes in the land wrought by parliamentary enclosure. In both
poetry and prose he marked the tracks, the wayside benches, the
names, the landmarks, the coppices and spinneys, the ponds and
streams, of the lost fields and meadows of his youth. Clare is
among English poetry's subtlest knowers of what the philosopher
Edmund Husserl calls 'thing-experience', *Dingerfahrung*. Clare's
world-horizon was the horizon of the things – the stones, animals,
plants, people – that he knew first and knew best. When he went
beyond that horizon, he no longer knew what he knew.

Clare's poetry is the record of his search for a home in the
world.

THE HOLLOW TREE

How oft a summer shower hath started me
To seek for shelter in a hollow tree
Old huge ash-dotterel wasted to a shell
Whose vigorous head still grew and flourished well
Where ten might sit upon the battered floor
And still look round discovering room for more
And he who chose a hermit life to share
Might have a door and make a cabin there

They seemed so like a house that our desires
Would call them so and make our gipsey fires
And eat field dinners of the juicey peas
Till we were wet and drabbled to the knees
But in our old tree-house rain as it might
Not one drop fell although it rained till night

I have found a language for my response to this poem in a book published in 1958 by the French philosopher and historian of science Gaston Bachelard. Entitled *The Poetics of Space*, its subject is what Bachelard calls the ontology of the poetic. He is interested in the way that through the brilliance of a poetic image, 'the distant past resounds with echoes, and it is hard to know at what depth these echoes will reverberate and die away'. For Bachelard, the poetic image has its distinctive being in this quality of reverberation, which is an overcoming of time. But we can only understand the being of the image by ourselves experiencing the reverberation. Bachelard thus calls for a mode of reading that is a listening rather than an interrogation. He considers himself a felicitous rather than a severe reader.

Bachelard's 'phenomenology' concerns itself with the moment of the onset of the poetic image in an individual consciousness. At that moment, 'the duality of subject and object is iridescent, shimmering, unceasingly active in its inversions'. The consciousness which experiences the poetic image becomes 'naive' in Schiller's sense of being at one with, not self-reflexively apart from, the world. Through the poetic image, oneness with the world can be experienced directly rather than yearned for elegiacally in nostalgia for the *temps perdu* of childhood or the imagined good life of primitivism.

The images which reverberate in *The Poetics of Space* are those of the spaces which we love: 'In this orientation, these investigations would deserve to be called topophilia'. *Topophilia* is a term derived from Greek *topos*, 'place', and *philos*, 'loving'. Bachelard's argument is that we especially love the spaces which afford us protection, first those within the house – secret rooms, drawers, chests, wardrobes – and then their equivalents in the world, especially nests and shells, the respective refuges of vertebrates and invertebrates. Bachelard is mesmerized by the interpenetration of indoor and outdoor spaces, interior and exterior ecologies, as when 'with the presence of lavender the history of the seasons enters into the wardrobe'. His central theme is what he calls *inhabiting*, which is what I call dwelling with the earth. 'In one short sentence, Victor Hugo associates the images and beings of the function of inhabiting. For Quasimodo, he says, the cathedral has been successively "egg, nest, house, country and universe".'

Though written in the medium of analytic prose, *The Poetics of Space* is itself poetic. It enacts the sense of 'poetic' which it describes. Read Bachelard on how we inhabit our childhood homes and your own childhood home creeps, almost unnoticed, into your memory. 'Our house is our corner of the world', writes Bachelard. 'The house shelters day-dreaming'. But he is not only concerned with bricks and mortar. 'All really inhabited space bears the essence of the notion of home'. When we truly inhabit the world, we are at home in it. True inhabiting necessitates a willingness to look at and listen to the world. It is a letting go of the self which brings the discovery of a deeper self.

'For a knowledge of intimacy, localization in the spaces of our intimacy is more urgent than determination of dates', writes Bachelard. John Clare's poetry is supremely committed to localization of the spaces of his intimacy with the world. 'The Hollow Tree' offers what Bachelard calls a 'primal image' which gives us back 'areas of being, houses in which the human being's certainty of being is concentrated', so that 'we have the impression that, in images that are as stabilizing as these are, we could start a new life, a life that would be our own, that would belong to us in our very depths'. In human terms, the hollow tree is both a communal shelter and a potential hermit's hut. For Bachelard, the hermit's hut derives its truth 'from the intensity of its essence, which is the essence of the verb "to inhabit." The hut immediately becomes centralized solitude, for in the land of legend, there exists no adjoining hut.' At the same time, in non-human terms, the hollow tree affords the protection of a shell. Bachelard again: 'A snail's shell, this house that grows with its inmate, is one of the marvels of the universe . . . The shell is the clearest proof of life's ability to constitute forms.' And Clare: he collected snail or 'pooty' shells, wondering delightedly at the variety and intricacy of their forms.

The hollow tree thus images not merely home, but home-in-the-world. A world, moreover, that is lived and worked with, not viewed sentimentally from without: the ash is a 'dotterel', which means a pollarded tree. That is to say, it has been felled at ten feet above the ground and then allowed to grow again, so as to produce successive crops of wood for the benefit of the local economy.

At the same time, however, the ash-dotterel in the poem remains an image: its being resides on paper, the trace of what was once wood-fibre, and in the poet's and reader's imaginations. Clare's other shell – which both protects him and cuts him off from his original dwelling-place – is the poem itself, constituted in the rounded form of an unpunctuated sonnet. Does Clare live in the place or the poem? The simultaneity of belonging and alienation, dwelling and writing, is the source of his profundity as a poet of both location and dislocation.

Clare's poems are round. The sonnet 'Emmonsails Heath in Winter' follows the motions of leaf and twig, and of bird-life that rises, dips and weaves in a composed landscape. The poem ends with the line 'And hang on little twigs and start again', the absence of a closing full stop inviting us to complete the circle and start reading again from the beginning. Through the rounding of the poem, the landscape is rounded and completed; because of the roundness, everything seems to be in repose even as it is in motion.

Birds are essential to the roundness of Clare's world. The 'Sand Martin', for instance, in the sonnet so called, drills its nest in the form of a small round hole in a quarry's side, and its motion in the air is of constant circling. Listen to Bachelard on roundness, as he set up reverberations between the language of a nineteenth-century French Romantic historian of natural forms and a twentieth-century German post-Romantic poet of place and displacement.

A bird, for Michelet, is solid roundness, it is round life. Michelet seized the bird's being in its cosmic situation, as a centralization of life guarded on every side, enclosed in a live ball, and consequently, at the maximum of its unity. All other images, whether of form, color or movement, are stricken with relativism in the face of what we shall have to call the absolute bird, the being of round life. Thus Rilke, who undoubtedly did not recall what Michelet had written on the subject, wrote:

> ... This round bird-call
> Rests in the instant that engenders it
> Huge as the sky above the withered forest
> Docilely things take their place in this call
> In it the entire landscape seems to rest.

To anyone who is receptive to the cosmicity of images, the essentially central image of the bird is the same in Rilke's poem as in the fragment by Michelet, only expressed in another register. The round cry of round being makes the sky round like a cupola. And in this rounded landscape, everything seems to be in repose. The round being propagates its roundness, together with the calm of all roundness.

And for the professor who has broken with every kind of 'being-there' (*être-là*), it is a joy to the ear to begin his course of metaphysics with the declaration: *Das Dasein ist rund.* Being is round.

Thus Bachelard, musing on Michelet's *L'Oiseau*. The closing allusion here is to the philosopher Martin Heidegger, to whom – together with Rilke – we will return in the final chapter.

There is an old French proverb that men can do everything except build a bird's nest. In the poetry of Clare, as in the vision of Bachelard, a nest is the small round thing which is the natural world's analogue of the human idea of home. 'Intimacy needs the heart of a nest', writes Bachelard. He explains that 'It is not the task of the phenomenologist to describe the nests met with in nature, which is a quite positive task reserved for ornithologists'. Rather,

A beginning of a philosophical phenomenology of nests would consist in our being able to elucidate the interest with which we look through an album containing reproductions of nests, or, even more positively, in our capacity to recapture the naïve wonder we used to feel when we found a nest. This wonder is lasting, and today when we discover a nest it takes us back to our childhood or, rather, to a childhood; to the childhoods we should have had. For not many of us have been endowed by life with the full measure of its cosmic implications.

John Clare was lucky and unlucky enough to have been endowed by life with the full measure of the cosmic implications of the bird's nest. In his many nest poems, he recaptures the wonder of the child finding a nest, but also recognizes the vulnerability of the nest, which becomes an analogue for the vulnerability of his own being-in-the-world.

Bachelard did not know Clare's work, but the following passage is a beautiful gloss upon 'The Fern Owl's Nest', 'The Wryneck's Nest', 'The Woodpigeon's Nest', 'The Robin's Nest', 'The Yellowhammer's Nest', 'The Pewit's Nest', 'The Nightingale's Nest', and a dozen other poems:

> It is living nests that could introduce a phenomenology of the actual nest, of the nest found in natural surroundings, and which becomes for a moment the center – the term is no exaggeration – of an entire universe, the evidence of a cosmic situation. Gently I lift a branch . . . This is a living, inhabited nest. A nest is a bird's house. I've known this for a long time, people have told it to me for a long time. In fact, it is such an old story that I hesitate to repeat it, even to myself. And yet I have just re-experienced it.

'When we examine a nest,' Bachelard remarks a few pages later, 'we place ourselves at the origin of confidence in the world'. For Clare, no bird has more confidence than the pettichap – the chiffchaff – which builds its nest by the open road. Let us walk with him:

THE PETTICHAP'S NEST

Well, in my many walks I rarely found
A place less likely for a bird to form
Its nest close by the rut-gulled waggon road

And on the almost bare foot-trodden ground
With scarce a clump of grass to keep it warm
And not a thistle spreads its spears abroad
Or prickly bush to shield it from harm's way
And yet so snugly made that none may spy
It out, save accident – and you and I
Had surely passed it on our walk today
Had chance not led us by it – nay e'en now
Had not the old bird heard us trampling by
And fluttered out – we had not seen it lie
Brown as the roadway side – small bits of hay
Pluckt from the old propt-haystack's pleachy brow
And withered leaves make up its outward walls
That from the snub-oak dotterel yearly falls
And in the old hedge bottom rot away
Built like an oven with a little hole
Hard to discover – that snug entrance wins
Scarcely admitting e'en two fingers in
And lined with feathers warm as silken stole
And soft as seats of down for painless ease
And full of eggs scarce bigger e'en than peas
Here's one most delicate with spots as small
As dust – and of a faint and pinky red
– We'll let them be and safety guard them well
For fear's rude paths around are thickly spread
And they are left to many dangers' ways
When green grasshopper's jump might break the shells
While lowing oxen pass them morn and night
And restless sheep around them hourly stray
And no grass springs but hungry horses bite
That trample past them twenty times a day
Yet like a miracle in safety's lap
They still abide unhurt and out of sight
– Stop, here's the bird. That woodman at the gap
Hath put it from the hedge – 'tis olive green
Well I declare it is the pettichap
Not bigger than the wren and seldom seen
I've often found their nests in chance's way
When I in pathless woods did idly roam

But never did I dream untill today
A spot like this would be her chosen home

It is difficult to write about a small, exquisite, complete poem such as this. The interpreter is all too like that woodman, entering at the end to disturb the bird from its nest. With his poking finger, he breaches the 'snug entrance' of the rounded female space. The work of the human economy – the woodman, the animals husbanded as agricultural produce – will always be around us, disturbing the processes of nature. At another level, the work of interpretation will always be, in Schiller's terms, the sentimental intruding upon the naive. Still, just by reading the poem and thinking about it, we may conclude that, though there is a necessity for us to work over nature in order to survive, there is also a necessity for us to find time for idleness, time to contemplate the miracle embodied in both the construction and the survival of a nest.

The pettichap's nest is a tiny thing, yet it shelters the principle of life itself, the egg. The shell may be so fragile that even a grasshopper's jump might break it. 'The Pettichap's Nest' is a poem about trust. The pettichap does not guard its nest with warlike instruments such as spear-grass and thistle. Not all the eggs in every nest will hatch, but it may repay us to repay the pettichap's trust and leave alone the nest upon which we could so easily trample. After all, there may come a time when we ourselves are vulnerable, a time when we may need to remember that even an exposed place sometimes has to be made into a home. Clare discovered as much when he set off to walk in the direction of home to Northamptonshire after escaping from the lunatic asylum where he was confined in Essex: 'one night I lay in a dyke bottom and found one side wet through from the sock [soak, damp] in the dyke bottom'.

A human being can do everything except build a bird's nest. What we can do is build an analogue of a bird's nest in a poem. We can make a verbal nest by gathering and cherishing odd scraps of language, the words which stand in for the bits and pieces of hay, rotten leaf and feather that are the pettichap's material. We spend our time as well in gathering words as in working over things. Even if you have never found a bird's nest

Above: The spirit of
the rainforest carved in
stone: Epstein's *Rima*

Right: The melancholy
man in the landscape:
'Trevelyan at Casalunga'

Poet as seer amidst the sublime: John Martin's *The Bard*

Picturesque station overlooking Windermere, with railway encroaching

Lake District cottages in picturesque disrepair

THE TOUR

of

DOCTOR SYNTAX,

In Search of the

A Poem.

Ut Pictura, Poesis erit; quæ, si propius stes,
Te capiat, magis; et quædam, si longius abstes.
Hæc amat obscurum; volet hæc sub luce videri,
Judicis argutum quæ non formidat acumen;
Hæc placuit semel, hæc decies repetita placebit.

Horat. Ars. Poet.

In search of the PICturesque

The perils of the picturesque

'Thus I (which few, I think, can boast) / *Have made a landscape of a post*'

The aesthete bemuses the locals

Harmoniously arranged cows, from Gilpin's 'Northern Tour'

Not so harmoniously arranged cows, drawn 'after nature'

The abbey placed in an ideal landscape, from Gilpin's Wye Tour

The abbey drawn from nature, in Ireland's
Picturesque Views on the River Wye

Above: The abbey lost in the landscape: de Louterbourg's *The River Wye at Tintern Abbey*

Left: Not quite at one with the child of nature: Beerbohm's *Wordsworth in the Lake District – at cross-purposes*

and wondered at it, you may by means of Clare's poem begin to feel a sense of why bird's nests matter, why they are, in Bachelard's grand term, 'the center of an entire universe'. For Clare, as for Bachelard, to be drawn to a nest, to stoop towards it but still to let it live, is to be gathered into the fabric of the earth and in being so gathered to secure the identity of the self.

How are we to live fully but without profligacy upon our crowded earth? Perhaps we could begin by taking the time to listen to Clare as he catches at little things:

> A gate whose posts are two old dotterel trees
> A close with molehills sprinkled o'er its leas
> A little footbrig with its crossing rail
> A wood-gap stopt with ivy-wreathing pale
> A crooked stile each path-crossed spinny owns
> A brooklet forded by its stepping-stones
> A wood-bank mined with rabbit-holes – and then
> An old oak leaning o'er a badger's den
> Whose cave-mouth enters 'neath the twisted charms
> Of its old roots and keeps it safe from harms

('The Moorhen's Nest')

Each thing here is known and loved because it is small. The roots of the oak offer not the 'charms' of a sweeping picturesque prospect. Rather, they are like a miniature 'charm' worn against evil. They keep the badger safe from huntsman and baiter. Small holes and molehills – images of roundness – help Clare to dwell.

'The cleverer I am at miniaturizing the world,' writes Bachelard, 'the better I possess it'. The thought is beautiful and true, but the associations of 'clever' and 'possess' are wrong because they are evocative of Cartesian man. Let us rephrase: the more attuned I am as I miniaturize the world, the better I dwell upon the earth.

*

The above suggestions attempt to describe, with the aid of Bachelard, some of the reverberations in the consciousness of one reader of Clare. But the work of criticism also requires historical reflection – reflection upon Clare's personal history, the history of his beloved place, and his own place in literary history. All three histories bear the scars of alienation.

John Clare was born in the village of Helpston, Northampton-shire, in 1793. His barely literate father was a labourer; he himself worked as a ploughboy, reaper and thresher. But he also became a reader, discovering Thomson's *The Seasons* at the age of thir-teen. To read the seasons in a book was perhaps to begin to lose the ability to live at ease with the seasons of the working life of the farm. Alienation was compounded when Clare's first love, Mary Joyce, was taken from him; her memory haunted the rest of his days, like that of childhood itself.

In 1820, his *Poems Descriptive of Rural Life* were published, followed the next year by *The Village Minstrel*. His publisher brought him to London, where he was celebrated as 'the peasant poet'. John Taylor, the well-meaning publisher, not only per-suaded Clare from his place, he also wrenched his language from its own natural idiom, severely editing the long poem of seasonal work and play, *The Shepherd's Calendar* (1827). By this time, Clare was enduring periods of severe depression. In 1832, his patron and friends – meaning as well as Taylor, but judging as ill – persuaded him to leave Helpston and move to a better-appointed cottage, with its own garden, in the village of Northborough, some three miles away. To us the distance seems small, but for Clare – the miniaturist, the inhabiter of locality – removal to Northborough meant exile from all that he knew and all in which he felt secure:

> I've left mine own old home of homes
> Green fields and every pleasant place
> The summer like a stranger comes
> I pause and hardly know her face
> I miss the hazel's happy green
> The bluebell's quiet hanging blooms . . .
>
> I miss the heath its yellow furze
> Molehills and rabbit-tracks . . .
>
> I sit me in my corner chair
> That seems to feel itself from home . . .
>
>   ('The Flitting')

In 1837 Clare was admitted to a private asylum at High Beech in Epping. There is an acute irony that the place should have been located near an ancient forest, a traditional refuge. In 1841, he escaped and walked home to Northamptonshire, navigating by the sun. Shortly afterwards, he was again removed, this time to Northampton General Lunatic Asylum, where he lived and wrote for a further twenty-two and a half years until his death in 1864.

The inhabited spaces of his childhood had gone too. In 1809, Parliament had passed An Act for Inclosing Lands in the Parishes of Maxey . . . and Helpstone, in the County of Northampton.

> Moors, loosing from the sight, far, smooth, and blea,
> Where swopt the plover in its pleasure free
> Are vanished now with commons wild and gay
> As poet's visions of life's early day . . .
> Fence now meets fence in owners' little bounds
> Of field and meadow large as garden grounds
> In little parcels little minds to please
> With men and flocks imprisoned ill at ease . . .
> These paths are stopt – the rude philistine's thrall
> Is laid upon them and destroyed them all
> Each little tyrant with his little sign
> Shows where man claims earth glows no more divine
> But paths to freedom and to childhood dear
> A board sticks up to notice 'no road here'
> And on the tree with ivy overhung
> The hated sign by vulgar taste is hung
> As tho' the very birds should learn to know
> When they go there they must no further go
> Thus, with the poor, sacred freedom bade goodbye
> And much they feel it in the smothered sigh
> And birds and trees and flowers without a name
> All sighed when lawless law's enclosure came

('The Mores')

Here enclosure is imagined as an impediment to dwelling in the world. The 'littleness' is not that of miniature, but of the mean and grasping mind that encloses for the sake of economic gain. The birds are presented as victims of such minds every bit as much as the poor. The sign of the property-owner blocks the road to the freedom of the common land and in so doing also changes the configuration of the poet's mental space, severing the memory's way back to childhood. The two Rousseauesque states of nature – childhood and a relationship to the land that is anterior to the proprietorial – are simultaneously foreclosed.

And what of the third history, that of Clare's place in the literary canon? Anthologies have always been a key mechanism in the process of canonization, so there could be no more graphic index of the continued undervaluation of Clare through the late twentieth century than his exclusion – save for one brief, weak, uncharacteristic love-lyric – from the 1993 *New Oxford Book of Romantic Period Verse*. It was an exclusion all the more astonishing given Clare's centrality to two works which were seminal to the growth of late-twentieth-century ideological, socially oriented criticism of Romantic period texts, John Barrell's *The Idea of Landscape and the Sense of Place* (1972) and Raymond Williams's *The Country and the City* (1973). 'History is repeating itself', wrote Hugh Haughton and Adam Phillips in their introduction to the first major collection of modern critical essays on Clare: his life was a story of marginalization and exclusion and that has long continued to be the story of his reputation.

One reason for the neglect of Clare by those who interrogated the so-called 'Romantic ideology' was that his case disproves an argument much favoured by disenfranchised late-twentieth-century radical literary theorists, namely that the bond with nature is forged in a retreat from social commitment, that it is a symptom of middle-class escapism, disillusioned apostasy or false consciousness. For Clare, the most authentically 'working-class' of all major English poets, social relations and environmental relations were not set in opposition to each other in this way. He viewed the 'rights of man' and the 'rights of nature' as co-extensive and co-dependent.

John Barrell's book *The Idea of Landscape and the Sense of Place* provided a masterly demonstration of how enclosure was one of the keys to Clare's alienation. But the author's politics led him to subordinate place to social formation. Consider a characteristic reading. Barrell expresses his admiration for Clare's poem 'The

Lamentations of Round-Oak Waters', in which a brook complains about the effects of enclosure, but he regards the poem as structurally flawed because Clare supposedly failed to 'properly fuse together' his personal grief and that of the landscape:

> It is the landscape as itself, where it was, that is being regretted here; and from here onward the poem leaves Clare's melancholy behind, and becomes more like a direct political statement against the enclosure. And so the poem, as it gets better, falls in half; it could only be made whole again if we were made to feel that Clare's sadness is his personal share of a general sorrow at the enclosure; but this will hardly do. In the first half of the poem the genius of the brook has been emphasising Clare's apartness from the collectivity of the village, and although the cause of his sadness isn't explained, we are given good reason to think it is the result of his feeling unlike and indeed superior to the other villagers, and yet unable to rise above his social position and establish himself as a poet.

The Clare of this poem is indeed set apart from the collectivity of the village, but should we conclude from this that Clare's personal sadness is not part of a general sorrow at the enclosure? Surely it *is* part of a general sorrow, but the point is that the sorrow is felt more deeply by the land itself than by the other villagers. Is the voice of Round Oak Waters to be understood only as a metaphor, a traditional poetic figuration of the genius loci, or 'an extreme use of the pathetic fallacy'? Or can we conceive the possibility that a brook might really speak, a piece of land might really feel pain?

As inheritors of the Enlightenment's instrumental view of nature we cannot. But if we imagine the poem from the point of view of someone who has not inherited the Enlightenment view of nature, it will not fall into two halves, the first of ecological and the second of social protest. How would the poem be read by, say, an Australian Aboriginal who has walked some of the invisible pathways which criss-cross the land, which are known to Europeans as Dreaming-tracks or Songlines and to the Aboriginals themselves as Footprints of the Ancestors or the Way of the

Law? Are we 'to understand the sorrows of the brook as an echo of Clare's own?' asks Barrell. No, the Aboriginal reader will reply, instinct with the knowledge that the land itself is always singing. It may just be the other way round: the sorrows of Clare are an echo of the brook's own.

Paul Klee spoke as an artist, not a critic: 'In a forest, I have felt many times over that it was not I who looked at the forest. Some days I felt that the trees were looking at me, were speaking to me ... I was there listening ... I think that the painter must be penetrated by the universe and not want to penetrate it.' (An ecofeminist would pause here over the language of penetrating and being penetrated.) Maurice Merleau-Ponty, a phenomenological philosopher in a similar mould to Bachelard, quoted Klee in 'Eye and Mind', an essay written late in his life on the theme of creative artists' power to break down science's divisions of subject and object, observing mind and mathematized world. For Merleau-Ponty, 'We speak of "inspiration," and the word should be taken literally. There really is inspiration and expiration of Being.' The poet breathes in the being of the world. Clare's inspiration was the expiration of his beloved places. His melancholy was his knowledge that after expiration comes death.

The traditional undervaluation of Clare on the part of Romanticists is also premissed on a valuation of what John Keats called the egotistical sublime. Clare merely *describes* nature, critics are always complaining, whereas Wordsworth reflects self-consciously on the relationship between mind and nature. Wordsworth is regarded as modern because he is, in Schiller's sense, sentimental; Clare is regarded as primitive because he is a kind of Ab-original, because he is, in Schiller's sense, naive.

But the distinction does not hold so simply. The moment Clare writes his poems he ceases to be naive, he separates himself from the land. He reads the texts of nature – for instance the 'pen-scribbled' eggs in 'The Yellowhammer's Nest' – but as a writer he inhabits the environment of imagination. His texts are at several removes from the ecology of Helpston; they belong to the *logos* and not the *oikos*. Once fixed in print and disseminated beyond their place of origin, the words of the poet are always Schillerianly sentimental. The poet may, however, aspire to conjure into the reader a knowledge of the Schillerianly naive. Because we are post-Enlightenment readers, I will never convince you by rational argument that the land sings, that a brook may feel pain, but by reading Clare you might be led to imagine the possibility. In Adorno and Horkheimer's phrase, the poem might re-enchant the world. It can only do so if it is understood as an experiencing of the world, not a description of it. 'A house that has been experienced is not an inert box,' writes Bachelard. 'Inhabited space transcends geometrical space.' Clare is above all a poet of the experience of miniature inhabited environments.

Clare was not a naive poet because he was aware of the difference between the world and the text: he acknowledged that the yellowhammer's eggs only *resemble* writing. But exactly because of this awareness he began to lose his home in the land. That loss was compounded when his publisher John Taylor removed the poems from their place of origin, excised their dialect of locality and polished them into London English fit for the urban literary set. It was extended still further when Clare was paraded before that set in his hob-nailed boots. He functions for us as a scapegoat: only by alienating himself can he restore us to the *oikos*. His identity came from the place; I suspect that it began to slip as he became a reader and a writer; I am not sure that he could ever have kept his sanity once he had gone to London and returned.

What finally broke him was the move from Helpston to Northborough. I think I hear the snap in a letter to Taylor of 6 September 1832, in which Clare speaks of 'the Depressions that distress me': 'I have nothing as yet on the ground neither cow nor pigs nor any thing else & am in fact worse off th[a]n before I entered on the place.' If our minds are to be grounded in sanity, we need to have our feet 'on the ground'; we enter into our being only when we have 'entered on the place'. It is a first principle of scientific ecology that the survival of both individuals and species depends on the survival of ecosystems. Clare foreshadows scientific ecology in his knowledge that, as James McKusick puts it, 'an organism has meaning and value only in its proper *home*, in symbiotic association with all the creatures that surround and nourish it'.

·*

Our species originated around forty thousand years ago. Even as it has advanced itself, it has been preparing to destroy itself by destroying its ecosystems. This has been going on ever since the moment identified by Rousseau at the beginning of the second part of the *Discourse on the Origin of Inequality* when civil society was founded through the act of enclosure. It is the contention of Michel Serres, whose work I discussed in chapter four, that by writing a social contract instead of a natural contract Rousseau proved himself blind to his own insight. Serres and his followers regard the Enlightenment as quite possibly our species' greatest and last missed opportunity. The culmination of Enlightenment thought was the declaration of the universal rights of man; the American and French revolutions proposed an ordering of society according to abstract principles such as liberty and equality as opposed to an inherited idea of supposedly 'natural' degree. Given that a hierarchical model was ingrained in eighteenth-century natural science, it is understandable that progressive thinkers sought to abandon the model of nature, but the price of that abandonment was an acceleration of the ravage of the earth.

Robert Harrison's book *Forests* is dedicated to Serres. It addresses these matters in the section entitled 'What is Enlightenment? A Question for Foresters'. Harrison reminds his readers of Nietzsche's madman rushing into the marketplace with the announcement that God is dead. Suppose we stopped him, calmed him down, and asked him when and where God died. 'And suppose he were to answer: "In 1637, in part 4 of the *Discourse of Method*!" A madman, after all, can afford to be precise about such matters.' Descartes does have a God, but it is a cold metaphysical God, not a force immanent in nature. A God who doesn't, for instance, live in trees.

With the Enlightenment, the forest became a place neither of mystery nor sanctuary but rather something to be managed: 'One of the ways in which this dream of mastery and possession becomes reality in the post-Cartesian era is through the rise of forest management during the late-eighteenth and nineteenth centuries.' Trees were planted with Cartesian precision, in straight lines. Italo Calvino's novel *The Baron in the Trees* fantasizes into being an eighteenth-century nobleman who climbed a holm oak at the age of twelve and vowed never to set foot on the ground again. Baron Cosimo wrote a number of political and philosophical treatises which attracted the attention of the high priests of Enlightenment, Voltaire and Diderot, but they had no time for his most characteristic work, a *Constitutional Project for a Republican City with a Declaration of the Rights of Men, Women, Children, Domestic and Wild Animals, including Birds, Fishes and Insects, and All Vegetation, whether Trees, Vegetable, or Grass*. Imagine the species and the forests that would still be living if some of the principles of this project had found their way into the enlightened declarations of the American and French revolutionaries.

Baron Cosimo's treatise would have found an enthusiastic reader in Shelley, but then he was always a marginal man. The one *philosophe* who might have understood it was Rousseau himself, for he stood Janus-faced at the edge of the Enlightenment wood: as author of the 'Project for the Constitution of Corsica', which proposed an 'exact policemanship of the forests', he was the incarnation of his age, whereas in the second *Discourse* and the frequent passages concerning rural regeneration in his other works – notably the Bois de Boulogne section of the *Confessions* and Saint-Preux's walks in the Valais in *La Nouvelle Héloïse* – he kicked against modernity and embarked upon an anti-Enlightenment quest for the old meanings of the forest. Harrison's book is an eloquent analysis of those old meanings, but it is equally a passionately argued case for the continuing necessity – social and psychological, as well as ecological – of the forest: 'Today we are witnessing the consequences of those one-sided declarations of the right of a single species to disregard the natural rights of every other species.'

The *Constitutional Project* of Calvino's 'Baron in the Trees' was, according to the novel's wry narrator, 'a very fine work, which could have been a useful guide to any government' – 'but which no one took any notice of, and it remained a dead letter'.

The Baron's book remained a dead letter because the Enlightenment style of discourse – the systematic, theoretical 'project' – encouraged such hierarchical descriptions of nature as the Linnaean system of classification. It did not provide a way of thinking which allowed for the possibility of extending the universal rights of man into a proclamation of the universal rights of nature. The handful of ideologues who proposed such an extension were dismissed as eccentrics. A book such as John 'Walking' Stewart's *Apocalypse of Nature* (circa 1790), which argued that man must do no violence to any part of animate nature, had absolutely no influence in comparison with Tom Paine's *Rights of Man*.

Calvino's fantastic Baron Cosimo tries to compose a treatise on the laws and government of an ideal arboreal state, 'but as he wrote, his impulse to invent complicated stories intervened and out poured a rough sketch of adventures, duels and erotic tales'. Which is to say: the universal rights of nature cannot effectively be *declared* in a systematic treatise; they can only be *expressed* by means of celebratory narrative. They require not an Enlightenment project but a Romantic riot of sketches, fragments and tales – narratives of community, reminiscences of walking and working, vignettes of birds and their nests, animations of children and insects and grass. Which is to say: the dead letter of the Baron's constitutional project is brought to life in the poetry and prose of John Clare – who was accordingly hostile to the Linnaean system of classification. If I may adapt a remark of John Berryman's about Shakespeare's sonnets: when Clare in the 'Lamentations of Round-Oak Waters' wrote of the stream, 'You'll find an equal there', reader, he was *not kidding*.

Equal carries the full weight of the Enlightenment discourse on rights. Clare extends *égalité* from mankind to the non-human world. When out walking on the first day of the open season for shooting he is 'forcd to return home fearing I might be shot under the hedges'; he thus puts himself into a bond of *fraternité*, fellow-vulnerability, with 'the poor hares partridges and pheasants'. He considers a fallen elm tree to be a 'Friend not inanimate', the word *friend* suggestive of radical philanthropy. And he seeks *liberté* for all living things, as in the following passage about a peregrine falcon:

I saw one of these which a man had wounded with a gun; he
had stupefied it only, for when he got it home it was as fierce
& as live as ever ... but at a dog it seemd rather scard & sat
on its tail end in a defensive posture with its wings extended
& its talons open, making at the same time a strange earpierc-
ing hissing noise which dis mayd the dog who would drop his
tail & sneak out as if in fear. They tyd a piece of tar marling
to one of its legs & tetherd it in a barn w[h]ere they kept it 3
or 4 days when it knawd the string from its leg & effected its
liberty.

Clare relished the bird's escape from the Bastille of that barn as
sharply as he would later lament his own incarceration in what he
called the 'English Bastille' of the madhouse.

'The Lament of Swordy Well' is a ballad of complaint, but
instead of being Wordsworthianly spoken by a discharged soldier
with 'limping leg' or a blind beggar with troubles pinned to his
breast, it is written in the voice of 'a piece of land'. 'Though I'm
no man yet any wrong / Some sort of right may seek', says
Swordy Well: the land may be wronged and may seek rights. It is
not only the poor but also the earth who is made to bow and sigh
under the weight of 'oppression's iron strife'. Swordy Well was
previously integral to a community of reciprocal respect, in which
it gave rights to the vagrant in return for its own freedom. If a
modest Utopia, it was nevertheless an effectively regulated ecosystem. Until, that is, enclosure replaced mutuality, community
and freedom, with exploitation, possession and enslavement:

> There was a time my bit of ground
> Made freemen of the slave
> The ass no pindar'd dare to pound
> When I his supper gave
> The gipsey's camp was not affraid
> I made his dwelling free
> Till vile enclosure came and made
> A parish slave of me.

('The Lament of Swordy Well')

The rights of the land, the ass and the gipsy are interlinked;
it is this interlinking which refutes the position of those who

regard Romantic 'Love of Nature' as a retreat from 'Love of Mankind'.

Phrases like 'The rights of freedom' and, conversely, 'Self-interest', 'cant of tyranny in stronger powers' and 'To wrong another by the name of right' are the common stock of radical pamphleteering and rural protest in the years between Waterloo and the Great Reform Bill. Clare, however, uses these phrases with regard to the treatment not of the poor but of a tree, 'The Fallen Elm'. He proclaims the right to life of every living thing. He recognizes that to hold such a belief will be regarded as a foolish 'indisposition', but he is impassioned in his assertion of it, even to the point of turning the language of tyranny against those who tyrannize over the environment for the sake of economic gain and of acknowledging that his position is incompatible with worldly (material) progress:

> my two favourite Elm trees at the back of the hut are condemned to dye [–] it shocks me to relate it but tis true [–] the savage who owns them thinks they have done their best & now he wants to make use of the benefits he can get from selling them – O was this country Egypt & was I but a caliph the owner shoud loose his ears for his arragant presumption & the first wretch that buried his axe in their roots shoud hang on their branches as a terror to the rest – I have been several mornings to bid them farewell – had I £100 to spare I woud buy their reprieves – but they must dye ... was People all to feel & think as I do the world coud not be carried on – a green woud not be ploughd a tree or bush woud not be cut for firing or furniture & every thing they found when boys would remain in that state till they dyd – this is my indisposition & you will laugh at it.

Taylor quoted this passage in his introduction to Clare's second collection of poems, *The Village Minstrel* (1821), as an example of the 'things which were the landmarks of his life'. 'Landmarks' is an excellent choice of word: without trees and hedges to orient himself, Clare has no inner map. What is psychosis if not the loss of such a map?

Even the supremely sane William Wordsworth sometimes

had to reach out and grasp a tree in order to prevent himself from falling into the abyss of idealism. To experience the play between inner and outer maps, between the tree which grounds the sanity of the mind and the tree that is planted upon the earth, we may listen once more to Bachelard, as he reads Rilke and discovers that the tree needs us every bit as much as we need the tree:

> Poets will help us to discover within ourselves such joy in looking that sometimes, in the presence of a perfectly familiar object, we experience an extension of our intimate space. Let us listen to Rilke, for instance, give its existence of immensity to a tree he is looking at:
>
>> Space, outside ourselves, invades and ravishes things:
>> If you want to achieve the existence of a tree,
>> Invest it with inner space, this space
>> That has its being in you. Surround it with compulsions,
>> It knows no bounds, and only really becomes a tree
>> If it takes its place in the heart of your renunciation.

The tree, like every genuine living thing, is taken in its being that 'knows no bounds.' Its limits are mere accidents. Against the accident of limits, the tree needs you to give it your super-abundant images, nurtured in your intimate space, in 'this space that has its being in you.' Then, together, the tree and its dreamer, take their places, grow tall. Rilke wrote: 'These trees are magnificent, but even more magnificent is the sublime and moving space between them, as though with their growth it too increased.' The two kinds of space, intimate space and exterior space, keep encouraging each other as it were, in their growth.

Thus *The Poetics of Space*.

For Clare, as for Bachelard in this extract, the interior order of the human mind is inextricable from the environmental space which we inhabit. Sanity depends upon grounding in place. But it also depends upon grounding in time. To reiterate the claim of my fourth chapter: our identities are constituted by a combination of environment and memory. For Clare, the elm tree is a temporal as well as a spatial landmark. Because it was there when he was a boy, it guarantees the continuity of his own life. 'Old favourite tree thou'st seen time's changes lower / But change till now did never injure thee.' When the tree goes, Clare's assuredness about his past, his self, goes too. So it is that in the asylum poem 'Child Harold', survival means a desperate attempt to hold on to both a place and a time: 'I'll be free in a prison and cling to the soil / I'll cling to the spot where my first love was cherished'. Might it not then be the case that nature's rights correspond to humankind's needs?

Democratic revolutions have always been underpinned by a rhetoric of rights – the right of the people to choose a government, and so forth – but the extent of their implementation has always been a matter of pragmatics. The people have usually been given just sufficient rights to keep the peace. Assuming that Hobbes was correct and Godwin was incorrect about the nature of civil society, no amount of abstract principled argument concerning the natural justice of animal or vegetable rights will be sufficient to bring into being Baron Cosimo's arboreal Utopia. But what the life and work of John Clare can show us is that even in terms of pragmatic self-interest it is to our benefit to care for nature's rights – our inner ecology cannot be sustained without the health of ecosystems.

In the first book of *The Prelude*, the boy Wordsworth climbs to a raven's nest and experiences the egotistical sublime ('While on the perilous ridge I hung alone'). But the raven's nest in Clare is a repository of communal, not individual memory. Each generation of village boys has attempted to climb the huge oak tree to reach the nest at the top. When old men watch the young boys try, they see themselves as they once were and gain assurance of their collective identity. An oral tradition of reminiscence creates a local history which identifies the village as a viable ecosystem, constantly evolving but with necessary continuity. The ravens return each spring and repair the nest:

> where still they live
> Through changes winds and storms and are secure
> And like a landmark in the chronicles
> Of village memorys treasured up yet lives
> The hughe old oak that wears the raven's nest.

But if the 'landmark' nest were to be destroyed, the village would lose its memory.

The lament of the piece of land ends with the words 'My name will quickly be the whole / That's left of Swordy Well'. That is true: Swordy or Swaddy Well is now partly a stone quarry and partly a refuse dump, but its name is left in the printed texts of John Clare's poetry. To name a place is to allow that place its being. Merleau-Ponty writes: 'The denomination of objects does not follow upon recognition; it is itself recognition ... For pre-scientific thinking, naming an object is causing it to exist or changing it; God creates beings by naming them and magic operates upon them by speaking of them.'

Ecopoetics reawakens the pre-scientific magic of naming. 'There remains,' wrote Heidegger in his *Holzwege*, or *Forest Paths*, 'the song that names the earth.' Postmodernity proclaims that all marks are textmarks; ecopoetics proposes that we must hold fast to the possibility that certain textmarks called poems can bring back to our memory humankind's ancient knowledge that without landmarks we are lost.

7

Poets, Apes and Other Animals

for
(Let deeper sages the true cause determine)
  He had a kind of inclination, or
Weakness, for what most people deem mere vermin –
  Live animals.

(Byron, *Don Juan*, 10.50)

EARLY IN THE *Discourse on the Origin of Inequality*, Jean-Jacques Rousseau, under the influence of René Descartes's proposition that an animal is nothing more than a sophisticated machine, writes as follows:

> I see in every animal merely an ingenious machine to which nature has given senses to keep it going by itself and to protect itself, up to a certain point, from everything likely to distress or annihilate it. I see precisely the same things in the human machine, with the difference that nature alone does everything in the activities of a beast while man contributes to his own, in his capacity as a free agent. The beast chooses or rejects by instinct, man by free action, meaning that the beast cannot deviate from the rule prescribed for it, even when it might benefit from doing so, whereas man often deviates from such laws to his own detriment.

It is Rousseau's argument, then, that animal behaviour is determined, whereas man is anti-nature in so far as he can determine his own destiny, even if it is harmful to himself. He can commit suicide, he can drink himself to death. 'Man is free enough to die of freedom', writes Luc Ferry, glossing this section of the second *Discourse*:

Seeing the best, he can choose the worst: this is the motto of the antinatural creature. His *humanitas* resides in his freedom, in the fact that he is undefined, that his nature is to have no nature but to possess the capacity to distance himself from any code within which one may seek to imprison him.

'Nor dread nor hope attend / a dying animal', wrote W. B. Yeats in his poem, 'Death': 'A man awaits his end / Dreading and hoping all . . . Man has created death'. Paradoxically, among the greatest glories of human life is the will to die. The Homeric warrior on the battlefield of *The Iliad* becomes most noble, most human in the blazing moment when he welcomes death. Likewise a tragic hero who has lost everything. 'My long sickness / Of health and living now begins to mend,' says Shakespeare's Timon, 'And nothing brings me all things.' The freedom to choose pain, to choose death, to seek another world of whose existence we have no sure knowledge: these are what make man the antinatural being. Negative freedom and secular transcendence: the claims of Enlightenment Man.

But is the distinction between man and the animals so sharp? It appears that whales can commit suicide. Birds as well as humans may put themselves in danger in order to protect their young. Rousseau himself argued in the preface to the second *Discourse* that although animals cannot participate in natural law, since they lack freedom, they must participate in natural right, 'and man is subject to some kind of duties toward them', since they have sensations. Since animals can feel pain, we have a duty not to inflict unnecessary pain upon them: from Rousseau onwards, this became a standard humanitarian argument, leading to the formation of such organizations as the Society for the Prevention of Cruelty to Animals (established in 1824). One of the Society's founders was William Wilberforce, among the most celebrated of anti-slavery campaigners. His pedigree reveals how the animal liberation movement is premised on the idea of an increasingly extended circle of rights: first the emancipation of the unpropertied and the poor, then that of women and children, next of slaves, and so to animals. The National Trust allowed the hunting of deer on its land in the west of

England until 1997, when a committee of scientists produced evidence that deer feel pain – or, more precisely, the level of their stress hormones sharply increases – when they are being chased at speed, then torn to pieces by hounds. In response to this information, the Council of the Trust immediately proposed a ban on the hunting. Presumably if some future committee of biologists produced evidence that trees feel pain when being chopped down, the circle of humanitarian obligation would be extended still further and the Trust would cease to manage its forests.

Homer's *Iliad* is Western literature's founding text for the idea of man as anti-nature, but his *Odyssey* offers a different picture. When Odysseus returns home from his long voyage, the first being to recognize him is not a human:

> While he spoke
> an old hound, lying near, pricked up his ears
> and lifted up his muzzle. This was Argos,
> trained as a puppy by Odysseus . . .
> Treated as rubbish now, he lay at last
> upon a mass of dung before the gates . . .
> Abandoned there, and half destroyed with flies,
> old Argos lay.
> But when he knew he heard
> Odysseus' voice nearby, he did his best
> to wag his tail, nose down, with flattened ears,
> having no strength to move nearer his master.

Having seen his master after twenty years' absence, Argos closes his eyes in death. This moment in the *Odyssey* supposes that a dog may stay alive not out of the instinct for self-preservation, but in order to await his reunion with a beloved other. In contradistinction to Rousseau's claim, this imagined dog chooses the moment at which he dies.

Values of home, community and loyalty are thus invested in an animal. Whether or not this investment is regarded as pure human projection, its function is to break down the distinction between human and animal being. Theodor Adorno and Max Horkheimer read Odysseus as the prototype of Enlightenment man, whose triumph is his overcoming of the Siren song of reversion to the animal: 'the estrangement from nature that he brings about is realized in the process of the abandonment to nature he contends with in each adventure.' But Argos's canine act of survival in the name of love does not consort with this reading. It invites us to think about what it might mean to dwell upon the earth in company with other species.

The critic Northrop Frye, never afraid of bold schemes and provocative generalizations, proposed that Homer established two paradigms for Western literature: the Iliadic, being the clash of human and social forces, centred upon the city; and the Odysseyan, being the struggle of human against natural forces, ranged across the sea. For Frye, the *Iliad* was the poem of war, the *Odyssey* of desire. Epic and tragedy are traditionally Iliadic, romance and comedy Odysseyan. Frye thought that all critics are either Iliad critics or Odyssey critics.

Not surprisingly, literary criticism in the war-torn twentieth century was predominantly Iliadic. The 'New Criticism' which dominated the mid-century began with T. S. Eliot in the immediate wake of the Great War; Eliot's epigone, F. R. Leavis, was an orderly on an ambulance train on the Western Front. New Criticism reached its zenith in the aftermath of the Second World War and was transformed into deconstruction during the Cold War. Formalism regarded texts as closed cities, waiting to be besieged by critics. With two-handed engines such as irony and ambiguity, the critics prised open the gates and the cities yielded up their riches. For all its talk about artworks as organisms, New Criticism typically treated texts as mechanisms – 'nature' was problematized or marginalized. Among the major influences on Eliot, Irving Babbitt and T. E. Hulme were notorious anti-romantics. In this respect, New Criticism was not the opposite but the cousin of the more overtly Iliadic, anti-natural, militaristic forms of analysis which flourished alongside it, from the Marxism of Christopher Caldwell in the 1930s through to the 'new historicism' and ideologism of the 1980s. As Karl Kroeber has written, the rhetoric of both deconstruction and ideologism 'springs from their common rootedness in a Cold War mind-set. Both "schools" reflect fundamental attitudes of superpower oppositionalism deriving from the global political situation produced by World War II.'

The twentieth century's two most nearly Odysseyan literary critics were Northrop Frye himself and his theoretical child, Harold Bloom. But the former's Christianity and the latter's Freudianism and Judaism led them to *internalize* romance. They thus regarded the forest of Arden, the mountain, the wilderness and the ocean primarily as exterior symbols of interior struggles. Once again, natural forces were displaced. An authentic Odysseyan criticism should accept that forests, mountains and oceans really are forests, mountains and oceans. It must find a place for the weather, the shifting of the continental plate and the quality of the air. It will be a criticism which speaks to the global crises of subsistence and environmental degradation which have been aggravated, not solved, by the end of the Cold War. It will be an ecological criticism.

The first book of explicitly ecological literary criticism was Joseph Meeker's *The Comedy of Survival: Studies in Literary Ecology* (1974). This study proposed that the truly ecological literary genre is comedy. The analysis fits the Homeric paradigm, for the roots of tragedy are to be found in the *Iliad* and of comedy in the *Odyssey*. The Trojan War gave the ancient Greek dramatists their principal tragic material, whereas the adventures of Odysseus on his journey home were often turned to comic account in the playfully defusing satyr plays, which were staged at the end of each group of three tragedies. Recognition, the key trope of the *Odyssey*, later became a driving-force of the classical 'new comedy' which – together with the Odysseus-like wanderings of the heroes of ancient 'romances' such as Apollonius of Tyre – made possible the comic art of the European and English Renaissance.

For Meeker, tragedy is a quest for transcendence. In the moment of death, the tragic hero somehow goes beyond the material world, rises to a plane of spiritual reconciliation. Comedy, on the other hand, is about survival. It grants us our animal being, relishes the materiality of the everyday world, concerns itself with the business of living and reproducing.

Hamlet meditates upon the double nature of humankind:

> What a piece of work is a man! How noble in reason, how
> infinite in faculty, in form and moving how express and
> admirable, in action how like an angel, in apprehension how
> like a god – the beauty of the world, the paragon of animals!
> And yet to me what is this quintessence of dust?

Our mental faculties make us into spiritual beings, yet we cannot
escape the mortality of the body. This is Hamlet's dilemma – the
tragic condition – bound within a nutshell. Comedy, by contrast,
accepts the body. It reckons that the best way to deal with the
problem of mortality is to find the right partner and set about
propagating the species. Hamlet rejects this option, with cruel
consequences for Ophelia. According to Meeker's argument,
which is developed from a way of thinking inaugurated by Hegel's
aesthetics, in the moment of tragic transcendence, humankind
seeks to become not so much 'the paragon of animals' as a Being
beyond the animal.

The principal value of Meeker's book is its recognition that
'literary ecology' must consider the question of our animal being.
In this chapter, I want to suggest that Romanticism as traditionally conceived may not be so ecologically attuned as the analysis
in my previous chapters may imply, for the aspiring spirit of the
Rousseauesque or Wordsworthian contemplative is sometimes
forgetful of the biological body. Coordinate with this occlusion
of the body is a deficiency in comedy. It is because of the absence
of self-deprecating humour in so many of his poems that Wordsworth is the most parodiable of major English writers: 'Wordsworth in the Lake District—at cross-purposes' (plate 15) is Max
Beerbohm's most accurate caricature. The intuitive Keats realized
that high Romanticism was readily mockable when he wrote in a
letter that his greatest ambition was to write fine things which
could not be laughed at in any way. Fortunately, though, British
Romanticism has a remedy for forgetfulness of – to use a word in
both its ancient and its modern senses – the humours. That
remedy is the life and work of George Gordon, Lord Byron.

*

Three bears are celebrated in the annals of English literature. One is fictional, one was real, the third may originally have been either, but has most frequently been reinvented as a human in animal skin. Each of them is a servant of Thalia, the Muse of Comedy. A. A. Milne's Winnie-the-Pooh is in the great tradition of *The Praise of Folly*: it is through a show of learning that Wol the owl reveals his ignorance, whilst Pooh, the Bear of self-confessed Little Brain, has that true wisdom which Erasmus ascribed to the *infans*. His is comedy's topsy-turvy knowledge. The bear in Shakespeare's *Winter's Tale*, meanwhile, is a sign of comedy's perpetual proximity to tragedy and its fascination with the interplay of art and nature. '*Exit pursued by a bear*': it is a bringer of death to Antigonus but of laughter to the theatre-audience, and at the same time a marker of the play's movement into the register of nature, but a nature complicated by art, for the animal's appearance is testimony to the human skill of either an actor and costume-designer or a trainer at the local bear-pit.

The other bear is part of a life, not a work – but a life that was projected into the works with peculiar magnification and self-consciousness. One of the two things which every schoolboy used to know about Lord Byron was that he kept a bear whilst an undergraduate at Trinity College, Cambridge. The knowledge gives us our first intimation that Byron was someone who, as John Keats put it, 'cut a figure'. We attach the lumbering beast to his owner and Milord has already become outrageous, larger-than-life. It is like Falstaff's first larded appearance: he does not have to speak a word – Byron does not have to pen a line of poetry – for us to know that he will fill his world, that he is life itself. 'Is it not *life*, is it not the *thing*?', we say, as Byron did of his own *Don Juan*.

The bear is also the occasion for comedy's necessary diet, the joke. Byron writes from college to Elizabeth Bridget Pigot:

> I have got a new friend, the finest in the world, a *tame Bear*, when I brought him here, they asked me what I meant to do with him, and my reply was 'he should *sit* for *a Fellowship*.' – *Sherard* will explain the meaning of the sentence if it is ambiguous. – This answer delighted them not, – we have

eternal parties here, and this evening a large assortment of *Jockies*, Gamblers, *Boxers*, *Authors*, *parsons*, and *poets*, sup with me. – A precious Mixture, but they go on well together, and for me, I am a *spice* of every thing except a Jockey, by the bye, I was dismounted again the other day. – Thank your Brother in my name, for his Treatise. I have written 214 pages of a novel, one poem of 380 Lines, to be published (without my name) in a few weeks, with notes, 560 Lines of Bosworth Field, and 250 Lines of another poem in rhyme, besides half a dozen smaller pieces . . .

What is the ambiguity of the sentence? Is it merely that Miss Pigot might not be expected to understand the idiom of sitting for a prize Fellowship? E. H. Coleridge thought that there was more to it, for he annotated the passage in his copy of Tom Moore's *Letters and Journals of Lord Byron* to the effect that 'Byron's dirty double entente has been quoted seriously as a piece of academic wit'. But Leslie Marchand footnotes his edition with a disappointed and disappointing 'No slang dictionary has yielded a double entendre for the phrase "sit for a fellowship."' We don't, however, need a slang dictionary to tell us that a bear adopts a sitting position in order to defecate. The double entendre is surely 'shit for a fellowship'. The qualification for becoming a Fellow of Trinity was to produce a load of shit.

This mockery of learning by means of scatological humour places Byron squarely in the tradition of *The Dunciad*. His generative, associative epistolary style maintains the allegiance to Pope. An evening party becomes the locus of writing; the poet mucks in with the gambler, sportsman and parson. Where the Lakers had made the poet into a Solitary, communing with the sublimities of nature, Byron puts him back into a world like that of the urbane Scriblerians of the London coffeehouses. Satire is the mode, rhyming couplets the form. That 'poem of 380 Lines' quickly grew and was published as *English Bards and Scotch Reviewers*, a brief *Dunciad* for the new century. Pope's theme of the degeneration of poetry is updated so that 'MILTON, DRYDEN, POPE, alike forgot, / Resign their hallow'd Bays to WALTER SCOTT'. Southey is mocked for trying to climb too high in his interminable epics, Wordsworth and Coleridge for sinking too low, as one of them 'both by precept and example, shows / That prose is verse, and verse is merely prose' while the other 'soars to elegize an ass' – 'So well the subject suits his noble mind, / He brays the Laureat of the long-ear'd kind!' The latter allusion is a dismissive reference to Coleridge's pathos-filled animal rights poem, 'To a Young Ass'.

A bear was not, however, the best creature through whom to turn the Lakers and their kind into asses. Byron's brisk assertion that the bear is the finest friend in the world is a satirist's dig at the frequent disloyalties of human friends, but not much more than that. What he needed was an animal that could entertain him while also demonstrating the cant of high Romantic claims about the uniqueness of humankind as manifested in the imaginative sublime.

William Hazlitt's *Lectures on the English Comic Writers* (1819) have the distinction of being the first critical history of English comedy. The very first words of the lecture-course offer a crisp inflexion of a traditional idea: 'Man is the only animal that laughs and weeps; for he is the only animal that is struck with the difference between what things are, and what they ought to be.' Romanticism thrives on a poetry of the difference between aspiration and actuality. 'We weep at what thwarts or exceeds our desires', continues Hazlitt: Romanticism aches with desire while always finding itself thwarted in the material world. But its faith in transcendence takes it beyond weeping towards what Wordsworth in his 'Intimations of Immortality' called 'Thoughts that do often lie too deep for tears'.

Hazlitt was of the view that 'To explain the nature of laughter and tears, is to account for the condition of human life; for it is in a manner compounded of these two! It is a tragedy or a comedy – sad or merry, as it happens.' Byron sometimes falls into line with this view, as when he writes in *Don Juan*, 'And if I laugh at any mortal thing, / 'tis that I may not weep', or when in both poems and letters he slips easily – 'as it happens' – from sadness to merriment. But on other occasions he complicates the matter. Had he read Hazlitt's lectures on comedy, he might have dissented from the opening proposition that 'Man is the only animal that laughs'. A good way of laughing at humankind's inflated sense of itself was to accept the possibility that animals might be capable of laughing at us. Byron liked geese, presumably because they cackled, and parrots because they mimicked. But it was not until 1819 in Venice that he acquired for his menagerie the genus that best fitted the bill:

> I have got two monkeys, a fox – & two new mastiffs – Mutz is still in high old age. – The Monkeys are charming. – Last month I had a business about a Venetian Girl who wanted to marry me – a circumstance prevented like Dr Blifil's Espousals not only by my previous marriage – but by Mr Allworthy's being acquainted with the existence of Mrs Dr Blifil.

It is clearly the monkeys that have caught his imagination.

The train of thought in this letter, from the monkeys to the business about the Venetian girl, is suggestive. The bear doesn't help us with the second thing that every schoolboy used to know about Byron, which is to say *the thing* that drives the letter on *Don Juan*: 'Could any man have written it – who has not lived in the world? – and tooled in a post-chaise? in a hackney coach? in a Gondola? against a wall? in a court carriage? in a vis a vis? – on a table? – and under it?' But the Monkey, that ancient symbol of randiness, is just the thing here. The comparison between Britain's two aristocratic poets is no less revealing for having become a cliché: the Earl of Rochester was painted with a monkey, whilst Lord Byron went better and owned two of them. It was by watching a lady of the town fondling her pet monkey – 'Kiss me, thou curious Miniature of Man' – that Rochester's Artemiza

> took this Time to think what Nature meant,
> When this mixt thing into the world she sent,
> So very wise, yet so impertinent.

For Byron, too, the monkey reveals that humankind is a 'mixt thing'. He watches his pair of them: 'all scratching – screaming and fighting – in the highest health and Spirits. – Fletcher is flourishing.' Like his servant Fletcher, they are part of the family; their vigour is an image of the kind of life into which Byron threw himself – only to draw back into periodic hours of idleness. Thus in a later letter, the news that 'the monkeys I have not looked to since the cold weather, as they suffer by being brought up' is swiftly followed by the chill of 'What is the reason that I have been, all my lifetime, more or less *ennuyé*?'

Byron was an acute observer and the remarks about his monkeys in the letters suggest that he would have noticed many of the behavioural traits which Charles Darwin described half a century later in *The Expression of the Emotions in Man and Animals*. The monkey is a sociable creature ('they perfectly understand each other's gestures and expression'); it can express pleasure and affection, but also dejection and anger; if tickled, a 'chuckling or laughing sound is uttered'; it may sulk. It loves to imitate and is of course a troublemaker, as Byron notes in a letter to Tom Moore: 'I have just been scolding my monkey for tearing the seal of her letter, and spoiling a mock book, in which I put rose leaves'. In all these particulars it resembles Byronic more than Wordsworthian man.

Oddly, in view of their love of all things 'natural', the Lakers and their followers didn't seem to have a particular affection for animals (though in one of Keats's visions in verse, Hazlitt is memorably glimpsed playing with Miss Edgeworth's cat). Wordsworth's world at its moments of intensity is strangely silent: the vision enters the boy when the owls *don't* reply. Nothing could be further from the chatter, screech and rapid movement of Byron's monkey-house. Wordsworth's Solitary and Wanderer could not be more different from Juan, that 'little curly-headed, good-for-nothing, / And mischief-making monkey from his birth', or Lambro on his travels, during which

> A monkey, a Dutch mastiff, a mackaw,
>   Two parrots, with a Persian cat and kittens,
> He chose from several animals he saw.

Primates also assisted Byron because they embodied a traditional metaphor for artistic imitation. In the section concerning Florentine Renaissance sculpture in *Childe Harold's Pilgrimage* there is a reference to 'the artist and his ape', and in *Don Juan* the Trimmer poet's mercenary mimicry includes a trip to Italy where 'he'd ape the "Trecentisti"'. Having accused the Trimmer, a figure closely related to the turncoat Lakers, of being an ape, Byron promptly apes that apeing in 'The isles of Greece, the isles of Greece!', a lyric so beautiful that we forget it is being sung by a genius of insincerity. The false poet becomes the poet in general: 'they are such liars, / And take all colours – like the hands of dyers.'

And if the poet is an ape, who is not? When Byron apes Wordsworth and Southey, he does so partly in order to have fun at their expense, in accordance with the general aim of *Don Juan* to show that it is possible to mix 'fun & poetry'. But he does so also in order to make the more serious point that all of us, including poets, share a lot with the monkeys and should not be ashamed of the fact.

Coleridge's poem 'To a Young Ass', with its emphasis on the suffering of the whipped beast of burden, is in the tradition of philanthropy leading to zoophilia, based on sympathy for the sentience of pain, which animates the animal rights tradition, the premiss of which was best articulated by Jeremy Bentham's 'The question is not, Can they *reason*? nor Can they *talk*? but, Can they *suffer*?' The unsentimental Byron, who seems to have had no qualms about confining his monkeys in small, dirty cages and dragging them round Europe, is emphatically not in this tradition. (He did, however, hate hunting and fishing, while his goose was originally bought for the table but then saved and kept as a pet.) My argument in this chapter is not about animal rights, but about how animals make us think about our own animalness, our embodiedness in the world.

In *The New Ecological Order*, Luc Ferry wittily dismantles the more excessive claims of the animal liberation movement, but then adduces from Immanuel Kant an eloquent argument in favour of respect for animals:

> Kant suggests a path for reflection when he writes the following: 'Because animals are an *analogue* of humanity, we observe duties toward humanity when we regard them as analogous to humanity, and thus we satisfy our obligations toward it.' Why? Simply because, as opposed to what Descartes and his

automata-makers thought, the living being is not a thing, the animal is not a stone, not even a plant. So what, one may ask? So life, defined as 'the faculty to act according to the representation of a goal,' is an *analogue of freedom. As such* (that is to say in its highest forms) and because it maintains a relationship of analogy with that which makes us human, it is (or should be) the object of a *certain* respect, a respect which, by way of animals, we *also* pay ourselves.

Analogously to this: by drawing attention to what we have in common with animals, Byron reminds us of the limitation of that ecopoetic of reverie which acknowledges only the self and the universe. Our selves only inhabit the universe in particular bodies, particular places and in the company of other species. What should follow from the recognition of this is respect for the environment which we share. That too is a respect which, by way of animals, we owe to ourselves.

*

Byron's *Don Juan* is among many other things an anti-Romantic manifesto. Its original preface parodies a notorious Wordsworthian 'note or preface (I forget which)', namely the explanatory note to 'The Thorn' in the second edition of *Lyrical Ballads*. In Byron's reworking, a small table with sherry on it replaces Wordsworth's bleak pool and thorn that are the external markers of dark human deeds. The parody is an implicit questioning of the whole Romantic ethos of solitude and sublimity, for it is a celebration of communal merriment, of story-telling for its own sake, of mundanity that is not invested with mysterious power. Like Fielding's Parson Adams, Byron's narrator likes a drink, a smoke and a chance to put his feet up; it is hard to imagine Wordsworth's Wanderer indulging himself thus. A certain amount of eating does go on in *The Excursion*, but the meals are frugal and the conversation is always elevated and purposeful, never Byronically desultory. Merriment upon the village green is sometimes observed, but is always from a distance – when the Poet suggests to his companion that they should linger amidst 'The simple pastimes of the day and place', the Wanderer replies that they must not, for it is necessary to toil on to the Solitary's cottage.

The matter of food, the need for which is part of our animal nature, is of the essence. If we visualize the typical Wordsworthian personae – Wanderer, Solitary, Pastor, narrator of 'The Thorn' – we are likely to find them gaunt. One or two might even have a touch of Malvolio about them. Byron's narrator, with his 'right sherris', is ample; he is Falstaff or Toby Belch. The epigraph to cantos six to eight of *Don Juan*, published in July 1823, is Sir Toby's '"Dost thou think, because thou art virtuous, there shall be no more cakes and ale?" – "Yes, by St Anne; and Ginger shall be hot i' the mouth too!"' – this despite the fact that two of these cantos concern the bloody siege of Ismail.

Crucially, Haidée is a practical girl who gives the near-drowned Juan a breakfast 'of eggs, coffee, bread, and fish' before she gives him her love. Indeed, there are two meals in the first dozen stanzas of the young lovers' relationship, for Haidée and her maid have already 'made a most superior mess of broth, / A thing which poesy but seldom mentions'. Eggs and coffee for breakfast or small tables with jugs of Malaga wine on them are things that matter in Byron's world, as rocks and stones and trees are things that matter in Wordsworth's.

'A thing which poesy but seldom mentions': in an essay called 'Tragedy and the Whole Truth', Aldous Huxley argued that (pure) tragedy does not tell the whole truth because in it people weep and grieve, whereas in real life 'even the most cruelly bereaved must eat', for 'hunger is stronger than sorrow' and 'its satisfaction takes precedence even of tears'. As an example of a writer telling the whole truth, Huxley cites the aftermath of Scylla's attack on Odysseus' ship in Homer, when the survivors expertly prepare and then eat their supper before they weep for their dead companions. Haidée making breakfast – and making a tasty job of it – on the beach is of those survivors' company; *Don Juan* as a whole tells this kind of truth, which may not be the 'whole truth' Huxley claims it to be, but which is a truth that the comedy of survival is especially good at telling.

When Haidée is dead, Byron knows exactly the moment to turn away from her grave and the hollow sea's mourning 'o'er the beauty of the Cyclades', knows just when to leave his 'sheet of sorrows on the shelf', and to change tack with Juan bundled below deck, to hurry his hero towards the harem. Which brings us to sex – another aspect of our animal, and in particular our simian, nature. There is love in Wordsworth's poetry, but it is a universal love, working most characteristically at the abstract level of the marriage between mind and nature. Falling in love and making love, the matter of comedy, are profoundly un-Wordsworthian. 'Vaudracour and Julia', the section of *The Prelude* based on his affair with Annette Vallon, is one of his principal failures. One reason why Shelley is such a fascinatingly complex figure – and perhaps why Byron tolerated him as he tolerated no other Romantic – is that in a poem like *Epipsychidion* he succeeds in embracing both the Wordsworthian marriage with nature and a Byronic celebration of sexual passion. Shelley at once endorses and modifies the Wordsworthian vision: where the Wanderer fuses himself with the universal 'pure principle of love' alone in the mountains, the speaker of *Epipsychidion* does so through his passion for his beloved Emily.

Byron's most acute criticism of Wordsworth may therefore be the sequence in the first canto of *Don Juan* (stanzas 90–94) in which the adolescent Juan falls in love for the first time: he wanders (a Wordsworthian thing to do), he thinks 'unutterable things' (the negative prefix, the sense of the inarticulable and the word 'things' are all Wordsworthian hallmarks), and the stanza ends with the line 'Unless, like Wordsworth, they prove unintelligible'. The next stanza begins, 'He, Juan, (and not Wordsworth)' – but it *is* Wordsworth, for the whole panoply of Wordsworthian Romanticism is there ('self-communion with his own high soul', the 'mighty heart', 'He thought about himself, and the whole earth'). Juan seems to be becoming a young Wordsworth, perhaps Keats under the influence of Wordsworth ('He thought of wood nymphs and immortal bowers, / And how the goddesses came down to men, / He miss'd the pathway . . .'), until the Byronic lower bodily stratum intervenes ('He found how much old Time had been a winner – / He also found that he had lost his dinner'). The unkindest cut of all is the couplet, 'If you think 'twas philosophy that this did, / I can't help thinking puberty assisted':

Romanticism's 'Longings sublime, and aspirations high' are reduced to the level of puppy love.

There is a serious critique here, and it is the same as Hazlitt's in his review of *The Excursion*: the line 'He thought about himself, and the whole earth' is so similar to Hazlitt's 'The power of his mind preys upon itself. It is as if there were nothing but himself and the universe' that it may well be one of Byron's many loose quotations. The point is that the egotism, the relishing of the solitary self, sits uneasily beside the aspiration towards universal love. He thought about himself and the whole earth, but not about the other humans and the animals who share the earth with him. By parodying the Wordsworthian vision in the form of adolescent love, Byron is implying that the goal might better be achieved by an adult love which keeps its feet firmly on the ground, its body well fed and its sexual needs satisfied. In *Don Juan* as a whole, the moral education offered by *The Excursion* is replaced by a comic education in the nature of desire.

At the beginning of canto eleven, Byron offers ironic praise of the philosophical idealism that lies behind the Romantic sublime:

> What a sublime discovery 'twas to make the
> Universe universal Egotism!
> That's all ideal – *all ourselves*.

The personae of *The Excursion* are ultimately all versions of Wordsworth himself: this is what Hazlitt saw in his lectures and Keats crystallized in his astonishingly apt phrase, 'the wordsworthian or egotistical sublime'. In opposition to egotism, Byron sets up a principle of *'Tuism'*, but it is emphatically a principle, not a system. Only in individual encounters is the principle lived out, and the encounter which offers the most intimate *tu* is that between two lovers in bed.

Romantic egotism is a form of post-Cartesian dualism which sets the mind against the world; it owes a substantial debt to Bishop Berkeley's argument that spirit is the only real cause or power. Erotic tuism, by contrast, grants that we inhabit the world with our bodies. Maurice Merleau-Ponty writes in a chapter called 'The Body in its Sexual Being' in his *Phenomenology of Perception*:

> Erotic perception is not a *cogitatio* which aims at a *cogitatum*;
> through one body it aims at another body, and takes place in
> the world, not in a consciousness ... There is an erotic
> 'comprehension' not of the order of understanding, since
> understanding subsumes an experience, once perceived, under
> some idea, while desire comprehends blindly by linking body
> to body.

Byron's principle, with its refusal to pass from the experience
to the idea, is a practical anticipation of this philosophical proposition.

'Tuism' is saying 'O, Thou!' to your lover, as Juan dreams of
saying to Aurora Raby. As her name suggests, Aurora represents
a new dawn for Juan; he loves her as he has only loved Haidée
before, but she is different from Haidée, for she lives not on a
paradisal island but in the fallen world of contemporary England
('She look'd as if she sat by Eden's door, / And grieved for those
who could return no more'). She seems to be the first woman
with whom Juan could have a truly adult and truly reciprocal
relationship. When the poem breaks off, it is 'her frolic Grace –
Fitz-Fulke' who has turned up in Juan's bedroom, and in all
probability, to judge from the sheepishness of the morning after,
his bed. But this is a digression: what we are eagerly anticipating
is the consummation of the hero's relationship with Aurora.

It is important that Tuism is not a 'system' because the attack
on system is fundamental to Byron's anti-Romanticism. Wordsworth's philosophical epic, despite its divagatory title, tries to
make all things one:

> And Wordsworth, in a rather long 'Excursion',
>   (I think the quarto holds five hundred pages)
> Has given a sample from the vasty version
>   Of his new system to perplex the sages.

'When a man talks of system, his case is hopeless', wrote Byron
in a letter to Tom Moore apropos of Leigh Hunt's 'cant' about
writing poetry according to a system. Juan's sexual adventures
make good anti-Romantic copy because they cannot be systema-
tized. In *The Excursion*, you walk a little way and then stop to
philosophize for a long, long time; in *Don Juan*, you travel at

speed by boat or coach, and are driven from scrape to scrape, bed to bed. Byron's mock-epic keeps on coming; it is insatiable, unstoppable, the very antithesis of Southey's epics, which strive and strive for thousands of lines but never make it, because ultimately they are sterile:

> And then you overstrain yourself, or so,
>   And tumble downward like the flying fish
> Gasping on deck, because you soar too high, Bob,
> And fall, for lack of moisture, quite adry, Bob.

That Southey's verse is like coition without emission (the 'dry bob') implies that sex is a question of style. Wordsworth's verse, especially that of *The Excursion*, is perhaps the chastest, most unyielding in the language; Byron's, especially that of *Don Juan*, is probably the most stylistically promiscuous. What Byron didn't like about *The Excursion* was its single-mindedness, its systematization and its concomitant lack of stylistic variety: 'A drowsy frowsy poem, call'd the "Excursion", / Writ in a manner which is my aversion'. It is not only the aspiration towards solitary communion with nature and the self, but also the style that gets in the way of the spirit of community, that sense of Horatian '*communia dicere*' which is Byron's ideal: Wordsworth's drowsy frowsy blank verse 'builds up a formidable dyke / Between his own and others' intellect'. The Byron of *Don Juan*, by contrast, is always crossing the dykes on the bridges of his rhymes. Those bridges are built between radically disparate territories; as Hazlitt remarked of the poem, 'the drollery is in the utter discontinuity of ideas and feelings . . . A classical intoxication is followed by the splashing of soda-water, by frothy effusions of ordinary bile. After the lightning and the hurricane, we are introduced to the interior of the cabin and the contents of wash-hand basins.'

Remembering Freud's view that dream-work and *Witz*-work share the same origin as means of discharging cathexis, we may say that humankind needs both the sublime and the ridiculous. We need to willingly suspend our disbelief in Romanticism's dream of the transformational power of reverie, but we also need to acknowledge, as Macbeth does tragically and *Don Juan* comically, that we are 'cabin'd, cribb'd, confin'd'. Macbeth will never be able to rest, since a Fleance will always 'scape; Juan's journey will always restart, even after Haidée's death. Haidée, like Duncan, 'sleeps well' in the grave. But Byron does not allow us to dwell on her, flipping instead to Juan in the cabin: 'The pun on "cabined" is atrocious and funny,' writes Bernard Beatty, 'hence the tragic allusion is now made to look ridiculous'. The joke effects a discharge of emotional tension in the exact manner of the Freudian paradigm.

Accepting 'the interior of the cabin and the contents of wash-hand basins', as the Byron of *Don Juan* does, is not just a matter of splashing the water around while we wait for death. As M. H. Abrams and other critics have repeatedly shown, Wordsworthian Romanticism was a profoundly religious phenomenon. The project of *The Recluse*, as outlined in the prospectus published with *The Excursion*, was to rediscover 'Paradise, and groves / Elysian, Fortunate Fields' in the form of 'A simple produce of the common day'. To bring humankind closer to the ape than the angel will at first seem to dampen this ambition. But it need not necessarily be so: confinement within the animal body may afford a kind of grace by returning us to the 'paradise' of the natural.

*

In an annotation to some letters of Shelley's published in *Fraser's Magazine* in 1860, Thomas Love Peacock wrote: 'Lord Byron told Captain Medwin that a friend of Shelley's had written a novel, of which he had forgotten the name, founded on his bear'. He went on to deny the identification: 'assuredly, when I condensed Lord Monboddo's views of the humanity of the Oran Outang into the character of Sir Oran Haut-ton, I thought neither of Lord Byron's bear nor of Caligula's horse. But Lord Byron was much in the habit of fancying that all the world was spinning on his pivot.'

But the denial is beside the point. What is significant is that Byron read Peacock's novel *Melincourt* (published in 1817) and imagined that the character of Forester, with his noble and companionable ape, was open to being read as an image of himself – he specifies the bear because it was his most famous pet and was large and hairy, but he could not have failed to think also of his monkeys. The association suggests that Byron found in the novel an image of his own way of thinking.

Like Peacock's other comic novels, *Melincourt* offers a series of dialogues on the great issues of the day, such as slavery in the West Indies, rotten boroughs in politics, and the characteristics of the Lake poets. The latter are parodied in the form of Mr Feathernest (Robert Southey, who had recently turned his coat from youthful radicalism to acceptance of the Laureateship), Mr Paperstamp (Wordsworth, who had accepted the minor government post of Distributor of Stamps for the County of Westmorland) and Mr Mystic (Coleridge, who had also swung to the right in politics, but without renouncing the impenetrable jargon of German metaphysics). The orangutan, meanwhile, has been educated by the wealthy young philanthropic philosopher, Mr Sylvan Forester. Sir Oran Haut-ton has developed all the gentlemanly virtues save speech. Forester has bought him a baronetcy and a seat in Parliament. A Member of Parliament who never speaks is welcomed as a delightful novelty.

The premise of *Melincourt* is Lord Monboddo's view that the orangutan is not a monkey at all, but rather 'a specimen of the natural and original man'. The Comte de Buffon's observations of an orang in Paris, who drank wine but preferred to lace it with milk or tea, were among Peacock's sources, but the great French naturalist is upbraided by Forester for classifying the orang 'among the *singes*, when the very words of his description give him all the characteristics of human nature'. In his *Natural History*, Buffon had been undecided as to whether the orang was best regarded as a supermonkey or a subhuman. The great apes have fascinated thinkers ever since Buffon because they mark the borderline between the human and the non-human. Western primatology's 'scene of origin', writes Donna Haraway, is 'the cradle of culture, of human being distinct from animal existence'.

Peacock's Forester – a character whose name suggests his own links with the natural man – points out that in his analysis of the biology and the behaviour of the orang, Buffon had emphasized the similarities with *Homo sapiens*, but in his final classification the naturalist had held back from crossing the barrier between human and animal. Lord Monboddo, on the other hand, reckoned that his own account of the orang had 'established his humanity by proof that ought to satisfy every one who gives credit to human testimony'.

Sir Oran, as Forester points out in a long quotation from Monboddo's *Ancient Metaphysics*, behaves

> *with dignity and composure, altogether unlike a monkey; from whom he differs likewise in this material respect, that he is capable of great attachment to particular persons, of which the monkey is altogether incapable; and also in this respect, that a monkey never can be so tamed, that we may depend on his not doing mischief when left alone, by breaking glasses or china within his reach; whereas the oran outang is altogether harmless; – who has so much of the docility of a man, that he learns not only to do the common offices of life, but also to play on the flute and French horn; which shows that he must have an idea of melody, and concord of sounds, which no brute animal has; – and lastly, if joined to all these qualities, he has the organ of pronunciation, and consequently the capacity of speech, though not the actual use of it; if, I say, such an animal be not a man, I should desire to know in what the essence of a man consists, and what it is that distinguishes a natural man from the man of art.*

To rephrase in modern terms: if we share 98.4% of our genome with the chimpanzee, 97.7% with the gorilla, and 96.4% with the orangutan, should we necessarily suppose that the essence of our humanity rests in the small residual percentages? Throughout Peacock's novel it is man who makes mischief, the orang-outang who behaves with grace, sincerity, openness, fearlessness and generosity. The orang is the true natural man, the utterly engaging contrary of the degenerate natural man imagined by Mary Shelley in that other Rousseauesque novel completed in 1817, *Frankenstein*.

As the French modulation of his surname implies, Sir Oran is a supremely uptown, *high-toned* creation. Peacock's central comic device is to give what he regards as the highest characteristics of mankind – affection, tender-heartedness, fierce loyalty, a sense of natural justice, a love of gardening, and, above all, music – not to a well-born human, but to the highest of the apes. If such an inversion had been made in the name of misanthropy, as it is when Swift gives reason to the Houyhnhnms and insults the apes by making man a Yahoo, the mode would have been satire. But it is not, for Sir Oran is the most philanthropic of creatures: he is violent only when the heroine Anthelia must be rescued from the corrupt representatives of aristocracy and Church, Lord Anophel Achthar and the Reverend Mr Grovelgrub, or when he loses patience with the corruption of electoral manipulation in the borough of Onevote. Finally, he saves Anthelia from being raped by Lord Anophel. Here, his simplicity and integrity are at one level those of Henry Fielding's natural man, the foundling Tom Jones, with Anthelia standing in for his beloved Sophie Western and Anophel for the corrupt urban aristocrat, Lord Fellamar. But the parallel which Peacock makes explicit in the text indicates that the mode of *Melincourt* is pastoral rather than Fielding's genre of comic epic in prose:

> They discovered in the progress of time, that he had formed for [Anthelia] the same kind of reverential attachment, as the Satyr in Fletcher forms for the Holy Shepherdess: and Anthelia might have said to him in the words of Clorin:
>
>> – They wrong thee that do call thee rude:
>> Though thou be'st outward rough and tawny-hued,
>> Thy manners are as gentle and as fair,
>> As his who boasts himself born only heir
>> To all humanity.

Thalia is the Muse of pastoral as well as comedy. Sir Oran, like Fletcher's Satyr and Spenser's Sir Satyrane, is a being who is courtly despite the expectation of savagery set up by his name and his nature. This is pastoral's use of the natural to show up the artifice and corruption of the sophisticated. Renaissance pastoral typically treats the sojourn in the green world as but an interlude before it swerves back towards the court as the shepherdess turns out to be a princess in disguise. *Melincourt*, by contrast, asks us to suspend our disbelief in Rousseau's and Monboddo's arguments that civilization is a decline from the original virtues of the natural. Rousseau's second *Discourse* is quoted twice in Peacock's footnotes to the chapter which introduces Sir Oran Haut-ton to the reader.

Monboddo's distinctive emphasis is upon language. In the passage from *Ancient Metaphysics* quoted above, and at great length in his *Origin and Progress of Language*, from which Peacock took most elements of Sir Oran's behaviour, Monboddo argued that speech is an artificial, not a natural, faculty and that it is therefore readily associated with the abuses of that decline away from the natural which we call progress. It was this argument which made his work a gift to Peacock. In his first novel, *Headlong Hall*, Peacock satirized what he took to be the worst excess of language in his age: the cant of fashionable theories about man and society, expressed in convoluted abstractions. But since he wrote in the form of Menippean dialogue, he found himself in the awkward position of using speechifying to debunk speechifying. Thus Mr Jenkison, the moderate man-in-the-middle who compromises between the Godwinian perfectibilism of Foster and the Malthusian deteriorationism of Escot, is linguistically no different from either of them.

Melincourt has its local parodies of the cant of theory, notably in the visit to Coleridge, alias the 'poeticopolitical, rhapsodicoprosaical, deisidaemoniacoparadoxographical, pseudolatreiological, transcendental meteorosophist, Moley Mystic, Esquire, of Cimmerian Lodge'. But at its centre, in place of Jenkison, is Sir Oran. He represents the alternative to theory. He has the capacity for language, but he chooses not to use it. His silence witnesses against cant with all the eloquence of Byron's wit. And when he breaks that silence, whether under the stress of society or solitude, it is not to speak but to harmonize art and nature in the best sound of which humankind is capable. 'His greatest happiness was in listening to the music of her harp and voice: in the absence of which he solaced himself, as usual, with his flute and French horn.' Where Byron's robust satire sometimes suggests that a poet may not be so different from a monkey, Peacock's life-affirming comedy allows us to imagine an ape who has the freedom to become an artist. In breaking the species barrier and thus forcing us to begin to rethink our relations to our non-human cousins, the imagined orangutan with a baronetcy extends the range of ecopoesis into a new comic sublime.

*

What is the distinctive contribution which the poet can make to the debate about our duties towards the non-human? Arguments for and against, say, the rights of great apes belong in the province of ethics. The role of ecopoesis is different: it is to engage *imaginatively* with the non-human. I have suggested in this chapter that comedy is an especially appropriate medium for such an engagement. The cause of ecology may not necessarily be best served by poets taking the high moral ground and speaking from the point of view of ecological correctness. Here is the self-consciously earth-aware Gary Snyder, in some stanzas of a poem called 'Mother Earth: Her Whales':

> Brazil says 'sovereign use of Natural Resources'
> Thirty thousand kinds of unknown plants.
> The living actual people of the jungle
>   sold and tortured –
> And a robot in a suit who peddles a delusion called 'Brazil'
>   can speak for *them*?
>
>   The whales turn and glisten, plunge
>   and sound and rise again,
>   Hanging over subtly darkening deeps
>   Flowing like breathing planets
>   in the sparkling whorls of
>   living light –
>
> And Japan quibbles for words on
>   what kinds of whales they can kill?
> A once-great Buddhist nation
>   dribbles methyl mercury
>   like gonorrhea
>   in the sea.

Worthy as the sentiments may be, they do not in any sense grow from the poetry. The poem has been written as an expression of a set of opinions, not as an attempt to transform into language an experience of dwelling upon the earth. In this respect, it is not what I call an 'ecopoem': it is not a thinking of the question of the making of the *oikos*. The language itself is not being asked to do ecological work. Though the compression and arrangement afforded by poetic form adds a certain rhetorical force to the statements, there is no relationship between vehicle and tenor; the medium for the message could as well have been a television panel discussion or a piece of journalistic prose.

Contrast this with the closing section of 'The Moose', Elizabeth Bishop's poem about a nighttime bus ride from Nova Scotia down through northern New England to Boston:

> . . .
> Suddenly the bus driver
> stops with a jolt,
> turns off his lights.
>
> A moose has come out of
> the impenetrable wood
> and stands there, looms, rather,
> in the middle of the road.
> It approaches; it sniffs at
> the bus's hot hood.
>
> Towering, antlerless,
> high as a church,
> homely as a house
> (or, safe as houses).
> A man's voice assures us
> 'Perfectly harmless . . .'
>
> Some of the passengers
> exclaim in whispers,
> childishly, softly,
> 'Sure are big creatures.'
> 'It's awful plain.'
> 'Look! It's a she!'
>
> Taking her time,
> she looks the bus over,
> grand, otherworldly.

Why, why do we feel
(we all feel) this sweet
sensation of joy?

'Curious creatures,'
says our quiet driver,
rolling his *r*'s.
'Look at that, would you.'
Then he shifts gears.
For a moment longer,

by craning backward,
the moose can be seen
on the moonlit macadam;
then there's a dim
smell of moose, an acrid
smell of gasoline.

Marianne Moore said of Bishop, 'At last we have someone who knows, who is not didactic'. The weakness of Snyder's 'Mother Earth: Her Whales' is its didacticism about the rights of whales and of the species and native inhabitants of the rainforest; the strength of Bishop's 'The Moose' is that it is a poem which *knows* why we need wild animals.

Moore's own animal poems were a key influence on Bishop. The following fine paragraph by the critic Guy Rotella could as well have been written of Bishop:

In her 'animiles' Moore describes creatures with an exactitude that 'honors' their separate and independent existences. In the process she employs without distress the subjective cultural 'filters' that protect us from the threat of wholly wild nature and that are essential to representation. She does so in ways that never presume completely to control or possess nature and that expose repeatedly but without anxiety the illusions of art. At the same time, Moore uses analogies with animal activities to chide, correct, and model human behavior, insisting all the while that 'as if' is different from 'is.' Moore is neither a taxidermist nor a field ecologist. Her poems are a menagerie with open habitats instead of cages, a place where the realms of art and nature meet, mingle, and separate, where conflicting claims cannot be reconciled but, at best, can coexist. She creates an artful, artificial space where 'unease' is not dispelled but restrained.

Bishop knows that we can only know nature by way of culture. The wood itself is 'impenetrable'. The moose is encountered on the road, a road being a piece of land that has been transformed by the demands of culture, a route from city to city. The moose comes to the bus, rather than vice-versa. This is a poem not about getting back to nature, but about how nature comes back to us. It is a poem of *wonder* in the face of the sheer physicality of the moose: its smell, its size. But also the ineffability of large mammals: in order to describe them we reach for similes out of culture – the church, the house – but somehow they are inadequate. The natural holiness of the moose reveals the insufficiency of a religion that confines itself to indoor worship; its presence reveals that our dwelling-place is the earth which we share, not the house which we own.

Though awe-inspiringly 'Grand, otherworldly', the she-moose elicits not fear but 'joy', a joy that in connecting us to nature connects us to each other: 'we feel / (we all feel)' the same sensation. The encounter lasts for no more than a moment, but it is a moment that is indescribably (save in poetry) precious. Our journeys go on, the 'smell of gasoline' signalling the inexorability of technological modernity. But it will serve us well if every now and then we crane backward to remember and to thank the moose in the moonlight.

Ever since ancient Rome, the dark forest has been a sign of untamed nature, the straight road the mark of civilization and empire. Only in our imagination and our dreams may we leave the road for long. History calls us back to the route-march of the political. Consider Seamus Heaney. Like Wordsworth, he sees into the life of things and he yearns for the rural places in which he grew up. But, like Yeats, he has been hurt into poetry by 'mad Ireland'. In *Seeing Things* (1991), his finest volume of mature work, he revisits Glanmore, the farm of his childhood, but he never fully gets back to nature. He squares up to the Januslike quality of the poet – singer of earth, exile from earth – and remains warily on guard as he crisscrosses between culture and nature.

Within the sequence 'Squarings', which constitutes part two of *Seeing Things*, there are a series of 'Crossings'. This is the first of them:

> Travelling south at dawn, going full out
> Through high-up stone-wall country, the rocks still cold,
> Rainwater gleaming here and there ahead,
>
> I took a turn and met the fox stock-still,
> Face-to-face in the middle of the road.
> Wildness tore through me as he dipped and wheeled
>
> In a level-running tawny breakaway.
> O neat head, fabled brush and astonished eye
> My blue Volkswagen flared into with morning!
>
> Let rebirth come through water, through desire,
> Through crawling backwards across clinic floors:
> I have to cross back through that startled iris.

As with Bishop's mingle of moose-smell and gasoline-smell, at the heart of the poem the speaker is entered by 'wildness' but cannot return to the wild because he is contained within his car. Furthermore, the fox is not Heaney's habitual animal. It belongs to his friend, and a key influence on his first volume, *Death of a Naturalist* (1966): Ted Hughes. Hughes was truly a feral poet, scavenging like a fox on the margins of urban modernity. His poetry has the hot stink of animal flesh, whereas this fox of Heaney's is cunningly hedged with literariness ('O neat head, fabled brush'). In the early 1960s, Hughes and Sylvia Plath embarked on an energized, vertiginous linguistic drive back to raw nature. For Plath, poetry was like riding at dawn on her horse named Ariel, 'Suicidal, at one with the drive / Into the red // Eye, the cauldron of morning'. The urbane Heaney, at the wheel of his Volkswagen rather than astride Ariel, cannot let himself flare fully into the cauldron of morning. His compulsion to cross back through the fox's startled eye is a symptom of his loss of unity with nature. We then turn the page and find the reason for that loss. The next poem begins:

Only to come up, year after year, behind
Those open-ended, canvas-covered trucks
Full of soldiers sitting cramped and staunch,

Their hands round gun-barrels, their gaze abroad
In dreams out of the body-heated metal.
Silent, time-proofed, keeping an even distance

Beyond the windscreen glass, carried ahead
On the phantasmal flow-back of the road,
They still mean business in the here and now.

Where the previous poem glimpsed a crossing of the border between culture and nature, the human and the animal, this one returns to business in the here and now, to the border-crossing between Northern Ireland and the South. Poets may sing the song that names the earth and all living things upon it, but sometimes they have to stop and ask who lays claim to sovereignty over their land.

8

The Place of Poetry

Rivers and mountains survive broken countries . . .

(Tu Fu, 'Spring Landscape', written in Ch'ang-an,
AD 757, after the rebellion of An Lu-shan.
Translator: David Hinton)

LORD BYRON'S community of species is a necessary antidote to
the Wordsworthian solitary. Yet William Wordsworth remains
the founding father for a thinking of poetry in relation to place,
to our dwelling upon the earth. His importance may be stressed
by way of a crude generalization: before Wordsworth, the poetry
of place tended to be inspired by *occasion* – a patron's request,
perhaps, or a historical event or association – whereas with
Wordsworth the poetry of place began to be inspired by place
itself.

He was the first English poet to record in detail the circumstances of composition of his own works, just as he was the first
to reflect publicly and at length upon his own art and its development. As testimony to 'the growth of a poet's mind', his
prefaces, notes, appendices and *obiter dicta* are of a piece with *The
Prelude*. Again and again in these reflections, he tells us *where* he
wrote a particular poem.

Although clouded by age and thus unreliable on certain matters
of detail, the body of notes which Wordsworth dictated to Isabella
Fenwick in 1843, intended for subsequent publication, constitute
the fullest commentary on himself by any major English poet. It is
from one of the Fenwick notes that this chapter will begin:

In the cottage of Town End, one afternoon in 1801, my
Sister read to me the Sonnets of Milton. I had long been well

acquainted with them, but I was particularly struck on that occasion by the dignified simplicity and majestic harmony that runs through most of them, – in character so totally different from the Italian, and still more so from Shakespeare's fine Sonnets. I took fire, if I may be allowed to say so, and produced three Sonnets the same afternoon, the first I ever wrote except an irregular one at school. Of these three, the only one I distinctly remember is 'I grieved for Buonaparté.'

For Wordsworth, poetry is something that happens at a particular time and in a particular place: 'In the cottage of Town End, one afternoon in 1801.' His need to ground the origins of his work would have been understood by Martin Heidegger, for whom human being is distinguished by its temporality and human dwelling by its particularity – by, one might say, its cottageyness.

The afternoon in question was in fact that of 21 May 1802, when, according to Dorothy's journal, William wrote two sonnets on Buonaparte after she had read Milton's sonnets to him. It is typical of Wordsworth to construct his own past in such a way that he discovers a new form on a particular afternoon, which almost takes on the intensity of what in *The Prelude* he called – in a phrase that crucially elides temporality and place – the 'spot of time'. The compact structure of the sonnet makes it an ideal form in which to crystallize a single idea. A good sonnet is nearly always a 'spot of thought', a realized moment. Often it is also an attempt to arrest time.

Wordsworth characterizes the difference between Milton's sonnets and those of Shakespeare and Petrarch as a matter of style: 'dignified simplicity and majestic harmony' as opposed to verbal ingenuity and structured play. But his practical response to the sonnet tradition reveals that the distinction which really counted for him was that of subject-matter. Where Shakespeare and his fellow-Elizabethans followed the Italians in making erotic desire the Leitmotif of the form, Wordsworth followed Milton in turning it to public account. It was such sonnets as those of Milton on Cromwell and Fairfax which led Wordsworth to write on Buonaparte. The importance of Milton's public theme for

Wordsworth is apparent from a letter to Walter Savage Landor in which he recollected that afternoon of 21 May 1802: he refers there not only to the sonnets' 'harmony' but also to their 'gravity' and 'republican austerity'. This letter was written in 1822, the year in which Wordsworth published his *Ecclesiastical Sonnets*, a national history in which the republican age of Milton is seen as a point of crisis.

Because he became Laureate and because the Victorians admired such effusions as 'Ode. The Morning of the Day appointed for a General Thanksgiving, January 18, 1816' and 'Occasioned by the Battle of Waterloo, February, 1816', Words-worth had enormous influence as a public poet. It is therefore easy to forget that he wrote no public poetry of any significance prior to 1802. This is not to say that his poems of the 1790s failed to address the great political issues of the day. Far from it. But they did so obliquely: the revolutionary desecration of the monastery of the Grand Chartreuse was the occasion not for an Ode, but for a picturesque incident in the loco-descriptive *Sketches* published in 1793. The character of the revolutionary was anato-mized theoretically in the drama of *The Borderers*, not overtly in an apostrophe to Robespierre or Danton. Instead of some poem entitled 'Ode on the eve of the ninth Anniversary of the Storming of the Bastille, July 13, 1798', we get 'Lines written a few miles above Tintern Abbey, on revisiting the banks of the Wye during a Tour. July 13, 1798'. Of the two genres signalled by the title of *Lyrical Ballads*, lyric is the essential private form and it quickly becomes apparent that the ballads offer seemingly inconsequential narratives about idiot boys and old men digging at roots, not historical tales of battles and heroes. The latter kind of ballad was being collected by Sir Walter Scott around this time, but it was not until such examples as Scott's own *Lay of the Last Minstrel* and *Marmion* were in print that Wordsworth turned to historical, and thus public, subject matter in *The White Doe of Rylstone; or, The Fate of the Nortons*.

In 1798, the year of the first volume of *Lyrical Ballads*, Coleridge published a volume containing three poems: the deeply personal 'Frost at Midnight', the very public 'France: An Ode', and the meditation which wonderfully links the personal and the public, the local and the national, 'Fears in Solitude'. But it was not until the reading of Milton's sonnets in 1802 that Wordsworth found a medium in which to write directly about contemporary history and national identity. He went on writing sonnets for the rest of his life, over five hundred of them, the vast majority Miltonic in form and public in matter. They make up his most sustained and accomplished body of public poetry. In contradistinction to the Petrarchan or Shakespearean sonnet which defines the poet's self in terms of love, time and fame, they transform Wordsworth into a national poet – but, crucially, a poet whose sense of nation is defined by a thoroughgoing regionalism. That regionalism sets him apart from the model of Milton, revealing him instead to be in a tradition that goes back to the antiquarian and chorographic prose and poetry of Queen Elizabeth's reign, which provided a precedent for the writing of nation through region.

*

It was in a sequence of sonnets written during the summer of 1802 that Wordsworth established himself as a poet of nation, having previously been pre-eminently one of nature. The force that led Coleridge to meditate upon love of country in 1798 was fear of invasion, of disruption of the peaceful landscape on which he looked down from the Quantocks in the West Country. For Wordsworth in 1802, it was – paradoxically – the lifting of the fear of invasion which gave him the opportunity to express his sense of his own Englishness. The Peace of Amiens, signed in March, enabled him to cross the Channel and revisit France for the first time since the early days of the Revolution. He arranged to meet Annette Vallon and his French daughter at Calais that August.

His earlier crossing of the Channel back to England, late in 1792, a few weeks before the birth of the daughter whom he would not see for nearly ten years, had precipitated his crisis-year of 1793. Committed to revolutionary France both politically and personally, he had felt utterly cut off from the country of his birth once war was declared in February 1793. His inner conflict then is recorded in a vital passage of *The Prelude*:

> I who with the breeze
> Had play'd, a green leaf on the blessed tree
> Of my beloved Country, nor had wish'd
> For happier fortune than to wither there,
> Now from my pleasant station was cut off
> And toss'd about in whirlwinds.

In this passage, patriotic belonging is imaged in pastoral terms. The country is figured organically in the blessed tree (in the later Wordsworth, imagery of this sort will be redolent of Burkean conservatism); the poet is a green leaf playing in the gentle correspondent breeze which is at once the inner imagination and the external spirit of place.

It is from this composed state in which the self is given ease by its commanding hold over the harmonious English landscape – 'pleasant station' is the language of the picturesque – that Wordsworth has been severed. The leaf is tossed in the revolutionary whirlwind. The conflicting pull of the word 'patriot' comes to the heart of a matter: it is a term for Wordsworth's bond with his native land (and in particular landscape), yet at the same time a key word in the radical lexicon – a patriot means a devotee of liberty and hence a staunch supporter of the revolution. The latter use of the term occurs in the previous book of *The Prelude*, when Wordsworth commits himself to the revolutionary cause in Orléans: 'and thus did soon / Become a Patriot, and my heart was all / Given to the People, and my love was theirs'. The ambivalence of the patriotic urge accounts for Wordsworth's sense of almost inexpressible alienation once he is back in England. A village church is part of the imagined organic English community in which he finds his home, yet in that church the villagers pray a prayer he cannot share for the defeat of liberated France:

> It was a grief,
> Grief call it not, 'twas any thing but that,
> A conflict of sensations without name,
> Of which he only who may love the sight
> Of a Village Steeple as I do can judge
> When in the Congregation, bending all

> To their great Father, prayers were offer'd up,
> Or praises for our Country's Victories,
> And 'mid the simple worshippers, perchance,
> I only, like an uninvited Guest,
> Whom no one owned, sate silent, shall I add
> Fed on the day of vengeance, yet to come?

The return to France in 1802 brings the healing of Wordsworth's bond with England. The sonnets composed there and on his immediate return were later gathered to make up the opening group of the section of his *Poems, in Two Volumes* of 1807 entitled 'Sonnets dedicated to Liberty'. He added to the group in successive editions, but the overall title remained the same until 1845, when it became *Poems dedicated to National Independence and Liberty*. This late change to the title is revealing: where the aged Laureate is explicit about his nationalism, in the editions from 1807 to 1843 the celebration of nation is implicit in that of liberty.

In thinking about what 'liberty' meant to Wordsworth in his middle years, we should not forget the terms in which Coleridge had defined it in 'France: An Ode'. 'O Liberty!' he wrote,

> Thou speedest on thy subtle pinions,
> The guide of homeless winds, and playmate of the waves!
> And there I felt thee! – on that sea-cliff's verge,
> Whose pines, scarce travelled by the breeze above,
> Had made one murmur with the distant surge!
> Yes, while I stood and gazed, my temples bare,
> And shot my being through earth, sea, and air,
> Possessing all things with intensest love,
> O Liberty! my spirit felt thee there.

The coordinates of Coleridgean liberty are a set of particular landmarks – a plantation of pines, a clifftop – which anchor the poet's dwelling as he extends his spirit towards the untrammelled being of sea, of sky, of the life of things.

And crucially, in this vision to *possess* means to love rather than to own. Each individual stanza of Coleridge's ode has an intensity of feeling and a rhyming intricacy loosely comparable to the structures of a sonnet. Under the influence of W. L. Bowles,

Coleridge had indeed been writing sonnets ever since his earliest work: sonnets political (on Burke, Pitt, Priestley, Erskine and others in a sequence of 'Effusions' written in 1794) and sonnets topographic ('To the river Otter', a summoning of childhood through place which begins 'Dear native Brook! wild Streamlet of the West!'). Many of Wordsworth's poetic innovations were developments of Coleridgean experiments. Put the variety of Coleridge's sonnets together with the impassioned linking of liberty, love and landscape in his ode recanting upon his initial equation of freedom with the French Revolution, and one has a possible origin for the 'Sonnets dedicated to Liberty'.

Wordsworth's brief stay in Calais coincided with the proclamation of Napoleon as consul for life. For the poet, this was confirmation that France could no longer be associated with freedom; liberty had to be reclaimed by England. Once it is seen that this was the project of the public poetry which Wordsworth began writing in 1802, it may also be seen why he chose the form that he did in which to write it: Milton's sonnets are defining texts of English liberty, written as they were in praise of martyrs to the cause of liberty such as the republican Vane and the proto-Protestant Waldenses massacred in Piedmont.

As they were arranged for publication, the 'Sonnets dedicated to Liberty' begin with 'Composed by the Sea-side, near Calais, August, 1802'. The origin of this poem is to be found in Dorothy's journal of the visit: 'We had delightful walks after the heat of the day was passed away – seeing far off in the west the coast of England like a cloud crested with Dover Castle, which was but like the summit of the cloud – the evening star and the glory of the sky.' This becomes:

> Fair Star of Evening, Splendor of the West,
> Star of my Country! – on the horizon's brink
> Thou hangest, stooping, as might seem, to sink
> On England's bosom; yet well pleas'd to rest,
> Meanwhile, and be to her a glorious crest
> Conspicuous to the Nations. Thou, I think,
> Should'st be my Country's emblem; and should'st wink,
> Bright Star! with laughter on her banners, drest

In thy fresh beauty. There! that dusky spot
Beneath thee, it is England; there it lies.
Blessings be on you both! one hope, one lot,
One life, one glory! I, with many a fear
For my dear Country, many heartfelt sighs,
Among Men who do not love her, linger here.

In Dorothy's journal, the coast is 'crested' with Dover Castle; in William's poem, the evening star is England's crest. The castle is not mentioned, though the allusion to banners implicitly evokes flags fluttering on its battlements. Wordsworth can assume that his readers will know it is Dover which may be seen from the French coast; he withholds the place-name and its resonances for a pair of sonnets to be written on his return. In this opening poem he guards the land not with a fortification built by man, but with a natural power, the light of the evening star. Its shining over the English coast mirrors the star that shone over Bethlehem and is thus made to mark the land out as blessed, as a place of special destiny. The poem is Wordsworth's first major statement of faith in England – a faith that came to be tested throughout the nineteenth century, most notably in Arnold's 'Dover Beach', which rewrites this poem from the other side of the Channel by turning England into a 'darkling plain' and replacing the star with a gleam of light from the French coast.

　　This first poem of Wordsworth's sequence is a love sonnet addressed to a land personified as female. Convert its tone from tender protectiveness to strident vaunting and you have a Romantic nationalism that will begin to lead you down the dark road to Germany in the 1930s. Stay true to the pull of the spot as opposed to the nation and you have a longing for belonging that is the essence of ecopoesis.

　　The second sonnet picks up from the end of the first, reversing the movement. Where Wordsworth lingers by the sea-side near Calais, as if magnetically drawn to England, other Englishmen – 'Lords, Lawyers, Statesmen, Squires of low degree' – hurry towards Paris, 'With first-fruit offerings crowd to bend the knee / In France, before the new-born Majesty'. The reference is to Charles James Fox and the other 'appeasers' of Napoleon, whose visits to France hot on the heels of the Treaty of Amiens were much mocked at the time. In Wordsworth's view it is a deep irony that his own headlong commitment to the newly liberated France of 1790–92 would have been viewed as seditious, whereas now that Paris was yoked to a tyrant others were eager to embrace it.

The contrast between 1790 and 1802 is the matter of the third sonnet in the sequence, 'To a Friend, composed near Calais, on the Road leading to Ardres, August 7th, 1802':

> Jones! when from Calais southward you and I
> Travell'd on foot together; then this Way,
> Which I am pacing now, was like the May
> With festivals of new-born Liberty:
> A homeless sound of joy was in the Sky;
> The antiquated Earth, as one might say,
> Beat like the heart of Man: songs, garlands, play
> Banners, and happy faces, far and nigh!
> And now, sole register that these things were,
> Two solitary greetings have I heard,
> '*Good morrow, Citizen!*' a hollow word,
> As if a dead Man spake it! Yet despair
> I feel not: happy am I as a Bird:
> Fair seasons yet will come, and hopes as fair.

This sonnet is exact about its time and place of writing because its effect depends upon a reanimation of the past which defines the compositional present by contrast. Of all Wordsworth's political sonnets, it is the one which comes closest to being a 'spot of time' like those in *The Prelude*. In terms of the sequence it is of great importance because it is the only poem to locate 'Liberty' in France, not England. As Wordsworth re-walks the road to Ardres, ghosts of his revolutionary youth return to him. He marks himself out as a 'patriot' in the radical sense of that word: the title 'To a Friend' evokes the spirit of *fraternité*, conjuring up the English Jacobin catch-phrase, 'Friends of Liberty'. The information that the two friends 'Travell'd on foot together' identifies them as of the people, in sharp contrast to the lords, lawyers and statesmen of the previous poem who 'Post forward' to Paris by carriage. The memory of 1790 buys into the full range of revolutionary iconography: the festival, the songs and garlands, the renewing of the 'antiquated Earth', the sense that the revolution entails a reuniting of man with nature in the Rousseauesque style. The hollowness of the *citoyen*'s greeting, the one remaining revolutionary icon on the silent road, proclaims the end of the dream. The 'dead Man' who speaks it symbolically becomes the poet's own youthful self. The figure revisiting the spot can do no more than comfort himself with the vague, distant hope of some future renewal.

The next part of the sequence lays out the evidence in support of the argument that liberty has been extinguished in France. There are two sonnets on Buonaparte, the one written back in May after hearing Dorothy read Milton and another on how 'his is henceforth an established sway, / Consul for life'. Then there is 'On the Extinction of the Venetian Republic', a response to Napoleon's conquest of what Wordsworth viewed as the model republic of the post-classical world, 'Venice, the eldest Child of Liberty'. To a far greater extent than Robespierre's Terror, it was Napoleonic expansionism that turned English Jacobins against France. In Coleridge's 'France: an Ode', the invasion of the model democracy, Switzerland, is the turning-point; the extinction of Venice has the same effect on Wordsworth. Later in the sequence, he follows Coleridge in citing Switzerland. 'Two Voices are there; one is of the Sea' (Britain), 'One of the Mountains' (Switzerland), 'each a mighty Voice', and each the 'chosen Music' of 'Liberty'. Now that the mountain voice has been silenced by the 'Tyrant', Liberty must cleave to the maritime one.

Another symptom of the end of liberty in France was the return of slavery. The eighth sonnet in the sequence concerns Toussaint L'Ouverture, the black leader of the Haitian uprising, who became governor after the French Convention's enfranchisement of slaves in 1794; he resisted Napoleon's edict reestablishing slavery, was arrested and sent to France. He was in prison when Wordsworth was in France in August 1802 and within a year would die in captivity. In the sonnet on Jones, the forces of nature had sung in harmony with the revolution; in that on Toussaint, they are reduced to a remnant in which the spirit of liberty can live on after the man who incarnated it has been destroyed:

> Thou hast left behind
> Powers that will work for thee; air, earth, and skies;
> There's not a breathing of the common wind
> That will forget thee.

Not only did Napoleon reintroduce slavery, he also banished all negroes from France. Wordsworth's ninth sonnet, simply entitled 'September 1st, 1802', describes the dignity of a negro woman going into exile as a fellow-passenger with Wordsworth and Dorothy on the boat out of Calais. One begins to see with what extraordinary care the sequence has been organized. The sonnet on the negro woman is appropriate both to follow that on Toussaint and to chart Wordsworth's own voyage. She is described in her own right with plain and unpatronizing sympathy, but she is also another of the poet's doubles: where the voice who speaks the hollow fraternal greeting is the dead revolutionary self, the negro woman is also Wordsworth driven from France, from his formative years there and from his daughter.

It should by now be apparent that Wordsworth's patriotism is complex, thought through and hard won. It is no knee-jerk jingoism. This must be recognized if we are to do justice to the next poem, which is the turning-point – or rather the landing-point – not merely in the sequence but in the whole configuration of Wordsworth's public poetry. He has come home to the peace of an English pastoral, to the protection of a womblike vale. This return does not replicate the ambivalence of the landing ten years before. Sonnet ten of the sequence is entitled 'Composed in the Valley, near Dover, on the Day of landing':

> Dear fellow-Traveller! here we are once more.
> The Cock that crows, the Smoke that curls, that sound
> Of bells, those Boys that in yon meadow-ground
> In white-sleev'd shirts are playing by the score,
> And even this little River's gentle roar,
> All, all are English. Oft have I look'd round
> With joy in Kent's green vales; but never found
> Myself so satisfied in heart before.

Europe is yet in Bonds; but let that pass,
Thought for another moment. Thou art free
My Country! and 'tis joy enough and pride
For one hour's perfect bliss, to tread the grass
Of England once again, and hear and see,
With such a dear Companion at my side.

In the previous poem, the negro woman was a 'fellow-Passenger';
here Dorothy is the dear 'fellow-Traveller'. 'Fellow' retains the
discourse of *fraternité* – or perhaps in these instances we should
say *sororité* – but removes it from France. Liberté has now crossed
the Channel with the Wordsworths, leaving behind the Europe
that is 'yet in Bonds'. As for *égalité*, it is to be found not in a
social agenda but in the composition of the landscape, the life-
giving bond whereby humankind (playing children, curling smoke
that is metonymic of a cottage home) is integrated with nature.
Wordsworth is moving here towards an image of organic England
which may well be construed as Burkean. But the precise location
in Kent sets Wordsworth apart from Burke.

It is here that regional specificity begins to play its part in
Wordsworth's construction of national identity. Burke had argued
in favour of evolution over revolution, of the organic, unwritten
English constitution over the mechanical, formalized codes of
France with its revolutionary proclamations and codified declaration of the rights of man. Tom Paine's most telling dismantling
of this argument came at that moment in the *Rights of Man* when
he asked from where this evolving English constitution came, to
whom the line of the monarchy could be traced back. The answer
was the invading, marauding Norman, William the Conqueror.
1066 has always been a problem for those who want to see England
as set apart in the silver sea, as an inviolable chosen nation. The
need for that myth of uniqueness became especially acute with the
Reformation: the Norman inheritance was not such a problem
when England was part of Catholic Europe, but with Henry VIII's
break from Rome history had to be rewritten. That task fell to the
Elizabethans, as they worked to secure the Anglican settlement
so as to ensure that there would never be another Counter-
Reformation like that of Bloody Mary. The creation of an English

national identity was one of the tasks of literary culture functions of writing in Elizabethan England. One thinks immediately of Holinshed's *Chronicles*, of Shakespeare's *Henry V*, Spenser's *The Faerie Queene*, William Warner's *Albion's England*.

The apogee of this kind of writing was William Camden's *Britannia*, published in 1586 and expanded in successive editions in 1587, 1590, 1594, 1600, 1607 and 1610 (when it was translated into English by Philemon Holland). '*Britain*, called also *Albion*,' Camden begins, 'the most famous Island of the whole world, is divided from the Continent of *Europe* by the Ocean.' The sea encloses the island and creates the conditions for national individuation, which, according to Camden, is effected by a combination of geography, language and mode of government. Camden's method of inventing national identity may be described as history-through-topography. He aimed 'to restore Britain to its Antiquities, and its Antiquities to Britain'. He did this by undertaking a county by county survey, emphasizing points of local historical interest. Much of his material was taken from John Leland, who had begun a similar survey on behalf of Henry VIII, but another model for Camden's county-based approach was the first published English chorography, William Lambarde's *Perambulation of Kent*. In Lambarde, Kent has particular associations with liberty: 'The yeomanrie, or common people . . . is no where more free, and jolly, then in this shyre'. This is principally because of a distinctive form of land tenure. 'There were never any bondmen (or villaines, as the law calleth them) in Kent',

> Neither be they here so much bounden to the gentrie by copyhold, or custumarie tenures, as the inhabitants of the westerne countries of the realme be, nor at all indangered by the feeble holde of tenant right, (which is but a discent of a tenancie at will) as the common people in the northren parts be: for Copyhold tenure is rare in Kent, and tenant right not heard of at all. But in place of these, the custome of Gavelkind prevailing every where, in manner every man is a freeholder, and hath some part of his own to live upon.

Kent is set up as an ideal commonwealth in which every man is like a freeholder because all sons, not just the eldest, inherit land.

And, crucially for Lambarde's account, the county is said never to
have been forced under the Norman yoke: 'the communaltie of
Kent was never vanquished by the Conquerour, but yeelded itself
by composition'.

From Lambarde, via Camden, the idealization of Kent reached
the key poetic text of chorography, a book well known to the
Wordsworth circle, Michael Drayton's *Poly-Olbion. Or A Chorographicall Description of Tracts, Rivers, Mountaines, Forests, and other
Parts of this renowned Isle of Great Britaine, With intermixture of the
most Remarquable Stories, Antiquities, Wonders, Rarityes, Pleasures,
and Commodities of the same* – a title which reveals that Drayton is
following Camden in the writing of history-through-topography.
As it was originally published in 1612, *Poly-Olbion* ended with a
marriage of Kentish rivers. The Stour praises his own county:

> O noble *Kent*, quoth he, this praise doth thee belong,
> The hard'st to be controld, impatientest of wrong.
> Who, when the *Norman* first with pride and horror sway'd,
> Threw'st off the servile yoke upon the *English* lay'd;
> And with a high resolve, most bravely didst restore
> That libertie so long enjoy'd by thee before.
> Not suffring forraine Lawes should thy free Customes bind,
> Then onely show'dst thy selfe of th' ancient *Saxon* kind.
> Of all the *English* Shires be thou surnam'd the Free,
> And foremost ever plac't, when they shall reckned bee.

Wordsworth's distinction between the bonds of Europe and
the freedom of Kent is in a line of descent from Drayton's
juxtaposition of the Norman yoke against Kentish independence
and liberty. 'To the Men of Kent', the twenty-third of the twenty-
six 'Sonnets dedicated to Liberty' in Wordsworth's *Poems* of 1807,
alludes explicitly to the Kentish yeoman's history in the vanguard
of English liberty:

> Ye, of yore,
> Did from the Norman win a gallant wreath;
> Confirm'd the charters that were yours before.

The genealogy of Wordsworth's perception of Kent gives the
'Valley, near Dover' sonnet a different kind of patriotism from

Burke's, a patriotism rooted not in evolving Westminster institutions ultimately of Norman origin, but in a tradition of local defence of liberty. It should be remembered here that Richard Price's controversial sermon which provoked Burke to write the *Reflections* was on the subject of the love of country and argued that England should welcome the French revolution as an extension across the Channel of liberties long won at home.

It is to the history of English liberty, and the fearful effects of a decline from its high ideals, that Wordsworth then turns his sequence. First, he remembers the example of the heroes of English republicanism: 'The later Sydney' (Algernon, that is), 'Marvel, Harrington, / Young Vane, and others who call'd Milton Friend'. Then he laments how the 'most famous Stream' of 'British freedom' is in danger of perishing 'in Bogs and Sands' (Sonnets 15, 16). The controlling image of the river, also in the tradition of Drayton, will recur in later sequences. Drayton's Stour and Wordsworth's Duddon serve as pure sources of locally grounded national identity, but when the greatest of English rivers nears the sea, it becomes, as Blake saw in his lyric 'London', 'the chartered Thames' – licensed out for commercial use, sullied in the pursuit of gain. London is the root of England's ill, so it is in the sonnet 'London, 1802' that the presiding genius of English republican virtue and freedom must be invoked. At the exact midpoint of his sequence Wordsworth places a model Miltonic sonnet – apostrophic, flexible in caesura, magniloquent in overflowing syntax – on Milton. The octave consists of two sentences, broken not at the end of the first quatrain, as they would be in a Shakespearean sonnet, but irregularly, in the middle of the sixth line, in homage to the presider:

> Milton! thou should'st be living at this hour:
> England hath need of thee: she is a fen
> Of stagnant waters: altar, sword, and pen,
> Fireside, the heroic wealth of hall and bower,
> Have forfeited their ancient English dower
> Of inward happiness. We are selfish men;
> Oh! raise us up, return to us again;
> And give us manners, virtue, freedom, power.

The sestet then begins with the famous line, 'Thy soul was like a Star and dwelt apart'. In the context of the sequence, this echoes the first lines of the first sonnet, 'Fair Star of Evening, Splendor of the West, / Star of my Country!' Milton has become the star of England and the extinction of his spirit – the embodiment of 'manners, virtue, freedom, power' – is proof that England is no longer true to itself. Wordsworth implicitly sets himself up as Milton Redivivus, calling England to return to its heritage of virtue and freedom. Where the star harks back to the opening of the whole sequence, the image of England as 'a fen / Of stagnant waters' is a variation on the recurring motif of the nation as a stream. The point here is that the water is no longer flowing and there is accordingly a nasty smell coming from the institutions evoked by altar, sword, pen, fireside and hall (Church, army, clerisy, family, gentry). In two later sonnet sequences Wordsworth set the stream flowing again.

But before turning to them, let us pause for a moment on the other London sonnet written in 1802 and published in 1807 (though not within the sequence of 'Sonnets dedicated to Liberty'), 'Composed upon Westminster Bridge':

> Earth has not any thing to shew more fair:
> Dull would he be of soul who could pass by
> A sight so touching in its majesty:
> This City now doth like a garment wear
> The beauty of the morning; silent, bare,
> Ships, towers, domes, theatres, and temples lie
> Open unto the fields, and to the sky;
> All bright and glittering in the smokeless air.
> Never did sun more beautifully steep
> In his first splendor valley, rock, or hill;
> Ne'er saw I, never felt, a calm so deep!
> The river glideth at his own sweet will:
> Dear God! the very houses seem asleep;
> And all that mighty heart is lying still!

Usually in Wordsworth the city is a place of alienation, but here it is transfigured because it is 'calm' and 'still'. Like the 'Jones' sonnet, the poem arrests a magical 'spot of time'. In the smokeless light of a silent dawn, Wordsworth is able to imagine the very being of a city in which human institutions – 'Ships, towers, domes, theatres, and temples' – are not set against nature but *open* to it. When the houses are asleep, they rest upon their earthly foundations. In this moment, the human mode of being seems no different from that of other creatures who dwell upon the earth. But Wordsworth knows that such stillness can only be for a moment. When the day's work begins, the river will no longer glide at its own sweet will. The fields will be covered by new buildings and the sky blackened with smoke. The ships of commerce will set themselves against the tide.

*

The River Duddon, conceived as a sequence and published in 1820, is a public counterpart to the private fluvial movement of *The Prelude*. As is now well known to Wordsworthians, *The Prelude* in its earliest recognizable form – the two-part version of 1798–9 – began with the Derwent:

> Was it for this
> That one, the fairest of all Rivers, lov'd
> To blend his murmurs with my Nurse's song
> And from his alder shades and rocky falls,
> And from his fords and shallows sent a voice
> That flow'd along my dreams? For this didst Thou,
> O Derwent! travelling over the green Plains
> Near my sweet birth-place, didst thou, beauteous Stream,
> Make ceaseless music through the night and day . . .

The Derwent, which ran by Wordsworth's birthplace in Cockermouth, becomes a figure for the poet's developing mind, and the autobiographical epic keeps wandering back to it. Where this is a personal connection, the Duddon sequence makes a general one: it is built upon a sustained correspondence between the course of the river and the course of human life. The river has a 'Foster-mother' in the form of the Earth; it is a 'cradled Nursling of the mountain'; it insensibly grows from rill to brook; in its maturity it undergoes changes of mood, passing through both open prospects and deep chasms; it looks outward geographically (as far away as the Oroonoko in the sonnet 'American Tradition') and backward historically (to Roman Britain in the sonnet 'Return'); its 'Tributary Stream' is like a child; near the end of its course it finds a 'resting-Place'; it is finally released from the bodily constraints of its banks 'to mingle with Eternity' in the sea.

But the sonnet 'Conclusion', in which the river passes into the sea, is not the conclusion. It is followed by the celebrated 'After-Thought' in which the poet deconstructs, then reconstructs, the analogy between human life and the life of the river:

> I thought of Thee, my partner and my guide,
> As being past away. – Vain sympathies!
> For, backward, Duddon! as I cast my eyes,
> I see what was, and is, and will abide;
> Still glides the Stream, and shall for ever glide;
> The Form remains, the Function never dies;
> While we, the brave, the mighty, and the wise,
> We Men, who in our morn of youth defied
> The elements, must vanish; – be it so!
> Enough, if something from our hands have power
> To live, and act, and serve the future hour;
> And if, as toward the silent tomb we go,
> Through love, through hope, and faith's transcendent dower,
> We feel that we are greater than we know.

The poet reaches the mouth of the river and looks back. If the analogy with human life holds, the Duddon should have drained into the sea, died into eternity. But it hasn't: the stream still glides and will for ever glide. For ever? Wordsworth could not have been expected to anticipate the combination of drought and profiteering privatized water companies which has drained dry so many of the English rivers that had flowed uninterrupted since the time not just of Drayton but of the Romans and even the Druids who inhabit the seventeenth Duddon sonnet. Nor indeed the 'Surfactants, ammonia, phosphates' which Ted Hughes found along the River Taw in his poem '1984 on "The Tarka Trail"'.

The analogy between human and fluvial time breaks down because, as we are reminded by Wyman Herendeen, a practitioner of what might be called the New Geographism in literary studies, 'the river challenges our epistemological concepts':

> What is a river? ... Is it the water between its banks, or the banks which embrace that protean element? ... If the banks, created by the furrowing water, is it not also the meadows, fields, and forests which are no less the product of their movement, as it is in [Andrew Marvell's] *Upon Appleton House*? ... And when is a river? How does one locate it in time, as one must, since it is in constant movement, and since it has a history, just as any other object involving human beings has?

Wordsworth's 'After-Thought' sonnet reconstructs the analogy by shifting it from the individual human who 'must vanish' to human aspiration in the largest sense. 'We Men' do not personally have the same kind of life as the stream, but humankind does. But to make this move from the individual to the universal is to elide the specified features which throughout the sequence serve to link the fluvial and the human: the surrounding meadows, the buildings on or near the banks and the history they bring with them. Through topographic specificity, Wordsworth makes the local and the national into necessary stepping-stones between the individual and the universal. Halfway through the sequence, occupying the same pivotal position as the apostrophe to Milton in the earlier collection, are a pair of sonnets which bind the Duddon to national history: 'Return', in which 'the imperial Bird of Rome invokes / Departed ages', and 'Seathwaite Chapel', an address to 'Sacred Religion!'. That for Wordsworth it is religion which provides the ultimate answer to the problem of mortality is obvious from the line in 'After-Thought' on love, hope, and faith's transcendent dower, but it will become apparent in the poet's next sonnet sequence that for him true religion is the national religion.

On its way to being an emblem of all human life, the river is an emblem of the nation. The nation is, however, grounded in the region. In his footnote to the pair of pivotal sonnets, Wordsworth included 'a prose account of the Duddon, extracted from Green's comprehensive "Guide to the Lakes,"' and when the sequence was published it was accompanied by Wordsworth's own *Guide to the Lakes*. Taken together, the sonnets, with their historical excursions, and the *Guide*, with its detailed mapping of place, constitute a new form of history-through-topography in the tradition of Camden and his Elizabethan peers.

At this point we need to ask: why this particular river? The Derwent, the river with the strongest personal associations for Wordsworth, is a much longer, more prominent river. In the Fenwick note to the sonnet sequence, Wordsworth spoke of the pleasure he had taken over the years in wandering by the Duddon, but the same could have been said of the Derwent and especially the Wye. A more significant comment to Isabella Fenwick is the following:

> It is with the little River Duddon as it is with most other rivers, Ganges and Nile not excepted, – many springs might claim the honor of being its head. In my own fancy I have fixed its rise near the noted Shire-stones placed at the meeting-point of the counties, Westmoreland, Cumberland, and Lancashire. They stand by the wayside on the top of the Wrynose Pass, and it used to be reckoned a proud thing to say that, by touching them at the same time with feet and hands, one had been in the three counties at once.

Lancashire extends well to the west and north of Lancaster itself; the Duddon appears on the map of that county which was published in *Poly-Olbion* with Drayton's twenty-seventh song, as well as on the map of Cumberland and Westmorland prefixing the thirtieth song. Wordsworth's notion that the source is at the confluence of three counties is by no means altogether fanciful. If national identity is to be grounded in regional identity, county boundaries, being markers of regional differentiation, are pressure-points. In crossing them one sacrifices a certain racination. As a child I was always ill at ease when I left the borders of my native Kent. But to stand at a point where one is in three counties at once is to retain one's root while also reaching out to the totality of counties which make up the nation. It is in this very specific sense that Wordsworth's Duddon binds.

Drayton's *Poly-Olbion* holds all Albion together through a network of rivers, each with its animated genius loci. The marriage of great rivers is his key symbol. Fluvial espousal, a topos learnt by Drayton from Spenser's *Prothalamion*, *Faerie Queene* and lost 'Epithalamion Thamesis', serves as a naturalized counterpart to the marriage of great landed families, which for the dominant culture of Elizabethan England was a means of perpetuating national unity and avoiding fragmentation into the feuding of baronial times (Drayton also wrote a poem, which Wordsworth knew, on *The Barrons Wars* – it represents the admonitory flipside of *Poly-Olbion*). Wordsworth eschews the great southern rivers, such as Thames and Medway, proposing instead that the smallest river – 'the little River Duddon' – in the corner of England most distant from London is the truest source.

Radical patriots of the 1790s argued that love of country was a foundation for love of all mankind, not an imperial ambition with an investment in the denigration and even extinction of other countries. Wordsworth shared this view in the early 1790s, but once it was apparent that the idealizing, cosmopolitan patriotism of the revolution, with its declaration of *universal* human rights, had given way to the imperial ambitions of Napoleon, he moved in the opposite direction. Instead of treating patriotism as a foundation for cosmopolitanism, he sought the foundations of true patriotism and found them in localism. If you respect the local origins of patriotism, he implies, then your patriotism will not take a Napoleonic, expansionist turn. Whilst the Napoleonic army prepared to extend itself across Europe, Wordsworth dug in to defend his region: in 1803 he joined the Grasmere Volunteers.

What would a united Europe look like? The question is as pressing in our time as it was in Wordsworth's. There are two possible models, which could be described as the imperial and the federal – or alternatively, the Napoleonic and the Wordsworthian. The imperial or Napoleonic takes a constitutional and legal model from one place – Paris in the early nineteenth century, Brussels in the early twenty-first – and imposes it on the broad geographical mass of Europe, with scant regard for the variety of local customs. The federal or Wordsworthian begins from the periphery, not the centre. It respects the distinctiveness of regions.

The difference between Wordsworth in 1792 and Wordsworth in 1802 has a lot to do with the different effects of his
residence in France in 1791–2 and his residence in Germany
in 1798–9. From William the Conqueror to the Bourbon court
to the revolutionary project of Robespierre to the imperial
ambitions of Napoleon – perhaps even to the dreams of M.
Jacques Delors, the most ardent unifier yet to hold the office of
President of the European Commission – the French have
tended towards the model that imposes from the centre. Paris
has always regarded itself as supreme; directives are issued from
the capital. Wordsworth saw the process at first hand in the
immediate aftermath of the revolution. His winter residence in
pre-Bismarckian Germany later in the 1790s provided him with
an alternative model: there being no over-arching German
nation state, loyalty was to the region, the *Land*. In Germany,
federalism means respecting regional difference, beginning from
locality rather than the centre. True federalism will be suspicious of the entity of the nation state, grounded as that entity is
in institutional structures as opposed to features originating in
geography.

There are a lot of buildings in Wordsworth's sonnets. Those
he likes best are of an architecture which is fitting to its environment. Alongside our model of the imperial against the federal,
we might also place two architectural styles: international modernism and critical regionalism. The modernist skyscraper or
Le Corbuserian living-space can be plonked down anywhere.
Modernism was a style with imperial, Napoleonic ambitions.
To an extraordinary degree, it has homogenized the cities of
the world. Critical regionalism, on the other hand, argues that
what is fitting in Manhattan may not be appropriate in Sydney,
say, or Edinburgh:

> Critical regionalism is a highly self-critical approach to archi-
> tecture and planning. It recognizes the importance of context,
> but this recognition is not limited to the acknowledgement of
> existing architectural forms. It also appreciates the signifi-
> cance of local culture, social institutions, political issues,
> building techniques, climate, topography and other elements

of the regional context. . . . the critical regionalist seeks to
enhance the identity of places.

Wordsworth's sonnets are meditations upon national identity
only in so far as that identity is thoroughly informed by the values
of critical regionalism.

The concept of critical regionalism does much to explain
Wordsworth's investment of faith in the Anglican establishment,
with its network of little parishes and its regionally distinctive
churches, each of them at the hub of the wheel of village life.
Anti-Catholicism was an inevitable consequence of this position,
Catholicism being another imperial, universalizing tendency with
its origins not in a region but a distant city. It was the coming
together of the codes of Rome and Paris in the Pope's coronation
of Napoleon that marked Wordsworth's final, absolute disillu-
sionment with French dreams. Perhaps one needs a Protestant
imagination in order to be a critical regionalist.

Alarm over Catholic Emancipation in 1820 led Wordsworth
to begin his third sonnet sequence, the *Ecclesiastical Sketches*.
The introductory sonnet to that collection links all three series
by means of the river motif: 'I, who accompanied with faithful
pace / Cerulean Duddon from its cloud-fed spring . . . I, who
essayed the nobler Stream to trace / Of Liberty . . . Now seek
upon the heights of Time the source / Of a HOLY RIVER'.
The sequence traces the course of religion in Britain from Druidic
and Roman times, through Augustine and Bede, through Norman
degeneration and the Reformation, the Civil War and on to the
present. Its argument is that the Anglican Church is true to the
origins of Christianity upon the island, and that both Rome and
Puritanism were aberrations (the hostility to Puritanism leads
Wordsworth into the paradox of writing Miltonic sonnets in
praise of Laud, latitudinarianism, and even Charles II). The
sequence is unified by the image of the river, as it begins with a
quest for source and ends with 'THAT STREAM' of the true
Church 'Floating at ease while nations have effaced / Nations,
and Death has gathered to his fold / Long lines of mighty Kings'.
The stream of the Church flows through the land which is the
nation. At times of crisis in the historical account, such as during

the 'Troubles of Charles the First', Wordsworth adverts to 'the Land's humblest comforts'; then in the third part of the sequence there is a particular emphasis on the rootedness of ecclesiastical buildings in the land.

A crucial sonnet for this latter idea was included not in the main body of the sequence but in a footnote to the sonnet 'Pastoral Character', which concerns a 'learned Pastor'. The note speaks of 'the residence of an old and much-valued friend in Oxfordshire'. It then prints the poem which Wordsworth subsequently published independently among his 'Miscellaneous Sonnets', with the title 'A Parsonage in Oxfordshire':

> Where holy ground begins – unhallowed ends
> Is marked by no distinguishable line
> The turf unites – the Pathways intertwine
> And wheresoe'er the stealing footstep tends
> Garden and that domain where Kindred[,] Friends
> And neighbours rest together, here confound
> Their several features, mingled like the sound
> Of many waters, or as evening blends
> With shady night – soft airs from shrub and flower
> Waft fragrant greetings to each silent grave
> And ever as those lofty poplars wave
> Their parting summits open out a sky
> Bright as the glimpses of eternity
> To saints accorded in their mortal hour.

There is no distinguishable line between the holy ground of the churchyard and the vicarage garden beyond because for Wordsworth the land itself is now sacred. A community of the living and the dead is gathered together, at peace in a particularized yet archetypal English landscape. This is the quietist patriotism to which Wordsworth has come thirty years after his first visit to France.

Just how closely it is tied to that first visit, how it is a laying to rest of it, will become apparent if we record the identity of the pastor whose garden it was, and the place and date of composition. We need to note here that the sonnet addressed to Robert Jones, 'Composed near Calais, on the Road leading to Ardres', was furnished in the edition of 1815 with a footnote identifying the day of the remembered first walk southward from Calais as July 14, 1790. 'A Parsonage in Oxfordshire' was not actually written on the spot at Souldern, between Bicester and Banbury: it was a memory of an English spot written on the Continent during the Wordsworths' tour of 1820. In the 'Continental Journal' of Mary Wordsworth, we find the following entry, dated July 14, 1820: 'Rose at five o'clock . . . but with disturbed mind[,] for I had left W. in bed hurting himself with a sonnet. . . . [later] I joined W. in our carriage, and have here written down the sonnet, Jones' Parsonage, so I hope he will be at rest'. The parson was Jones, the date was July 14. It hurt Wordsworth to remember the road to France, but in composing the Oxfordshire idyll his imagination came home and found rest.

*

'The ultimate irony of organic evolution', writes Edward O. Wilson, is that 'in the instant of achieving self-understanding through the mind of man, life has doomed its most beautiful creations'. Twenty-first-century *Homo sapiens* is unique among species not only in its knowledge of evolution but also in the degree and the speed with which it is able to alter the course of evolution. Indeed, these two powers are closely inter-related: the human claim to understand nature has led to Western humankind's understanding of itself as apart from nature and therefore able to use and reshape nature at will. All species influence their ecosystems; only our species has a conception of ecosystems and that conception brings the capacity to destroy whole ecosystems.

By rewriting Darwinian evolution at the level of the gene, modern biology has come close to answering the question of how we and the rest of the living world came to be as we are. As well as moving inward from the species to the gene, biologists have also moved outward from the species to the environment. They have begun to ask how evolution operates at the level of the ecosystem. At one level, the unit of natural selection is the gene, but at another it is the ecosystem; the species which destroys its ecosystem destroys itself.

The key to the continuation of life in any ecosystem is

biodiversity: 'Life in a local site struck down by a passing storm springs back quickly because enough diversity still exists. Opportunistic species evolved for just such an occasion rush in to fill the spaces.' When the sea otter was hunted to near-extinction off the Pacific coast of North America, sea urchins – the otter's prey – went unchecked and overconsumed the marine kelp forest, rendering barren large stretches of the ocean floor. When conservationists reintroduced the sea otter, the kelp forest duly grew again and the barren sea was reanimated, reinhabited by a full range of aquatic life from plankton to whale. The point of this story is that if you don't have what Edward Wilson calls 'keystone species', such as the sea otter, a site once destroyed may remain barren. One cannot know which will be the keystone species in any particular environment, so nature has evolved a profligate diversity – among every multitude of apparently expendable species, there is one which will be the keystone on which new ecosystems will be built.

Biodiversity means that for most of time the number of species on earth expands; the fossil record suggests that the normal 'background' extinction rate is one species per million each year. At a conservative estimate, the current extinction rate in the tropical rainforests alone is at least a thousand species a year. The order of this is akin to that of the catastrophic extinction spasms of the paleozoic, mesozoic and cenozoic eras, the last of which wiped out the dinosaurs.

In his book *The Diversity of Life*, Wilson argues with extraordinary eloquence for the beauty as well as the necessity of biodiversity. He has sufficient faith in humankind to believe that if we can be made to understand the importance of biodiversity, we might do something to slow down the rate at which we are eroding it. An anatomist of interlocking ecosystems such as Wilson gives us a technical language with which to understand the inter-relatedness of all living things, of species and environment. But few are the scientists with Wilson's elucidatory and linguistic power to engage the non-specialist reader in their anatomies. And, if we accept Heidegger's argument – to be considered in my next chapter – that the scientific mode of understanding is dangerous exactly because it is representational rather than presencing, because it presupposes a Cartesian subject challenging forth the world of objects, then the anatomy of the world in a language of scientific explanation is itself part of the problem. If only half-consciously, Wilson realizes this: through his use of words like 'beauty', through the quasi-poetic power of his evocation of a storm in a tropical rainforest, through his resort to actual poetry (the sentence about the irony of organic evolution is immediately preceded by Virgil's lines on the descent to Avernus), he implicitly yokes the scientific to the aesthetic and recognizes that we need poets to do the work of dwelling.

Could the poet be a keystone sub-species of *Homo sapiens*? The poet: an apparently useless creature, but potentially the saviour of ecosystems.

One controlling idea invoked in *The Diversity of Life* is that of the bioregion. Common ecosystems may be thought of as united into bioregions which are bounded by great rivers and mountain ranges. A bioregion is a place that has its own distinctive natural economy. It has, in Heidegger's language, its *Dasein*. Neither ecosystems nor social customs are co-extensive with national boundaries; acid rain and nuclear fallout do not respect the lines that are drawn on human maps. A map divided according to bioregions will look very different from one bounded according to nation states, and that may be why politicians, who think in terms of national interest, seldom think bioregionally. What, then, might it mean to think bioregionally?

For a hundred years ecology has been both a biological science and a politico-economic value system. There are environmental ethics as well as environmental data. A scientific ecologist will map a bioregion; a political ecologist will ask what it is to live in a bioregion, will address the question of how advanced human society can accommodate itself to bioregional rhythms. No bioregion is strictly stable (aeolian plankton move in on every wind, natural borders shift minutely with every storm), but at human levels of temporal and spatial perception every bioregion is by definition unique unto itself. A bioregion is a self-sustaining, self-sufficient natural *oikos* for a diverse body of co-habiting species. From seeing this, one does not have to travel far to reach the 'small is beautiful' economics of E. F. Schumacher, to see that bioregions may adapt to intermediate technology but, again by definition, are singularly vulnerable when they are set upon by multiregional capitalism.

'To become dwellers in the land,' says Kirkpatrick Sale in a Schumacher Lecture, 'to come to know the earth, fully and honestly, the crucial and perhaps only and all-encompassing task is to understand the place, the immediate, specific place, where we live.' Sale goes on to cite Schumacher himself – 'In the question of how we treat the land, our entire way of life is involved' – before he modulates his voice into a tone of ecopiety: 'We must somehow live as close to [the land] as possible, be in touch with its particular soils, its waters, its winds; we must learn its ways, its capacities, its limits; we must make its rhythms our patterns, its laws our guide, its fruit our bounty.' This, he concludes, is the essence of politicized bioregionalism.

The bioregion, as I have said, tends not to be co-extensive with the modern nation state. Gary Snyder is a poet who grounds himself regionally in the watershed of the Pacific north-west of the place which most people call the United States of America, but which he calls, after one of its names in indigenous myth, 'Turtle Island'. The distinction between the power-hungry nations of modernity and the distinctive, diverse bioregions which have evolved over thousands of years is crucial to his vision:

> The little nations of the past lived within territories that conformed to some set of natural criteria. The culture areas of the major native groups of North America overlapped, as one would expect, with broadly defined major bioregions. That older human experience of a fluid, indistinct, but genuinely home region was gradually replaced – across Eurasia – by the arbitrary and often violently imposed boundaries of emerging national states. These imposed borders sometimes cut across biotic areas and ethnic zones alike. Inhabitants lost ecological knowledge and community solidarity. In the old ways, the flora and fauna and landforms are *part of the culture*. The world of culture and nature, which is actual, is almost a shadow world now, and the insubstantial world of

political jurisdictions and rarefied economies is what passes for reality.

But to know your place and to celebrate the biota among which you have lived and grown is not necessarily to reject cultural difference. Snyder's work looks to the wisdom of the Buddhist traditions of the East – he is a committed practitioner of Zen and imitator of the Chinese ideogrammatic style of poetry – as well as to Native American household lore. The poet of biodiversity will also celebrate cultural diversity.

The writer and traveller Elizabeth Bishop is a marvellous exemplar in this respect. Both geographically and culturally, her work respects the difference between 'North and South'. There is no home for the monolithic nation state in Bishop's shifting, glimmering world. Always an outsider, she is perpetually fascinated by meetings on the border and unexpected encounters, such as that between the bus smelling of gasoline and the moose smelling of moose. She is intrigued by maps, those reminders of the arbitrariness of the location of national boundaries. Historians tell temporal stories with an emphasis on the growth and decline of great nations. The spatial approach of the geographer articulates, as Bishop has it, a more 'delicate' knowledge:

> Mapped waters are more quiet than the land is,
> lending the land their waves' own conformation:
> and Norway's hare runs south in agitation,
> profiles investigate the sea, where land is.
> Are they assigned, or can the countries pick their colors?
> —What suits the character or the native waters best.
> Topography displays no favorites; North's as near as West.
> More delicate than the historians' are the map-makers' colors.

Recent cultural analysis has made much of the role of litera-ture in the ideological state apparatus and the construction of literary canons in the furtherance of ideologies of nationhood. Historically, it has certainly been the case that literature has been central to the formation of national identity; one thinks of Augustan Rome, Elizabethan England and early nineteenth-century Germany. In the twentieth century this pattern began to break down. Institutionally, our structures of literary study remain largely bound by the nation state – English Literature, French Literature, Russian Literature, American Literature – but we now recognize that a movement such as high Modernism was profoundly, indeed intrinsically, cosmopolitan. One might even argue that as the nineteenth-century canon was wedded indissolubly to the nineteenth-century notion of (imperial) nation, so the Modernist canon was wedded indissolubly to twentieth-century multinational capitalism. The freefloating Modernist found him- or herself in those cities in which stock markets and currency exchanges fuelled international capital accumulation: New York, London, Paris, Zurich. Notoriously deracinated, the high Modernist is the very antithesis of the bioregionally grounded poet.

Could this be one reason why Basil Bunting has been excluded from the high Modernist canon, even though Ezra Pound championed him almost as vociferously as he did T. S. Eliot? It is because Bunting at his best was a bioregional poet that we need to reclaim him now. If a mode of dwelling answerable to the order of nature is one grounded in regional particularity, so the literary tradition in our language needs to be opened up to regional diversity. The canon has been controlled for too long by those whom Bunting called Southrons, by metropolitan interests, literary London (Bloomsbury), Oxford and Cambridge. Bunting's bioregion, by contrast, is resolutely northern. When interviewed, he was unequivocal: '"Did you always think that you would return to Northumbria and write a specifically Northumbrian poem?" Bunting: "Yes."'

The Northumbrian poem is Bunting's masterwork, *Briggflatts* (1966), a poem which speaks its regional dwelling in dialect ('The spuggies [baby sparrows] are fledged'), place-name (Rawthey, Garsdale, Hawes, Stainmore), local myth and history (Bloodaxe, Lindisfarne). It is a deeply Wordsworthian autobiographical meditation on loss and recovery in which identity is forged in place. The narrator awakens into identity through a childhood sexual encounter; the girl he lies with is, like Wordsworth's Lucy, an embodiment of the land. His departure from her is, as Bunting's best critic, Peter Makin, writes, 'the abandoning of the North for the South, which is also the abandoning of a hard field for an easy one'. The poem tracks a return to the north; it traces the complex web of relations between things in 'an ecology of fox, slow-worm, rat, blow-fly, and weed; sheepdogs and pregnant sheep; light on water and foam on rock: things seen'. It reaches a climax in these lines from the fourth section:

> Columba, Columbanus, as the soil shifts its vest,
> Aidan and Cuthbert put on daylight,
> wires of sharp western metal entangled in its soft
> web, many shuttles as midges darting;
> not for bodily welfare nor pauper theorems
> but splendour to splendour, excepting nothing that is.
> Let the fox have his fill, patient leech and weevil,
> cattle refer the rising of Sirius to their hedge horizon,
> runts murder the sacred calves of the sea by rule
> heedless of herring gull, surf and the text carved by waves
> on the skerry. Can you trace shuttles thrown
> like drops from a fountain, spray, mist of spiderlines
> bearing the rainbow, quoits round the draped moon;
> shuttles like random dust desert whirlwinds hoy at their
>   tormenting sun?
> Follow the clue patiently and you will understand nothing.

The author himself offers a valuable gloss in a letter of 18 May 1965, close to the time of composition:

> I have been talking of the Anglo-Celtic saints who 'put on daylight', represented as a brocade in which wires of 'western metal' are woven. . . . Now the brocade is woven by shuttles, woven with extreme intricacy, for indeed it is nothing less than the whole universe: shuttles like midges darting, like drops from a fountain, like the dust of the little whirlwinds which continually form in the desert. It bears the rainbow and the moon's halo, things beautiful but hard to define, and it opposes the sharp sun that wants all things to be chained to the dictionary or the multiplication table. It gives, not so much tolerance as enthusiastic acceptance of a world in which things are not measured by their usefulness to man.

The movement thus proceeds from the intricacy of Anglo-Celtic metalwork – metonymic of the poet's own art – to the weaving of the material universe. 'Nature' is an interpenetration of organic and inorganic forms, not all of them the traditional matter of poetry; 'nothing that is' can be excepted from the dance, neither midge nor 'patient leech and weevil'. The passage promulgates Bunting's version of the Wordsworthian 'one life', the motion and the spirit 'that impels / All thinking things, all objects of all thought, / And rolls through all things'. But *Briggflatts* resists the Wordsworthian attempt explicitly to unify all things, to go beyond the things themselves towards a transcendental signified, whether that signified be the great spirit of the universe or the poet's own unifying imagination.

Basil Bunting stands somewhere between the Wilson of biodiversity and the Heidegger of dwelling, who has been shadowing me throughout the writing of this book (we will finally confront him squarely in a few pages' time). Like Wilson, Bunting celebrates the diversity of fox, leech and weevil, enthusiastically accepting a world – like that of the tropical rainforest – in which things need not necessarily be 'measured by their usefulness to man'. Unlike Wilson, he is not interested in the scientific description of biodiversity. To use the language of enumeration, say by calculating the number of species in a single patch of rainforest, is to be 'chained to the dictionary or the multiplication table'. 'Follow the clue patiently and you will understand nothing': or rather, you may re-present, but you will not dwell.

To dwell you must be content to listen, to hear the music of the shuttle. *Briggflatts* begins by inviting a 'sweet tenor bull' to 'descant' on the 'madrigal' of a place as 'A mason times his mallet / to a lark's twitter': the poem's essential lexis is aural. There is a distinctive sound to every bioregion, whether Bunting's Northumbria, with its herring gull and running beck, or Wilson's rainforest, with its honking leptodactylid frog and echoing howler monkey. But there is also an undersound, a melody heard perhaps only by the poet, which harmonizes the whole ecosystem. Let us listen for a moment to the seashore ecology of the fifth section of *Briggflatts*:

> Conger skimped at the ebb, lobster,
> neither will I take, nor troll

roe of its like for salmon.
Let bass sleep, gentles
brisk, skim-grey,
group a nosegay
jostling on cast flesh,
frisk and compose decay
to side shot with flame,
unresting bluebottle wing. Sing,
strewing the notes on the air
as ripples skip in a shallow. Go
bare, the shore is adorned
with pungent weed loudly
filtering sand and sea.

But again we must pause. These lines are far removed from any actual Northumbrian ecology. That phrase in section four, 'the text carved by waves / on the skerry', reminds us of Shelley's knowledge that the poet can only give us a trace, not the thing itself. Locked in the prison-house of language, dwelling in the *logos* not the *oikos*, we know only the text, not the land. Unless, that is, we could come to understand that every piece of land is itself a text, with its own syntax and signifying potential. Or one should say: come to understand once again, as our ancestors did. For the idea that the earth itself is a text is a very old one. And there used to be an agreed answer about who the author is.

*

'There'll always be religion around while there is poetry / or a lack of it', writes Les Murray in 'Poetry and Religion', a poem which reasserts the intimacy, the uneasy but vital interdependence, of two ancient human instincts:

Both are given, and intermittent,
as the action of those birds – crested pigeon, rosella parrot –
who fly with wings shut, then beating, and again shut.

In his essay 'Some Religious Stuff I know about Australia', Murray makes some suggestive connections:

In the native religion of Japan, deity (*kami*), sometimes indi-
vidualised into deities of a polytheistic sort, is held to be
present in all sorts of existing objects, in certain mirrors,
wells, rocks, swords, mountains, in special shrines and the
like. These bearers of immanent divinity are called *shintai*
('god-bodies') or *mitamashiro* ('divine-soul-objects') ... It
appears to be a formalisation, surviving surprisingly long in a
developed form, of a pretty widespread early response of man
to intimations of the Spirit's presence. In the West, Wordsworthian romanticism, the 'sense of something far more
deeply interfused' in things is a modern analogue.

Murray implies that the vastness and untamability of Australia
mean that the peculiar power and sacredness of that land may still
be sensed. He christens this religious sense 'Strine Shinto'. His
own poetry – though tempered with wryness, irony and self-
deprecation – undertakes a complex integration of the ancient
idea that nature is the book in which a transcendent God writes
his presence with a kind of secular Shinto which serves as the
ground for an environmental ethic.

Murray heartily dislikes critics who hitch poets to the bandwagon of politics and Causes, but there is a case for viewing him
as the major ecological poet currently writing in the English
language. That he is Australian provides a bioregional emphasis.
He and his schoolmates didn't like poetry, he says, because it
'was for us a remote and unreal form of writing which referred to
the seasons and flora and class-ecology of an archipelago off the
north-west coast of Europe'. To interpose his antipodean voice
into the English literary canon is to force awareness of biodiversity upon us: for a reader accustomed to Keats's autumn or the
shepherds' calendars of Edmund Spenser and John Clare, it is a
peculiar and peculiarly liberating experience to read 'The Idyll
Wheel: Cycle of a Year at Bunyah, New South Wales, April
1986–April 1987' and discover spring coming in September. But
what is most important about Murray is his yoking of the religious
sense to the sense of place.

Poems like 'The Returnees' and 'The Buladelah-Taree Holiday Song Cycle' are loving celebrations of Australian people in

Australian places. Like Bunting, Murray hears the undersound of ecosystems – 'wild sound', he calls it, 'that low, aggregate susurrus which emanates from living landscape' – but his human agents do not stand in a state of what Heidegger would call 'thrownness'. They are robustly active. In the 'Holiday Song Cycle' urban trippers enjoying the great outdoors jostle with insects and ibis, sharing the land. The mosquito may be a pest, but it is also to be wondered at, to be recognized as the life-blood of the place:

> Forests and State Forests, all down off the steeper country;
>   mosquitoes are always living in there:
> they float about like dust motes and sink down, at the places
>   of the Stinging Tree,
> and of the Staghorn Fern; the males feed on plant-stem fluid,
>   absorbing that watery ichor;
> the females meter the air, feeling for the warm-blooded
>   smell, needing blood for their eggs.
> They find the dingo in his sleeping-place, they find his
>   underbelly and his anus;
> they find the possum's face, they drift up the ponderous
>   pleats of the fig tree, way up into its rigging,
> the high camp of the fruit bats; they feed on the membranes
>   and ears of bats; tired wings cuff air at them;
> their eggs burning inside them, they alight on the muzzles of
>   cattle,
> the half-wild bush cattle, there at the place of the Sleeper
>   Dump, at the place of the Tallowwoods.
> The males move about among growth tips; ingesting
>   solutions, they crouch intently;
> the females sing, needing blood to breed their young; their
>   singing is in the scrub country;
> their tune comes to the name-bearing humans, who dance to
>   it and irritably grin at it.

These are lines which wonderfully combine biological accuracy with a joyfulness that glories in all creation. Mosquito and human share the same dance.

That fruit-bat, with its tired wings cuffing air at the mosquito, is a species for which Murray has a particular sympathy:

Both Coolongolook River and the red-headed fruit bat are important sponsors of my writing. It was while sitting in the now-vanished timber mill at Coolongolook and contemplating the river, one evening in the mid-fifties, that I first realised that I was going to be a writer; rivers in my work often have a lot of Coolongolook water in them. The metaphoric appropriateness of the flying fox, a nocturnal creature who sleeps upside down during the day and flies out for miles at night in search of 'grown and native fruit', to the general situation of poets in this country has a compelling force for me. I examined this in a poem written in 1974 and entitled 'The Flying-Fox Dreaming, Wingham Brush, NSW'. That poem connects the metaphor with the ancient ritual and economic significance of the flying fox in my country. Along the Manning in pre-white days, there seems to have been a seasonal ecology of native figs, flying foxes and Aborigines. The fruit bats are very nearly my 'dreaming', in the half-serious, half-joking way that Douglas Stewart identified his totem animal as the bandicoot while claiming David Campbell's was a big red fox.

Like his fruit-bat, Murray often inhabits a 'high camp', but he is more than half-serious about the idea of this nocturnal creature as his 'dreaming', his totemic ancestor. The major vision of his late work is entitled 'Presence: Translations from the Natural World' (1992). 'Translations' is a recognition that the poet's home in the *logos* is a different place from the natural world itself, but 'presence' proclaims poetry's capacity to reveal the being of things. The sequence consists of lyrical dreamings of a huge diversity of living things from 'Cell DNA' to 'Cockspur Bush' to 'Mollusc' to 'Eagle Pair' to 'The Octave of Elephants'.

Strine Shinto draws strength from the Aboriginal creation myth of the beings who walked the dreaming-tracks, singing animals, birds, plants, rocks and pools into existence. Most British and American readers first learned of that myth from Bruce Chatwin's *Songlines*:

the Ancestors had been poets in the original sense of *poesis*, meaning 'creation'. No Aboriginal could conceive that the

created world was in any way imperfect. His religious life had
a single aim: to keep the land the way it was and should be.
The man who went 'Walkabout' was making a ritual journey.
He trod in the footprints of his Ancestor. He sang the
Ancestor's stanzas without changing a word or note – and so
recreated the Creation.

The assertion that the Aboriginal sings the Ancestor's stanzas
without changing a word or note is false – like all traditions of
oral poetry, Aboriginal song involves a large measure of improvisation – but Chatwin's apprehension of the inextricability of the
dreaming and the land is profoundly true.

In one sense, Murray is an aboriginal kind of creator or
recreator. But he is also a worldly wise poet, who recognizes that
the land is now marked not only by songlines but by property
boundaries, mappings of territorial possession. Rousseau remarked in his second *Discourse* that you may be justified in
claiming that you own a wall. But then he asked: by what right
do you claim to own the boundary-line that the wall is supposed
to mark?

Consider, to close, Murray's sonnet 'Thinking About Aboriginal Land Rights, I Visit the Farm I Will Not Inherit':

Watching from the barn the seedlight and nearly-all-down
currents of a spring day, I see the only lines bearing
consistent strain are the straight ones: fence, house corner,
outermost furrows. The drifts of grass coming and canes
are whorled and sod-bunching, are issuant, with dusts.
The wind-lap outlines of lagoons are pollen-concurred
and the light rising out of them stretches in figments and wings.
The ambient day-tides contain every mouldering and oil
that the bush would need to come back right this day,
not suddenly, but all down the farm slopes, the polished shell barks
flaking, leaves noon-thin, with shale stones and orchids at foot
and the creek a hung gallery again, and the bee trees unrobbed.
By sundown it is dense dusk, all the tracks closing in.
I go into the earth near the feed shed for thousands of years.

The regimented demarcations of property are broken down by
the grass and pollen that drift in on the wind, a motion enacted

in the flow of the syntax across the lines of the metrical structure. The bush will eventually repossess the place. The poet is thus disinherited, as the Aborigine has been. The land rights question became a public issue in Australia as a result of a classic liberal concern for social justice, but it developed into something else: a rediscovery of the Aborigine's sacral relationship with the land. Seeing this, the speaker of the poem recognizes that dwelling in the land is not a matter of putting up a sign saying 'Murray's Farm', of legally inheriting it. By letting the 'ambient day-tides' drift over him, he lets the place absorb him. He becomes the farm's dreaming. Long ago, that dreaming 'went into the earth near the feed shed for thousands of years'. The poet sings it back to life until at dusk he returns it into the earth.

Will the dreaming emerge again thousands of years in the future? That will depend on whether the bush is humming with undersound or silent with extinction. John Keats had his own phrase for Murray's 'wild sound' or 'low, aggregate susurrus which emanates from living landscape': that phrase was 'The poetry of earth'. In his sonnet 'On the Grasshopper and Cricket' Keats wrote of how earth's own poetry 'is ceasing never' – whether in the heat of a still summer noon or the chill of a frosty winter night, the well-tuned ear will always hear insect sound. 'The poetry of earth', the sonnet confidently begins, 'is never dead'.

But in another poem, 'La belle dame sans merci', Keats imagined a silent landscape in which 'The sedge is withered from the lake / And no birds sing.' He imagines a nature that has died because man is in thrall to desire. In 1962 Rachel Carson alerted the world to the consequences of modern man's desire for more efficient agricultural production. The elimination of insect life by means of pesticides had the unintended but inevitable consequence of also eliminating birdsong – of creating a *Silent Spring*. Forty years on from Carson, the silencing continues. Go and stand on the chalk downs of Wiltshire where a century ago W. H. Hudson roamed with the shepherd Caleb Bawcombe. You will not hear the grasshopper, let alone the skylark. The agribusinesses of mass arable production, fed by the giants of the chemical industry, have seen to that.

9

What Are Poets For?

> But to have been
> this once, completely, even if only once:
> to have been at one with the earth, seems beyond undoing.

(Rainer Maria Rilke, ninth *Duino Elegy*, trans. Stephen Mitchell)

THERE WAS A TIME, we may assume, when *Homo sapiens* was driven above all by the will to survive. Like other mammals, we sought to keep ourselves warm and well fed, we had an instinct to reproduce, we protected ourselves and our young from predators. In the state of nature, wrote Rousseau, 'the only goods in the world' known to man 'are food, a female, and repose, and the only evils he fears are pain and hunger'. But over the last few thousand years we have come to consider ourselves different from other mammals. The difference is made by the very act of considering: to think and talk about our distinctiveness as a species is to mark our distinctiveness as a species.

The ancient Greeks regarded the faculties of reasoning and of speech – what their successors the Romans called *ratio* and *oratio* – as uniquely human powers. Modern science may have taught us to be less confident in making such distinctions. Chimpanzees not only learn by trial and error, which is a form of reasoning, they also apparently recognize that thoughts are the agents of actions and they accordingly behave in ways which are intended to influence the states of mind of other individuals. As for language, even less advanced primates such as vervet monkeys use different vocalizations to represent different predators: they have distinctive cries to warn their companions of leopard, eagle and snake. But there is still much about humankind which seems to set us apart from the rest of nature: we are the only species to have advanced technology, to have a religious sense, to have values like justice and liberty, to have scientists, philosophers and poets. We alone are 'sophisticated', interested in the pursuit of abstract wisdom (*sophos*) as opposed to that practical knowledge which helps a species in its quest for survival.

Students of the ancient cultures of Africa, of the Far and Near East, of Sumeria, China, Egypt, Greece, will go on arguing about where, when and why that sophistication came into being. Thinking about humankind's thinking of itself as apart from nature is as old as culture; such thinking is indeed one important definition of culture. But, as has been argued at various points in this book, advanced Western culture has a distinctive and perhaps exceptionally divisive understanding of humankind's relationship to nature, an understanding which may for convenience be traced back to Baconian empirical science and Cartesian philosophical dualism, and which was further developed in Kantian idealism.

Ironically, at around the time the Kantian revolution gave philosophic supremacy to the mind of man, a revolution in biology inverted the age-old model of a hierarchy in nature extending down from the supreme being through man to the higher animals to the insects to vegetable matter. Lamarck's theory of evolution began with the protozoa, the single-celled organisms at the bottom end of the old chain of being. The great divide between the humanities and the sciences is one result of these twin revolutions: if you are an artist you are likely to begin with the creations of the human mind, whereas if you are a scientist you are likely to begin with particles, elements, genes or organisms. This division further exacerbates the crisis of environment. The values with which the humanities have taught us to regard humankind have rarely been extended to the material world which the sciences examine and technology transforms. The Enlightenment had a discourse of *rights*, taken up in moral and political science, and a discourse of *nature*, taken up in the natural sciences. But, as was seen in chapter six, only on its margins did it have a discourse of the rights *of* nature. Romanticism frequently proclaims those rights, but under the rule of technology its cry has been heard only in the (diminishing) wilderness.

The dominant strand of twentieth-century philosophy did little to heal the rift which Cartesianism opened between what Percy Shelley called 'the human mind's imaginings' and what William Blake called 'the things of Vegetative & Generative Nature'. By arguing that philosophical thinking must begin with language, that there is indeed no knowledge prior to language, modernity and postmodernity have shifted the emphasis from *ratio* to *oratio*. But whether we begin with the mind or the word, we are not beginning with the external world. The major philosophical revolutions since the seventeenth century have constituted a progressive severance of humankind from nature that has licensed, or at least neglected, technology's ravaging of the earth's finite resources.

It has been the principal argument of this book that writers in the Romantic tradition which begins in the late eighteenth century have been especially concerned with this severance. Romanticism declares allegiance to what Wordsworth in the preface to *Lyrical Ballads* called 'the beautiful and permanent forms of nature'. It proposes that when we commune with those forms we live with a peculiar intensity, and conversely that our lives are diminished when technology and industrialization alienate us from those forms. It regards poetic language as a special kind of expression which may effect an imaginative reunification of mind and nature, though it also has a melancholy awareness of the illusoriness of its own utopian vision. I have redescribed this broadly conceived Romanticism as an 'ecopoetic', a *poiesis* (Greek 'making') of the *oikos* (Greek 'home' or 'dwelling-place').

Since poetry is a product of culture whereas ecology is a science which describes nature, it may seem perverse to bring the two fields together. But there has always been a network of intimate relations, as well as an apparent hostility, between culture and nature. The science of ecology was made possible by Darwin's theory of natural selection, which was itself made possible by the application to the biological sciences of Malthusian principles derived from the social sciences of economics and human population study. Why not, then, fold the principle of natural selection back into the realm of culture? We may then ask: Given what fragile, elusive and impractical things poems are, is it not surprising that they survive at all? Might those poems that survive do so because, like naturally selected species within evolving ecosystems, they successfully perform necessary work within our distinctively human ecology?

Gary Snyder, the most ecologically self-conscious of twentieth-century poets, draws an analogy between poetry and a key concept in scientific ecology, that of 'climax':

> The communities of creatures in forests, ponds, oceans, or grasslands seem to tend toward a condition called climax, 'virgin forest' – many species, old bones, lots of rotten leaves, complex energy pathways, woodpeckers living in snags, and conies harvesting tiny piles of grass. This condition has considerable stability and holds much energy in its web – energy that in simpler systems (a field of weeds just after a bulldozer) is lost back into the sky or down the drain. All of evolution may have been as much shaped by this pull toward climax as it has by simple competition between individuals or species.

In a climax ecosystem, a high proportion of energy comes from the recycling of dead biomass (fallen leaves, dead animals and so on): 'Detritus cycle energy is liberated by fungi and lots of insects.' And so to Snyder's analogy:

> as climax forest is to biome, and fungus to the recycling of energy, so 'enlightened mind' [in the Zen sense] is to daily ego mind, and art to the recycling of neglected inner potential. When we deepen or enrich ourselves, looking within, understanding ourselves, we come closer to being like a climax system. Turning away from grazing on the 'immediate biomass' of perception, sensation, and thrill; and re-viewing memory, internalized perception, blocks of inner energies, dreams, the leaf-fall of day-to-day consciousness, liberates the energy of our sense-detritus. Art is an assimilator of unfelt experience, sensation, and memory for the whole society. When all that compost of feeling and thinking comes back to us then, it comes not as a flower, but – to complete the

metaphor – as a mushroom: the fruiting body of the buried threads of mycelia that run widely through the soil, and are intricately married to the root hairs of all the trees. 'Fruiting' – at that point – is the completion of the work of the poet, and the point where the artist or mystic reenters the cycle: gives what she or he has done as nourishment, and as spore or seed spreads the 'thought of enlightenment,' reaching into personal depths for nutrients hidden there, back to the community. The community and its poetry are not two.

The idea is that poetry – perhaps because of its rhythmic and mnemonic intensity – is an especially efficient system for recycling the richest thoughts and feelings of a community. Every time we read or discuss a poem, we are recycling its energy back into our cultural environment. That is how the process of survival and modification functions in the realm of art.

For Snyder, then, there is a powerful analogy between poetry and climax ecosystem. His own belief in a Zen theory of the interconnectedness of all things means that he does not have to worry that the analogy is *merely a metaphor*. He would reply that metaphor is a way of understanding hidden connections, of reunifying the world which scientific understanding has fragmented. He would argue that the poet is supremely important precisely because he believes in the power of metaphor.

But from the point of view of most modern literary theory, this will never do. Among intellectuals, Snyder's analogy would generally be regarded as mere mystification. Theorists are very suspicious of any claim that poems are the verbal equivalents of anything in nature, let alone a climax ecosystem. Language and imagination have come to be defined as realms that are split off from nature because they only function by means of representation. What is produced by representation is by definition something other than the thing-in-itself (Kant's *Ding an sich*).

This 'crisis of representation' or 'hermeneutic of suspicion' is at the core of all versions of 'postmodern' literary theory. Ecopoetics, with its affirmation of not only the existence, but also the sacredness, of the-things-of-nature-in-themselves seems naive in comparison. It needs to find a path through scepticism, to reach a clearing beyond the dense undergrowth of the proposition that language is a self-enclosed system. As in chapter three we worked our way towards a new ecopoetic by going through a 'post-colonial' mode of reading, so let us try to pass from hermeneutics to ecopoetics. My starting-point for this endeavour is one of the more accessible foundation-texts of fin de siècle literary theory, Paul Ricoeur's essay 'Writing as a Problem for Literary Criticism and Philosophical Hermeneutics'.

'To the extent that hermeneutics is a text-oriented interpretation, and that texts are, among other things, instances of written language,' Ricoeur begins, 'no interpretation theory is possible that does not come to grips with the problem of writing.' Our problem, then, is that the environmentalist's loving gaze upon 'nature' entails a forgetting that 'nature' is a word, not a thing. Snyder's claim for poetry as a form of renewable energy failed to come to grips with the problem of writing, the gap between 'presence' and 'representation':

> For contemporary philosophy, representation is a great culprit. Some philosophers even speak of a representative illusion, just as Kant spoke of a transcendental illusion. This representative illusion allegedly stems from the impossible claim of uniting the interiority of a mental image in the mind and the exteriority of something real that would govern from outside the play of the mental scene within a single entity or 'representation.' The illusory nature of this claim is said to be even clearer if one says that the interior presence and the exterior presence can be made present to each other through some process of adequation which would define the truth of the representation. Representation, accordingly, it is said, should be denounced as the reduplication of presence, as the re-presenting of presence.

Since the literary theory of the late twentieth century was locked into the hermeneutic circle described here, it could not look out from the text to the planet. It was too busy worriedly manipulating the words 'nature' and 'man' to pay any attention to man's manipulation of nature through technology.

Yet Ricoeur himself proposed a way out of the linguistic bind.

Having acknowledged that writing is a 'problem', he proceeded by way of an elegant dialectic to make poetic writing into a solution. The problem of writing is that it detaches the 'said' from the act of 'saying', the 'meaning' of an utterance from the 'event' of utterance. In speech, meaning can be checked because of the presence of the sayer. 'Open the window.' 'Do you mean this window [*pointing*] or that one [*pointing*]?' 'This one [*pointing*].' The act of inscription complicates affairs, for it severs the link with the immediate life-world of the speaker. The written text thus takes on a semantic autonomy. Whereas a speech-act occurs in a moment of time, a piece of writing occupies space and may endure through time. The space and time of writing are not the same as the space and time of reading. The text is given over to whoever may read it. In the case of a classic literary text, the differing interpretations offered by successive generations of readers become part of the work's history.

Here, however, Ricoeur warns us against two opposing fallacies. We are equally in error when we moor a text solely to its author (that is to neglect its semantic autonomy) *and* when we cast it adrift utterly from its author (that is to neglect its human origin). Bad interpretation is either that which insists on always checking back with the author (to do so is to deprive writing of the peculiarity that makes it different from speech) or that which claims we can say anything we like about a text (to do so is to hypostasize the text as an authorless entity, which is not the condition of any text). Good interpretation is a synthesis of the two parts of the dialectic constituted by author and reader.

In this synthesis, the author's and the reader's horizons of experience come to overlap with one another – to overlap, but not to be overlaid one exactly upon another. This overlapping allows for an overcoming of the problem of reference to the world.

My fragment of dialogue about opening a window refers to a *situation*. A piece of writing, by contrast, is severed from its originary situation. According to Ricoeur, all that an animal knows is its immediate situation, whereas

> Thanks to writing, man and only man has a world and not
> just a situation. This extension is one more example of the

spiritual implications of the substitution of material marks for the bodily support of oral discourse. In the same manner that the text frees its meaning from the tutelage of the mental intention, it frees its reference from the limits of situational reference.

'World' for Ricoeur is knowledge, history, memory, imagination, all those aspects of our being which allow us to transcend the here-and-now of our bodies. Most writing tells us about 'world': travellers' reports, geographical textbooks, historical monographs and other 'descriptive accounts of reality' serve to 'restructure for their readers the conditions of ostensive reference'.

Literary and especially 'poetic' writings, however, seek to do something different. Save in exceptional limiting cases such as the poetry of Stéphane Mallarmé, literature does not abolish reference – 'In one manner or another poetic texts speak about the world' – but its manner of speaking is not descriptive. This is the peculiar power of literary works:

> The effacement of the ostensive and descriptive reference liberates a power of reference to aspects of our being in the world which cannot be said in a direct descriptive way, but only alluded to, thanks to the referential values of metaphoric and, in general, symbolic expression.

Following Martin Heidegger, Ricoeur proposes that what we understand first in a literary discourse is

> not another person, but a 'project', that is the outline of a new way of being in the world. Only writing . . . in freeing itself, not only from its author and from its originary audience, but from the narrowness of the dialogical situation, reveals this destination of discourse as projecting a world.

When we respond to an artwork, we open ourselves to another person's 'project', to an alternative way of being in the world. (I disagree with Ricoeur's claim that only writing confers this freedom: surely something similar happens when we look at a painting or a performance-work.) This idea may then be given an ecological inflection: works of art can themselves be imaginary states of nature, imaginary ideal ecosystems, and by reading them, by inhabiting them, we can start to imagine what it might be like to live differently upon the earth.

Snyder's argument that poetry functions ecologically may be recuperated, provided it is understood as a form of what Ricoeur calls 'symbolic expression'. Symbolic expression is one of the peculiar systems that our species has evolved for coping with the world; it is one of our survival-mechanisms.

For Ricoeur, a 'world' is a horizon of possibilities which constitutes an environment, a dwelling-place. Ricoeur glosses:

> I like very much this notion of Heidegger when he links these three terms: constructing the house [building], and dwelling, and thinking. So we are dwellers in a world. The relation of dwelling has its counterpart in the notion of a world. The world is where we dwell.

But there is a problem here. Ricoeur's 'world' – the abstract, disembodied zone of possibility – is a building inside the head. It is not synonymous with any actual dwelling-place upon the earth.

In order to overcome this obstacle, we must confront a paradox. Heidegger himself distinguished between 'world' and 'earth'. If 'world' is, as Ricoeur has it, a panoply of possible experiences and imaginings projected through the infinite potentiality of writing, then our world, our home, is not earth but language. And if writing is the archetypal place of severance – of alienation – from immediate situatedness, then how can it speak to the condition of ecological belonging? Heidegger replies with the other half of the paradox: there is a special kind of writing, called poetry, which has the peculiar power to speak 'earth'. Poetry is the song of the earth.

*

What are poets for? They are not exactly philosophers, though they often try to explain the world and humankind's place within it. They are not exactly moralists, for at least since the nineteenth century their primary concern has rarely been to tell us in homiletic fashion how to live. But they are often exceptionally lucid or provocative in their articulation of the relationship between internal and external worlds, between being and dwelling. Romanticism and its afterlife, I have been arguing throughout this book, may be thought of as the exploration of the relationship between external environment and ecology of mind.

'What are poets for?' (*'Wozu Dichter?'*) asked Martin Heidegger in the title of a lecture delivered on the twentieth anniversary of the death of Rainer Maria Rilke. In his later philosophy, Heidegger meditated deeply upon three questions. 'What are poets for?' was one of them, 'What does it mean to dwell upon the earth?' was the second, and 'What is the essence of technology?' was the third. Heidegger's answers to the three questions turn out to be closely inter-related.

On 18 November 1953 Heidegger lectured to the Bavarian Academy of Fine Arts on 'The Question concerning Technology'. Technology itself, he argued, is not the essence of technology. 'We shall never experience our relationship to the essence of technology so long as we merely represent the technological, put up with it, or evade it. Everywhere we remain unfree and chained to technology, whether we passionately affirm or deny it.' Technology is traditionally defined as the mechanical art; it is associated with the application of machinery to production. Its origins may be dated to the beginnings of tool-use; its apotheosis is the modern age, which may be dated from the advent of steam power in eighteenth-century England. In these customary terms, technology is a means to an end: it is *instrumental*. Manipulate technology correctly as a means and we will be masters of it. So says the instrumental understanding. But for Heidegger, this account does not come to the *essence* of technology.

He goes a step further and asks: 'What is the instrumental itself?' The instrumental is premised on the ancient idea of causality. Imagine a silver chalice. According to the traditional interpretation, the material cause of the chalice is the silver out of which it is made, its formal cause is its chalicey shape, its final cause is the use appropriate to a chalice, and its efficient cause is the work of the silversmith who makes it. The silversmith is the key cause: he is instrumental in the creation of the chalice. But Heidegger, in a manner utterly characteristic of what he called his deconstruction (*Destruktion*) of Western metaphysics, says exactly the opposite. The primordial meaning – the Being, or, more accurately, the being-there (*Dasein*) – of the chalice is its chaliceness. Its material, its form and its function are all part of that meaning, whereas the work of the silversmith, though instrumental towards it, is detached from it.

In the *Symposium* Plato has Socrates say that there is more than one kind of '*poiesis*', in the true sense of the word. Whenever something is called into existence that was not there before, there is '*poiesis*'. Heidegger thus glosses '*poiesis*' as synonymous with 'bringing-forth into presence':

> It is of utmost importance that we think bringing-forth in its full scope and at the same time in the sense in which the Greeks thought it. Not only handicraft manufacture, not only artistic and poetical bringing into appearance and concrete imagery, is a bringing-forth, *poiesis*. *Physis*, also, the arising of something from out of itself, is a bringing-forth, *poiesis*. *Physis* is indeed *poiesis* in the highest sense. For what presences by means of *physis* has the irruption belonging to bringing-forth, e.g. the bursting of a blossom into bloom, in itself (*en heautoi*). In contrast, what is brought forth by the artisan or the artist, e.g. the silver chalice, has the irruption belonging to the bringing-forth, not in itself, but in another (*en alloi*), in the craftsman or artist.

The work of the craftsman is thus a splitting apart of *poiesis* and *physis*. That is what renders technological making different from the *poiesis* of nature. For Heidegger, 'bringing-forth' is a bringing out of concealment into 'unconcealment'. When a tree brings itself forth into blossom, it unconceals its being as a tree, whereas the unconcealing of the being of a chalice is the work not of the chalice but of the craftsman.

Unconcealment is a 'revealing', for which, according to Heidegger, the Greek word is *aletheia*. That word also means 'truth'. 'The possibility of all productive manufacturing lies in revealing'. Technology is therefore not merely instrumental: it is *a mode of revealing*. It 'comes to presence in the realm where revealing and unconcealment take place, where *aletheia*, truth, happens'.

Technology is a mode of revealing: Heidegger implies that it is one of the distinctively human ways of being-in-the-world. As such, it cannot be avoided and is not to be casually condemned. We have no choice but to be technological beings. But something changed with the scientific revolution and the evolution of the distinctively modern form of technology:

> the revealing that holds sway throughout modern technology does not unfold into a bringing-forth in the sense of *poiesis*. The revealing that rules in modern technology is a challenging [*Herausforden*], which puts to nature the unreasonable demand that it supply energy which can be extracted and stored as such.

A windmill derives energy from the wind, but 'does not unlock energy from the air currents *in order to store it*'. The peasant works with the soil of the field; he does not 'challenge' the earth in the way that land is challenged in the mining of coal or ore, in the way that uranium is challenged to yield atomic energy.

Heidegger took the example of a hydroelectric plant on the River Rhine. It sets the Rhine to supplying energy. Its relationship to the Rhine is different from that of an ancient bridge across the river. The bridge does not affect the being of the river, whereas when the Rhine is dammed up into the power plant the being of the river ceases to be its riverness: 'What the river is now, namely, a water-power supplier, derives from the essence [not of the river, but] of the power station.' Does not the river nevertheless remain a river in a landscape? asks Heidegger. He answers: 'In no other way than as an object on call for inspection by a tour group ordered there by the vacation industry.' According to this argument, it is not a coincidence that picturesque tourism emerged in the eighteenth century, at exactly the same time as modern technology. Modern technology turns all things into what Heidegger calls 'standing-reserve' (*Bestand*). When a mountain is set upon, whether it is made into a mine or a nature reserve, it is converted into standing-reserve. It is then revealed not as a mountain but as a resource for human consumption – which may be tourism's hungry consumption with the eye as much as industry's relentless consumption of matter.

Modern technology is a mode of being which has the potential to convert even humans into standing-reserve:

The forester who measures the felled timber in the woods and who to all appearances walks the forest path in the same way his grandfather did is today ordered by the industry that produces commercial woods, whether he knows it or not. He is made subordinate to the orderability of cellulose, which for its part is challenged forth by the need for paper, which is then delivered to newspapers and illustrated magazines. The latter, in their turn, set public opinion to swallowing what is printed, so that a set configuration of opinion becomes available on demand.

Heidegger's diagnosis here is very similar to that in the leftist tradition embodied by Adorno and Horkheimer, who placed at the centre of their *Dialectic of Enlightenment* a critique of mass media and the 'culture industry'. Herbert Marcuse's account of 'one-dimensional man' and his alienation from nature has the same pedigree.

In Heidegger's theory, when man is driving technology, he does not become standing-reserve. Technological man orders the world, challenges it, 'enframes' it. 'Enframing' (*Ge-stell*) is the essence of modern technology. Enframing means making everything part of a system, thus obliterating the unconcealed being-there of particular things. Enframing is a mode of revealing which produces a styrofoam cup rather than a silver chalice. The chalice's mode of being in the world, its *Dasein*, embraces aesthetic and social traditions – it is shaped so as to be beautiful, it is associated with customs such as sacrificial libations and the sharing of a communal cup. The styrofoam cup has no such associations. Its being is purely instrumental. The styrofoam cup is a symptom of modern technology's forgetting of *Dasein*. 'Above all, enframing conceals that revealing which, in the sense of *poiesis*, lets what presences come forth into appearance ... Enframing blocks the shining-forth and holding sway of truth.' The *techne* of the craftsman, though it was not internal to the *physis* of the chalice, nevertheless revealed the presence, the shining-forth, the truth of the chalice. The enframing of modern technology conceals the truth of things.

Both Plato and Aristotle said that philosophy begins in wonder.

The history of technology is a history of the loss of that wonder, a history of disenchantment. Bruce Foltz explicates Heidegger's version of the story:

> The need that [philosophy's original] astonishment engenders is that entities, emerging of their own accord (*phusei*), must stand in unconcealment. The completion or fulfillment, then, of the necessity arising from this fundamental astonishment lies in *techne*, which keeps in unconcealment the rule of *phusis*. Yet precisely in *techne* as the fulfillment of this fundamental mood lies the danger (*die Gefahr*) of its distraction and ultimately its destruction; that is, there is a possibility that *techne*, originally allowing *phusis* to hold sway in unconcealment, could become detached from the mood of astonishment before entities in their self-emergence and hence become willfull and arbitrary in its independence from *phusis*. It is through such a 'defection from the beginning' that unconcealment could become distorted into correctness, that the 'letting-reign' (*Waltenlassen*) of *phusis* in unconcealment could become a demand for constant presence, that thinking could become metaphysics, and that the *techne* of the Greeks could be utterly transformed into modern technology.

Wonder is a response to a momentary presence, not a constant one. The original *techne* of the Greeks was attuned to the natural unfolding of things. Heidegger claims that the history of metaphysics, from the Christian demand for the constant presence of a transcendent God, to the Cartesian move in which the human subject comes to stand over against (*Gegen-stand*) the realm of objects, inevitably led to modern technology's all-encompassing enframing and the loss of that original *poiesis* in which the *Dasein* of things is unconcealed. This argument seems to have been first articulated by Heidegger in his 1934–5 seminars on Hölderlin's hymns, 'Germany' and 'The Rhine', where he proposed that the original Greek sense of nature was twice 'de-natured' by 'alien powers':

> Once through Christianity, whereby nature was, in the first place, depreciated to [the level of] 'the created,' and at the same time was brought into a relation with super-nature (the

realm of grace). Then [it was denatured] through modern natural science, which dissolved nature into the orbit of the mathematical order of world-commerce, industrialization, and in a particular sense, machine technology.

From here, Heidegger has put himself in the position to reveal what he regards as the true 'danger' of technology:

The threat to man does not come in the first instance from the potentially lethal machines and apparatus of technology. *The actual threat has already afflicted man in his essence.* The rule of enframing threatens man with the possibility that it could be denied to him to enter into a more original revealing and hence to experience the call of a more final truth.

So how may we recover the original revealing and experience the call of the primordial truth of things?

Heidegger's answer is to go back to the original Greek sense of *techne*:

There was a time when it was not technology alone that bore the name *techne*. Once the revealing that brings forth truth into the splendor of radiant appearance was also called *techne*.

There was a time when the bringing-forth of the true into the beautiful was called *techne*. The *poiesis* of the fine arts was also called *techne* . . .

[The poet Hölderlin] says to us:

poetically man dwells on this earth.

The poetical brings the true into the splendor of what Plato in the *Phaedrus* calls *to ekphanestaton*, that which shines forth most purely . . .

Could it be that revealing lays claim to the arts most primally, so that they for their part may expressly foster the growth of the saving power, may awaken and found anew our vision of, and trust in, that which grants?

Because the essence of technology is not technology itself, we must reflect upon *techne* in other realms as well as that of science. We cannot do without technology, not simply for technological reasons, but because it is our mode of being. But it need not be our only mode of being. In his *Discourse on Thinking* of 1955, Heidegger asserted that 'We can say "yes" to the unavoidable use of technological objects, and we can at the same time say "no," in so far as we do not permit them to claim us exclusively and thus to warp, confuse, and finally lay waste to our essence'.

'Revealing lays claim to the arts most primally': poetry is our way of stepping outside the frame of the technological, of reawakening the momentary wonder of unconcealment. For Heidegger, poetry can, quite literally, save the earth. Why poetry more than all the other arts? Because another distinctive feature of the human mode of being is that we are language-animals. For Heidegger, language is the house of being; it is through language that unconcealment takes place for human beings. By disclosing the being of entities in language, the poet lets them be. That is the special, the sacred role of the poet. What is distinctive about the way in which humankind inhabits the earth? It is that we dwell poetically (*dichterisch*).

The later Heidegger returned obsessively to the quotation that he attributed to the German Romantic poet Friedrich Hölderlin (1770–1843): 'poetically man dwells on this earth'. Michael E. Zimmerman explains:

> In a letter of June 4, 1799, Hölderlin wrote: 'the formative and artistic need is a true service that men render to nature.' Nature, in Heidegger's interpretation of Hölderlin, 'needs' humanity. Yet it is nature that first grants the 'open' in which the mortal poet can bring forth the 'saying' to ground the world needed for the historical encounter between gods and mortals, and for the self-disclosure of the earth.

In an affront to the modern way of looking at the world, Heidegger wrests Hölderlin to his own purposes and proposes that the language of poetry, not of science, is that which 'unconceals' the essence of nature.

The key quotation has a curious history. In 1823 a young Tübingen college student called Wilhelm Waiblinger, a passionate admirer of Hölderlin, published a novel entitled *Phaeton*. Its hero was a mad sculptor, a figure clearly based on Hölderlin, who was by this time regarded as insane and confined in a tower in the city wall of Tübingen under the care of a carpenter. The novel reproduces a supposed sample of the mad artist Phaeton's writing, a fragment of prose in the exact style of the later Hölderlin, beginning 'In lieblicher Bläue blühet mit dem metal-lenen Dache der Kirchthurm'. The narrator claims that the lines were originally laid out as verse. Waiblinger's connection with the real mad poet led the scholar Ludwig von Pigenot to recast the fragment in verse and attribute it to Hölderlin himself:

> In lovely blue the steeple blossoms
> With its metal roof. Around which
> Drift swallow cries, around which
> Lies most loving blue.

'In lovely blue' is a poem of simultaneous containment and release. At one level, the deranged mind is contained within the head of the poet, who is contained within his tower, which is surrounded by representatives of the biotic community (the cir-cling swallows), which are themselves contained beneath the blue of the sky. At another level, though, the act of writing takes the poet out of his self, out of his confinement, through windows which are like 'gates to beauty', out to a view of a church steeple and to the living world of birds and trees, things that are 'so simple' yet 'so very holy' that 'one fears to describe them'. The poet then asks:

> May a man look up
> From the utter hardship of his life
> And say: Let me also be
> Like these? Yes. As long as kindness lasts,
> Pure, within his heart, he may gladly measure himself
> Against the divine. Is God unknown?
> Is he manifest as the sky? This I tend
> To believe. Such is man's measure.
> Well deserving, yet poetically
> Man dwells on this earth.

Humankind alone among species has a knowledge of beauty, of kindness and purity, of the divine. We alone say that the sky is lovely and the forest trees are holy. In all this, we are 'well deserving'. But then humankind alone among species also knows those afflictions we call doubt, despair, derangement. Whereas the swallow *is* its biology, our knowledge of mind, our self-consciousness, brings the possibility of alienation from self and from nature. We only know the feeling of at-homeness-upon-the-earth because we also know the feeling of being lost in the world. Poetry is the medium through which Hölderlin – or Hölderlin as ventriloquized by Waiblinger – explores both his connection with, and his dislocation from, the earth.

'Dwells' (German *wohnet*) suggests a sense of belonging. But what is meant by 'yet poetically' (*doch dichterisch*)? A superficial answer might be 'yet linguistically': well deserving (because of his evolutionary superiority), yet as a language animal, man dwells on this earth. 'Dwelling' and 'well deserving' may be regarded as conditions apprehensible only in language. We understand the terms by means of an instant mental comparison with their linguistic opposites ('homelessness' and 'ill deserving'). Yet they may also be conditions which we convince ourselves we can feel pre-linguistically – instinctively, in the guts. This contradictory apprehension brings us directly to the central paradox of poetry. Poetry is merely language. Yet poetry is not merely language, because when we allow it to act upon us it seems able to conjure up conditions such as dwelling and alienation *in their very essence*, not just in their linguistic particulars.

Ludwig von Pigenot's arrangement of the lines into verse is crucial here.

In lovely blue the steeple blossoms with its metal roof.
Around which drift swallow cries, around which lies most
loving blue.

is not the same as

In lovely blue the steeple blossoms
With its metal roof. Around which
Drift swallow cries, around which
Lies most loving blue.

The space on the page, or the pause for breath in the reading, at the end of each line is essential to the difference. Space and pause are poetic, yet they are not linguistic. The white of the page or the second of silence after each 'around which' is an enfolding, like the blue of the sky which enfolds the cries of the swallows. To dwell poetically might mean to enter such spaces and to find that they are not only 'lovely' but 'loving'.

'Is God unknown? / Is he manifest as the sky?' When we feel especially at home or especially lost we may reach for poetry but we may also reach for 'God', a name for both the unknown and what we take to be our deepest knowings. We sometimes think of God as that which is beyond the sky, beyond the boundary of the knowable, but at other times we read his name in the beauty of human deeds and earthly things. Perhaps he may be manifest as – in the form of – the sky itself. To say this is to make a claim for the sacredness of the earth. Perhaps he may be manifest as – in the form of – the poem itself. To say this is to reiterate a very ancient claim for the sacredness of the poetic act. In his essays 'Hölderlin and the Essence of Poetry' and '. . . Poetically Man Dwells . . .', Heidegger began from 'In lieblicher Bläue' and swiftly found himself wrestling with intractable questions of the mortal and the divine, the linguistic and the earthly:

> dwelling occurs only when poetry comes to pass and is present . . . as taking a measure for all measuring. This measure-taking is itself an authentic measure-taking, no mere gauging with ready-made measuring-rods for the making of maps. Nor is poetry building in the sense of raising and fitting buildings. But poetry, as the authentic gauging of the dimension of dwelling, is the primal form of building. Poetry first of all admits man's dwelling into its very nature, its presencing being. Poetry is the original admission of dwelling.

What, then, for Heidegger is dwelling? It is the term he used in his later philosophy for that authentic form of being which he set against what he took to be the false ontologies of Cartesian dualism and subjective idealism. We achieve being not when we represent the world, not in *Vorstellung*, but when we stand in a site, open to its being, when we are thrown or called. The site is then gathered into a whole for which we take on an insistent care (*Besorgung*):

Only if we are capable of dwelling, only then can we build. Let us think for a while of a farmhouse in the Black Forest, which was built some two hundred years ago by the dwelling of peasants. Here the self-sufficiency of the power to let earth and heaven, divinities and mortals enter *in simple oneness* into things, ordered the house.

For Heidegger, poetry is the original admission of dwelling because it is a presencing not a representation, a form of being not of mapping. What he offers us might be described as a post-phenomenological inflection of high Romantic poetics. His late essays are growings from readings in the German Romantic and post-Romantic tradition, readings of Hölderlin, Trakl and Rilke. The contemporary poet whom Heidegger regarded as the true descendant of Hölderlin was Paul Celan, who was himself deeply influenced by Heidegger's theory of the poet's vocation to speak the earth. Further on in this chapter, I will discuss the poem that arose from the meeting of the poet and the thinker.

Heidegger asks us to suppose that the poem is like the peasant farmhouse in the Black Forest: it gathers the fourfold of mortals, gods, earth and heaven into its still site in simple oneness. It orders the house of our lives. By bethinging us, it makes us care for things. It overrides dualism and idealism; it grounds us; it enables us to dwell. In this account, 'earth' is crucially different from 'world': 'world' refers to the historical mode of living, which for modernity means living in an instrumental relationship to the earth. To be attuned to earth is to live in another way, to respect the difference, the 'self-concealing', of entities even as they are 'unconcealed' in poetry. To be so attuned is, for Heidegger, to dwell. 'Mortals dwell in that they save the earth ... Saving the earth does not master the earth and does not subjugate it, which is merely one step from spoliation'. This is in the strictest sense an ecopoetic.

Heidegger's later work should not be thought of as formal philosophy. He himself regarded it as 'thinking' and as thanking. He was especially thankful to the poets from whom he derived his way of thinking and many elements of his distinctive terminology. Foremost among those poets was Rainer Maria Rilke.

In a letter of 13 November 1925 to his Polish translator, Rilke explained his purpose in his masterwork, the *Duino Elegies*. He considered these meditations as responses to the transience of all earthly things. In the face of transience, the poet must undertake the work of transformation. Not, however, Christian transformation towards a Beyond, a spiritual other world. Rather, the aim was to instantiate 'what is *here* seen and touched' into a living whole 'in a purely earthly, deeply earthly, blissfully earthly consciousness'. With this ambition Rilke remains in the mainstream of Romanticism. The language of unification and transformation, the yoking of earth and consciousness, the divinization of the immanent world as against a withdrawal to a transcendent realm: these are all the moves which Wordsworth made in 'Tintern Abbey'.

The enigmatic 'angel' of Rilke's elegies is not a Christian spirit, a harbinger from heaven. The angel is the creature in whom the transformation of the visible into the invisible, of earth into consciousness, is already complete. Potentially, the poet – or perhaps the poem itself – is the angel. The mode of being to which Rilke aspired in poetry was that which he called the 'open' (one of the terms borrowed by Heidegger). The open is akin to Schiller's 'naive', where there is no division between nature and consciousness. In the eighth Duino elegy, this blessed state is enjoyed by a gnat, glimpsed by a child, and recovered in death. From a rational point of view, to aspire to a condition of which the exemplar is a gnat, or for that matter a corpse, must seem profoundly atavistic. But, as in a Romantic meditation on mortality such as Keats's 'To Autumn', the purpose is not to elevate 'naive' modes of being over thoughtful ones, but rather to seek to reconcile the two. Like the Romantics, Rilke is in search of a way of thinking and living which reconciles instrumental rationality with openness to 'the open'. This involves him in the acceptance of finitude and of mortality, but also in a letting-go akin to the experience he underwent in the garden of Schloss Duino in 1912 when, reclining against a tree, he felt himself entered by 'the open'. He seemed to become nature itself, to share his being with tree and singing bird as inner and outer were gathered together into a single 'uninterrupted space'.

For Rilke, precisely because nature is so vulnerable as we are, because the earth shares our provisionality, we must be attuned to nature, we must not 'run down and degrade' all that is here and now. The things of the earth must be our 'familiars', as they were for our ancestors. But the task of reciprocation and transformation has become supremely urgent in the age of technological modernity, for which Rilke's shorthand is 'America':

> And this activity is curiously supported and urged on by the ever more rapid fading away of so much of the visible that will no longer be replaced. Even for our grandparents a 'house', a 'well', a familiar tower, their very clothes, their coat: were infinitely more, infinitely more intimate; almost everything a vessel in which they found the human and added to the store of the human. Now, from America, empty indifferent things are pouring across, sham things, *dummy life* ... A house, in the American sense, an American apple or a grapevine over there, has *nothing* in common with the house, the fruit, the grape into which went the hopes and reflections of our forefathers ... Live things, things lived and conscient of us, are running out and can no longer be replaced. *We are perhaps the last still to have known such things.* On us rests the responsibility not alone of preserving their memory (that would be little and unreliable), but their human and laral value. ('Laral' in the sense of the household gods.) The earth has no way out other than to become invisible: *in* us who with a part of our natures partake of the invisible.

This brings us close to the deep meaning of Heidegger's claim that poets may save the earth. As the solidity of things is replaced by the evanescence of commodities, so the poets must stand in for the ancient Roman *lares*, those everyday gods who guarded hearth and home. On another level, as the realm of nature – the wilderness, the forest, that which is untouched by the human, the Being that is not set upon – has diminished almost to vanishing-point with the march of modernity, of technology and consumerism, so a refuge for nature, for the letting-be of Being, must be found in poetry.

Our grandparents were intimate with house and well. We

move from house to house and our water comes from reservoirs, not wells. That is progress, but it is also alienation. So it is that we need poetry which will haunt us with the lost feeling of what it might have been like to experience the 'laral worth' of house and well. In the ninth Duino elegy, Rilke writes of how 'Things that we might experience are vanishing'. The silver chalice was a vessel to experience and to live with, whereas the styrofoam cup is an object to use and to dispose of – in Rilke's and Heidegger's special sense, that which is mass produced is not a true 'thing'. The task of the poet is to sing of *things*: 'Sag ihm die Dinge', tell him of things, writes Rilke in the ninth elegy. We have been here before with Wordsworth's 'We see into the life of things', with Husserl's *Dingerfahrung*, and Heaney's *Seeing Things*. Poets let being be by speaking it:

> For when the traveler returns from the mountain-slopes into
>   the valley,
> he brings, not a handful of earth, unsayable to others, but
>   instead
> some word he has gained, some pure word, the yellow and
>   blue
> gentian. Perhaps we are *here* in order to say: house,
> bridge, fountain, gate, pitcher, fruit-tree, window, –
> at most: column, tower? . . . but to *say* them, you must
>   understand,
> oh to say them *more* intensely than the Things themselves
> ever dreamed of existing.

Gentian, house, pitcher and fruit-tree do not know their own being. For Rilke and Heidegger, earth 'apparently needs us' and 'in some strange way / keeps calling to us': things need us so that they can be named. But in reciprocation we must return from our experience of things, from Rilke's mountain, content with word and wonder. We must not set upon the earth – or each other – with ambitions of conquest and mastery. Perhaps that is why the ninth elegy hesitates over column and tower. Rilke himself was a wanderer and an exile. Born in Prague, he moved across Europe and watched the pillars of the Austro-Hungarian empire collapse. His attunement to earth was not synonymous with love of fatherland. He could embrace the being of trees because he had no roots of his own. With Heidegger, it was a different story.

*

The poet's way of articulating the relationship between human-kind and environment, person and place, is peculiar because it is experiential, not descriptive. Whereas the biologist, the geographer and the Green activist have *narratives* of dwelling, a poem may be a *revelation* of dwelling. Such a claim is phenomenological before it is political, and for this reason ecopoetics may properly be regarded as pre-political. Politics, let us remember, means 'of the *polis*', of the city. For this reason, the controlling myth of ecopoetics is a myth of the pre-political, the prehistoric: it is a Rousseauesque story about imagining a state of nature prior to the fall into property, into inequality and into the city.

But advanced Westerners are perforce of the *polis*. We live after the fall, in a world where no act of reading can be independent of the historical conditions in which it is undertaken. It is therefore not surprising that ecocriticism should have emerged at a time of ecological crisis; it is to be expected that those who practise this kind of reading should be sympathetic to some form of Green politics. Marxist, feminist and multiculturalist critics bring explicit or implicit political manifestos to the texts about which they write. They regard their work as contributing towards social change. Green critics have a difficulty in this respect: it would be quixotic to suppose that a work of literary criticism might be an appropriate place in which to spell out a practical programme for better environmental management. That is why ecopoetics should begin not as a set of assumptions or proposals about particular environmental issues, but as a way of reflecting upon what it might mean to dwell with the earth. Ecopoetics must concern itself with consciousness. When it comes to practice, we have to speak in other discourses.

The dilemma of Green reading is that it must, yet it cannot, separate ecopoetics from ecopolitics. In exploring this problem, the hardest case makes the best law. It is the case of Martin Heidegger himself.

So what is the problem? Bachelard writes in *The Poetics of*

Space: 'In the domain of poetic phenomenology under consideration, there is one adjective of which a metaphysician of the imagination must beware, and that is, the adjective *ancestral*.'

Begin by reflecting upon Heidegger's Black Forest peasant. What words might we hear in that reflection? Perhaps: blood, soil, *Volk*, belonging, fatherland, Germany, Reich. Crudely we may say: it's all very well for the Black Forest peasant dwelling in his farmhouse, but if proper living means dwelling, means remaining in one's own native region, what do we do with aliens, with those who migrate, who have no home, no fatherland? What, we might ask, Dr Heidegger, Nazi-approved Rector of Freiburg University, would you have had done with, say, gypsies and Jews? In books on Richard Walther Darré, advocate of organic farming and agricultural minister to Adolf Hitler, and on the broad political history of ecological thinking in the twentieth century, Anna Bramwell has demonstrated that the connections between deep ecology and fascism have been anything but accidental. At the centre of Luc Ferry's assault on *The New Ecological Order* is an alarming chapter called 'Nazi Ecology', which proposes that Hitler was the greenest political leader of the modern era. One might invoke Gandhi in immediate response to this claim, but what cannot be gainsaid is that disturbing connections between ecologism and extreme right-wing politics may be traced well back into the nineteenth century: to Social Darwinism, to Ernst Haeckel (the originator of the word 'ecology'), to the co-presence in the later work of John Ruskin of a prescient ecological awareness and an atavistic neo-feudalism.

Scientific ecology attempts a systematic explanation, on Darwinian principles, of 'the question concerning dwelling'. Political ecology attempts to translate the conclusions of scientific ecology into a set of principles and practices for human action. That both the considered anarchism of Peter Kropotkin, mentioned in chapter two, and the organic fascism of Darré, revealed by Bramwell, may be derived from ecological principles demonstrates that the path from scientific to political ecology is crooked and rocky. Green has no place in the traditional political spectrum which runs from Fascist Black to Conservative Blue to Labour Pink to Marxist Red. Nature is so various that no consistent political principles can be derived from it. Of course they cannot. To describe an ecosystem, you have to stand imaginatively outside it, you cannot be simply ('naturally', 'unthinkingly') dwelling within it. Concordantly, the very conception of a 'politics of nature' is self-contradictory: politics is what you get when you fall from nature. That is the point of Rousseau's second *Discourse*.

In an earlier chapter I quoted Lord Byron's exasperated remark about Leigh Hunt's poetical systematizing: 'When a man talks of system, his case is hopeless'. When ecopoetics is translated into political system, its case, too, is hopeless. It may become fascism (Darré), or romantic neofeudalism (Ruskin), or utopian socialism (William Morris, Murray Bookchin), or philosophical anarchism (William Godwin, Peter Kropotkin). Whatever it becomes, it ceases to be ecopoetics.

Histories, theories, political systems are all *enframings*. They treat their raw material as 'standing reserve'. The Rhine is enframed when it is dammed up into a power plant; then it becomes not 'The Rhine' as uttered by the art-work in Hölderlin's hymn of that name, but rather a standing reserve for the production of electricity. A poem is enframed when it becomes not an original admission of dwelling, but rather a cog in the wheel of a historical or theoretical system. To read ecopoetically is, by contrast, to find 'clearings' or 'unconcealments'. In the activity of *poiesis*, things disclose or unconceal themselves. For Heidegger, 'Wherever man opens his eyes and ears, unlocks his heart, and gives himself over to meditating and striving, shaping and working, entreating and thanking, he finds himself everywhere already brought into the unconcealed.' Ecopoetics seeks not to enframe literary texts, but to meditate upon them, to thank them, to listen to them, albeit to ask questions of them.

The question concerning Martin Heidegger: is the relationship between the Nazism which he never renounced and the theory of dwelling which he developed in his late essays contingent or necessary? The question has been addressed with great historical and philosophical cogency by a succession of Heidegger's critics, beginning from Adorno in his *Jargon of Authenticity*. It has by now been demonstrated conclusively that Heidegger was initially attracted to Nazism principally because he saw its apparent rootedness in the soil of Germany as the only viable alternative to what he regarded as the dehumanization wrought by American technology on the one hand and Soviet mass industrialization on the other.

The ecopoetic response to the question cannot, however, be a historical and social, or even logical, analysis of the problem. All such analyses are enframings. Ecopoetics renounces the mastery of enframing knowledge and listens instead to the voice of art. In this dark case, though, it would be evasive to hear a poem by an English or American writer. An honest address requires a German-Jewish voice.

Paul Celan's parents both died, his mother shot in the neck, in a Nazi internment camp in Transnistria. His 'Death Fugue' – 'death is a master from Germany his eyes are blue' – has become the quintessential Holocaust poem. Celan knew of Heidegger's complicity with the Master and yet he remained compelled by his philosophy and in particular his poetic of dwelling. In 1967, he visited the philosopher in his Black Forest home. Robert Altmann, a publishing friend of the poet's, reports that Celan's intention was to ask and to press upon (*'de poser et d'imposer'*) the philosopher the question of his position with regard to his pronouncements during the Nazi era. But the question seems to have gone unanswered: as far as we know, Heidegger kept his habitual silence on the matter. Celan, however, wrote a poem about the visit. Its title is 'Todtnauberg', the place-name widely recognized in intellectual circles as a synecdoche for the reclusive philosopher's rootedness (*Bodenständigkeit*) in the Black Forest. The title announces that the theme is to be Heidegger and the place of dwelling. Perhaps in its first three letters – 'Tod' – it also announces the presence of death, the blue-eyed master from Germany.

TODTNAUBERG

Arnica, eyebright, the
draft from the well with the
starred die above it,

in the
hut,

> the line
> – whose name did the book
> register before mine? –,
> the line inscribed
> in that book about
> a hope, today,
> of a thinking man's
> coming
> word
> in the heart,
>
> woodland sward, unlevelled,
> orchid and orchid, single,
>
> coarse stuff, later, clear,
> in passing,
>
> he who drives us, the man,
> who listens in,
>
> the half-
> trodden wretched
> tracks through the high moors,
>
> dampness,
> much.

The word arnica is used not only for the plant of that name but also for the medicinal tincture prepared from it that is especially valuable in the treatment of bruises. Eyebright, otherwise known as euphrasy, is a traditional remedy for weak eyes. The draft from the well suggests purifying water. The opening images, then, have connotations of healing, of the possibility of some soothing of the bruise of the Holocaust. In Nazi Germany Jews were forced to wear a star that was yellow, the colour of arnica; to Celan's eyes, the yellow star over Heidegger's well calls for some recognition on the philosopher's part of his short-sightedness back in the 1930s. If the blue-eyed master were to acknowledge his need for euphrasy, the fresh water of the well might make some atonement for the black milk of the death camps.

Once inside the house (or rather, the 'hut' which announces

itself as primitive, rooted like a forest peasant's dwelling), the poet inscribes in the visitors' book of the philosopher the hope that his host might find in his heart some word of penitence or sorrow. But no reply is forthcoming. The poem does not report a dialogue; it is itself a monologue. Heidegger is absent. The only voice is that of the poet, the only other human presence is that of the chauffeur who – like the reader – listens in, but is not granted any explicitly articulated knowledge.

The only source of insight is the change in environment. The poem begins with plants of hope and with clear water. After the writing in the book, it moves to plants which thrive in dank places, to woodland darkness, the bleakness of the high moors, 'dampness, / much.' The central metaphor of Heidegger's later philosophy is a path through a wood (*Holzwege*) to a clearing (*Lichtung*) in which truth is unconcealed (*a-letheia*). But the road which 'Todtnauberg' takes leads only into the darkness.

Heidegger gains his sense of identity from his forest dwelling-place, whereas Celan, the archetypal Wandering Jew, finds no home. The poet himself said that his place of origin was not to be found on any map. The only place from which he was not estranged was the place of *poiesis*. In this poem, his identity is asserted through an act of writing (though even here there is a displacement, since the name written in the book would have been 'Celan', not his inherited surname 'Ancel'). 'The Jew and nature', Celan wrote in his 'Conversation in the Mountains', 'are strangers to each other'. For Celan, 'What is earthy and material is language, not ground; what is cultivated is text not crops.'

Is this, then, to propose that the only possible response to the evil wrought by ideology is pure textualism, a hermetic sealing of the self in the world of language? Paul de Man's swerve from youthful Nazi fellow-travelling to mature linguistic deconstruction steals to mind. But this is not Celan's way. It is not, because of the orchids. Celan's writing is always marked by botanical exactitude, suggesting he was not such a stranger to nature as the 'Conversation in the Mountains' claims. Heidegger told Hans-Georg Gadamer 'that in the Black Forest, Celan was better informed on plants and animals than he himself was'. Orchids are frequently epiphytic – they grow upon other plants – whereas

Celan's are 'single'. In the world of the text, Celan has had no choice but to be parasitic: he has written in the book of the host in the language of the host. He is a *German* poet. But the single orchids demonstrate that organisms – and thus by extension human beings – can have an individual, free identity. Orchids are also characterized by the strangeness of the shapes and colours of their flowers: strangeness in the sense not of estrangement but of distinctiveness. They are singular, to be valued exactly because they are different from normative flora; they are testimony to that biodiversity upon which the survival of ecosystems depends.

Heidegger made an appalling error of judgement when in the 1950s he compared the mechanization of modern agriculture – battery farming and so forth – to the mechanization of mass extermination in the Nazi death camps. Coming from a former member of the Nazi party, the comparison served only to give the impression of a Heidegger who still refused to grasp the unique evil of the Holocaust. But when Celan, a Jew and a child of the camps, writes of the orchid he invites us to reflect on the sacredness of many diverse forms of life. He permits the comparison which says: without Jews the human race would have been diminished, without orchids the earth would be diminished.

Heidegger's poetics mattered to Celan because they proposed that the poet can unconceal the being of things, can reveal the essential orchidness of an orchid. The *poet* more than anyone else, because our distinctive being – our *Dasein* – is in language, and the poet is the guardian, the treasurer, the primary maker of language. The *Dasein* of the orchid is unconcealed in the *Dasein* of the poem, even after the visit to Todtnauberg offers no enlightenment on the question of Nazism. The very poem which tells of how the thinking man did not offer a word from the heart retains its allegiance to Heideggerian thinking in the directness with which it speaks a language of earth: arnica, eyebright, orchid and orchid.

Celan found no earth with which he could dwell. Just over two years after the poem was published, he threw himself to his own death by water. But the orchids which he saw on his journey away from the hut, which he memorialized in the poem, and which we imaginatively reanimate when we read the poem, effected for him and may effect for us an unconcealment. The distinction between the epiphytic and the singular is only one of many possible unfoldings of their presence in the poem. Celan's kind of poetry opens itself to many readings. It does not admit solution or fixed interpretation. What matters is not the conclusion which we draw about the orchid but the fact that we are made to attend to the orchid. The poem makes us ask the question concerning the orchid, the question concerning the earth. And that in itself is enough of a beginning. In Rilke's ninth Duino elegy, the wanderer does not bring a handful of earth from the mountain to the valley, 'but instead / some word he has gained, some pure word, the yellow and blue / gentian'. Celan brought back from the forest neither a word from Heidegger's heart nor a handful of orchids. But he won the word 'orchid', as Rilke prized the word 'gentian'.

*

There is no philosopher more self-consciously German than Heidegger in his Black Forest hut. There are few poets who have so frequently been regarded as 'English' as the Anglo-Welsh Edward Thomas. Thomas died in the first Great War against Germany; Heidegger's allegiance to Germany in the second war is notorious. And yet it seems to me that the work of Thomas calls to be read through Heidegger's ecological poetics.

HOME

Often I had gone this way before:
But now it seemed I never could be
And never had been anywhere else;
'Twas home; one nationality
We had, I and the birds that sang,
One memory.

They welcomed me. I had come back
That eve somehow from somewhere far:
The April mist, the chill, the calm,
Meant the same thing familiar
And pleasant to us, and strange too,
Yet with no bar.

The thrush on the oak top in the lane
Sang his last song, or last but one;
And as he ended, on the elm
Another had but just begun
His last; they knew no more than I
The day was done.

Then past his dark white cottage front
A labourer went along, his tread
Slow, half with weariness half with ease;
And, through the silence, from his shed
The sound of sawing rounded all
That silence said.

A home is a house in which one does not live but dwell. It is a place to which one comes; on arriving one knows that one has always been travelling there and that one can rest. Home is the place from where Coleridge's Ancient Mariner is estranged: 'In his loneliness and fixedness he yearneth towards the journeying Moon, and the stars that still sojourn, yet still move onward; and every where the blue sky belongs to them, and is their appointed rest, and their native country, and their own natural homes, which they enter unannounced, as lords that are certainly expected and yet there is a silent joy at their arrival.' Home and dwelling matter to humans because we also know homelessness and alienation. Other species dwell perpetually, are always at home in their ecosystem, their territory; those which migrate do not, as far as we are aware, have any consciousness of estrangement from their other home.

The poem quoted above is the second which Thomas called 'Home'. The first to which he gave this title is about the difficulty of finding home. Brought up in London and proud of his Welsh familial origins, Thomas never quite felt at home in the southern English countryside he grew to love. 'Home [1]' is a poem of restlessness. It looks to past and future, to then and now, to there and here, to going back – but 'I cannot go back, / And would not if I could' – and looking forward. Home may be nowhere save Hamlet's undiscovered country found only in the hereafter: 'That land, / My home, I have never seen; / No traveller tells of it, /

However far he has been'. Thomas can only write a poem of dwelling, such as 'Home [2]', because so many of his poems are about not-dwelling, about roads rather than homes ('I love roads', begins one of his key poems, 'Roads'), about going out in the dark and not in to the rest that seems 'the sweetest thing under a roof' ('The Owl').

'But now it seemed I never could be / And never had been anywhere else': the verb 'to be' takes on a full, a Heideggerian, weight here. Home is the place of authentic being. The birds welcome the poet; they and he have one memory. The April mist welcomes him: he is gathered into the place. His house is ordered because he has entered into the simple oneness of things. There is 'no bar' between the mind and nature, the self and the environment. The voice of the poem is a hearing as well as a speaking; the song is passed from thrush to thrush. 'They knew no more than I / the day was done': the negative form of the statement, very characteristic of Thomas's style, is a way of making the knowledge an acceptance, not a striving. The rhythms of the sky seem to be known naturally, not quested for: 'Mortals dwell in that they receive the sky as sky. They leave to the sun and the moon their journey, to the stars their courses, to the seasons their blessing and their inclemency; they do not turn night into day nor day into a harassed unrest.'

Both dark and white, the cottage is a dwelling not a house. The labourer's work has made him weary, but given him ease. We may say, as Heidegger does of the Black Forest peasant's home, 'A craft which, itself sprung from dwelling, still uses its tools and frames as things, built the farmhouse'. The wood sawn in the shed will be crafted well.

What kind of sawing is this? Humans must build to live; they must saw wood for their houses, chop it for their fires. Organic matter must be consumed, destroyed. But humans who dwell take only from their own locality; they know that if they uproot, they must also plant. 'The sound of sawing' is not that of a sawmill, of mass consumption and destruction, of the formless formation of advanced technology interposing itself. The silence speaks of the oneness into which the poem, the home, is gathered; that silence is not broken but 'rounded' by the sawing. The sawing is thus the same order of sound as the birdsong. 'Sawing' is also a word for thrush song; and a thrush, like a labourer, takes wood to make its dwelling.

The quiet voice of Edward Thomas does not elicit political shivers of the order of those that may be inspired by Heidegger's Black Forest musings. But nagging doubts remain. To have the same memory as the birds sounds good, but 'one nationality / We had, I and the birds that sang' seems wrong. Dwelling with the species of a place is not synonymous with belonging to a nation. As a poet of Anglo-Welsh origin, of country/city migration and of mobile class sympathy – children sent to liberal middle-class Bedales, but sympathy with 'Dad' Uzzell the poacher – Thomas negotiated his nationhood tentatively. His uniquely diffident war poetry is our gift from that negotiation, as in, for example, the third of his poems entitled 'Home', where the soldier's home-sickness is the means of meditating upon questions of belonging. But 'nationality' grates in 'Home [2]' because the thrush cannot speak for all of England, let alone Britain. Thomas is at his best when he is at his most provincial: the birds of Oxfordshire and Gloucestershire in 'Adlestrop' are heard in a regional circle; they do not sing of the nation. It may be that 'nationality' in 'Home' is best understood as an appropriation of the term, a deliberate distancing from the associations of flags and identity documents: to share a nationality with the thrushes is to declare allegiance to the species of a biologically demarcated region, not the institutions of a politically constituted state.

The poetry of dwelling may at first seem to lead naturally to Burkean conservatism. The word *conservation* is not irrelevant here. What strikes one about the vignette in Thomas's 'Home' is its immemorial quality. Such evenings, such birdsong, such returning labourers, seem to have always been there. It could be the eclogue-world of Theocritus or Virgil; it could be Gray's *Elegy*; it could be now and (diminishing parts of) England. The National Trust for Places of Historic Interest and Natural Beauty has been quite cunning in harnessing itself to the heritage indus-try as a way of furthering its conservationist aims. The way to save the earth for the future, the proposition goes, is to remind us that it is our inheritance from the past. The argument at the core of Burke's *Reflections on the Revolution in France* asks to be quoted at length:

> This policy appears to me to be the result of profound reflection; or rather the happy effect of following nature, which is wisdom without reflection, and above it. A spirit of innovation is generally the result of a selfish temper and confined views. People will not look forward to posterity, who never look backward to their ancestors. Besides, the people of England well know, that the idea of inheritance furnishes a sure principle of conservation, and a sure principle of transmission ... By a constitutional policy, working after the pattern of nature, we receive, we hold, we transmit our government and our privileges, in the same manner in which we enjoy and transmit our property and our lives. The institutions of policy, the goods of fortune, the gifts of Providence, are handed down, to us and from us, in the same course and order. Our political system is placed in a just correspondence and symmetry with the order of the world, and with the mode of existence decreed to a permanent body of transient parts; wherein, by the disposition of a stupendous wisdom, moulding together the great mysterious incorporation of the human race, the whole, at one time, is never old, or middle-aged, or young, but in a condition of unchangeable constancy, moves on through the varied tenour of perpetual decay, fall, renovation, and progression. Thus by preserving the method of nature in the conduct of the state, in what we improve we are never wholly new; in what we retain we are never wholly obsolete. By adhering in this manner and on those principles to our forefathers, we are guided not by the superstition of antiquarians, but by the spirit of philosophic analogy. In this choice of inheritance we have given to our frame of polity the image of a relation in blood; binding up the constitution of our country with our dearest domestic ties; adopting our fundamental laws into the bosom of our family affections; keeping inseparable, and cherishing with the warmth of all their combined and mutually reflected charities, our state, our hearths, our sepulchres, and our altars.

The 'philosophic analogy' according to which this argument works is Heideggerian in so far as it is anti-Enlightenment. For the Burke of 1790, the Enlightenment elevation of reason led to the framing of innovative constitutions which answered to the systems of the human mind and not the truth of nature. True wisdom is a kind of wise passiveness, a following of nature broadly akin to Heideggerian openness to being. Where Burke differs most signally from Heidegger is in the directness of his move from his perception of the order of nature to his ideal for the order of the state. Like Volney's contemporaneous *Ruins, or Meditation on the Revolutions of Empires*, but from the opposing end of the ideological spectrum, the *Reflections* translate into the realm of politics and history the language of the new geology of the late eighteenth century which was suggesting that the earth 'moves on through the varied tenour of perpetual decay, fall, renovation, and progression'. Where Volney linked geological catastrophe theory to revolution, Burke used the earth's perpetual decay and renovation as an argument for an evolutionary conduct of state affairs.

Yet once again we see the contradictions of an ordering of constitutions according to the order of nature. Historically, such an ordering has been a principal bulwark of hierarchical societies and conservative ideologies. From the *Politics* of Aristotle to the Tudor conception of 'degree' to Burke, the argument from nature has been used to support a model of society as a pyramid. But the argument has always been highly selective: a patriarchal image of the family – which comes across very strongly in Burke's invocation of the domestic – has been grounded in observation of male dominance in other species, whereas the hierarchical structure of the bee community has been used to support monarchy, not matriarchy. Arguments which seek in 'the pattern of nature' a 'just correspondence and symmetry with the order of the world' have a way of neglecting those asymmetries whereby nature's order does not correspond to the political order to which the arguer owes allegiance.

At the centre of Burke's argument is the view that 'we receive, we hold, we transmit our government and our privileges, in the same manner in which we enjoy and transmit our property and our lives'. That government should be transmitted as life is transmitted makes good evolutionary sense: our communities survive in the same way that organisms survive, the individual decaying and dying, the species regenerating and perpetuating. But Burke smuggles another element into his analogy from nature: 'we enjoy and transmit *our property* and our lives'. In Burke's time, property-owning was the prerogative of the elite; to 'transmit our property' means to maintain a system in which ownership of the land is confined to the rich, who pass their holdings from father to son and consolidate their proprietorial power through the assignment of marriage-portions. It was, of course, this unequal system which was threatened by the French Revolution.

There is no such thing in nature as what Thoreau in the section of *Walden* entitled 'Shelter' calls 'superfluous property'. The savage has his shelter, writes Thoreau, the birds their nests and the foxes their holes, but 'in modern civilized society not more than half the families own a shelter'. 'Civilization' creates laws which prevent the 'natural' process whereby shelter superfluous to the necessities of one individual animal or animal-family is swiftly occupied by others. Under the law of civilization, the few have large houses with many spare rooms, while the poor huddle together in one room or none. In the natural world, different species fight for territory between each other and among themselves, but each must share its ecosystem with other species. The whole thrust of the *Reflections* is a defence of the exclusive property rights of the wealthy. Burke's argument from nature ultimately boils down to an apology for 'the natural landed interest'. But a landed interest is not *natural*: ecosystems thrive on competition, but they do not have interests and inheritances in Burke's sense. Burke's great philosophical opposite, Rousseau, may have been nearer the truth on this matter, with his argument in the *Discourse on the Origin of Inequality* that the innovation of property marked the exact moment at which humankind ceased to live according to the economy of nature.

For Thoreau, property-ownership was not a right but an encumbrance. To inhabit is not to possess. Dwelling is not owning; you may legally own a house without it being a home;

you may find a dwelling-place which you do not legally own. Think back to John Clare: his legal relationship to the cottage in Helpston and that in Northborough was the same (tenancy), but the first was a home and the second was not. Think back to Thomas's labourer: his cottage would surely have been a tied one, not a freehold. The deed of title which is constituted by a poem of dwelling is not a legal document. Poets who find their home in a specific environment have an imaginative, not a proprietorial, interest in belonging. The ecopoetic vision is inclusive, not exclusionary.

In this chapter we have glanced at a rural landscape beyond the window of Hölderlin's tower, and we have read two poems about simple dwelling-places. The purpose has not been to propose that we should all try to find ourselves a remote tower like that of William Butler Yeats in the west of Ireland, a secluded hut like Heidegger's in the Black Forest or a snug homestead like that of Edward Thomas's agricultural labourer under the English Downs. The point is rather to reflect on the relationship with earthly things that is turned into language by the poetry of dwelling. Heidegger used a village cabinetmaker as an exemplar of dwelling, contrasting the craftsman's connectedness to wood with the disconnection of the factory-worker from the materials with which he works. I have contrasted Thomas's labourer sawing in his shed to the mass production of sawmills. 'The cabinet-maker's craft was chosen as an example,' writes Heidegger, 'and it was presupposed thereby that it would not occur to anyone that through the choice of this example is the expectation announced that the condition of our planet could in the foreseeable future, or indeed ever, be changed back into a rustic idyll.' Ecopoetry does not exist for the benefit of cabinetmakers and agricultural labourers; it exists, at the expense of wood, for those of us who do not know wood. The response it asks us to share is not that of the hand-worker but that of the imagination-worker, the poet – the response of Celan, of Thomas.

The poem is a clearing in that it is an opening to the nature of being, a making clear of the nature of dwelling. But such a clearing can only be achieved through a dividing and a destroying. The point of Edward Thomas's poem is that the labourer may be like the thrush, but the poet knows that he is not. He is called 'home' because he knows himself to be an outsider. When we hear the poem properly, so that even the silence speaks, we participate in the gathering. But when we reflect upon the poem, when (as I have done here) we interpret it rather than dwell in it, we cannot escape a Cartesian dualism. The experience evoked by the poem is that of feeling at home, being gathered into oneness with the surrounding environment. But the experience itself is what Shelley in the 'Defence of Poetry' called an evanescent visitation of thought and feeling, its footsteps 'like those of a wind over a sea, which the coming calm erases, and whose traces remain only as on the wrinkled sand which paves it'.

Thomas attempts to erase that erasure in his notebook entry of 12 April 1915: 'Evening of misty stillness after drizzly day – last thrushes on oaks – then man goes by a dark white cottage front to thatched wood lodge and presently began sawing and birds were all still'. He then attempts to reanimate and disseminate the experience in the poem. But the material process of dissemination effects clearings of its own. It can only occur through technology: the manufacture of paper and print, the commerce and consumerism which make the sale and reading of poetry possible. And the reanimation is displaced from its geographic origin in deep England. The primary experience belongs to Steep in Hampshire, a few miles down the road from Gilbert White's Selborne and Jane Austen's Chawton; the reanimation occurs in the human mind, the environment of the imagination.

The poetic articulates both presence and absence: it is both the imaginary recreation and the trace on the sand which is all that remains of the wind itself. The poetic is ontologically double because it may be thought of as ecological in two senses: it is either (both?) a language (*logos*) that restores us to our home (*oikos*) or (and?) a melancholy recognizing that our only home (*oikos*) is language (*logos*). In the closing words of Robert Harrison's *Forests*, a book that thinks hauntingly about wood, about the earth and about what poets are for:

Precisely because finitude is given over to us in language, we lose the instinctive knowledge of dying. Nature knows how to die, but human beings know mostly how to kill as a way of failing to become their ecology. Because we alone inhabit the *logos*, we alone must learn the lesson of dying time and time again. Yet we alone fail in the learning. And in the final analysis only this much seems certain: that when we do not speak our death to the world we speak death to the world. And when we speak death to the world, the forest's legend falls silent.

*

What are poets for in our brave new millennium? Could it be to remind the next few generations that it is we who have the power to determine whether the earth will sing or be silent? As earth's own poetry, symbolized for Keats in the grasshopper and the cricket, is drowned ever deeper – not merely by bulldozers in the forest, but more insidiously by the ubiquitous susurrus of cyberspace – so there will be an ever greater need to retain a place in culture, in the work of human imagining, for the song that names the earth.

Reader, allow me a final test of whether you believe in eco-poetics, whether you are willing to hear the voice of Ariel. Consider the following lines of Wallace Stevens and ask yourself whether you can accept that a poem is not only a making of the self and a making of the world, but also a response to the world and a respecting of the earth. As you read the poem, hold in your mind's eye a photograph of the earth taken from space: green and blue, smudged with the motion of cloud (of weather), so small in the surrounding darkness that you could imagine cupping it in your hands. A planet that is fragile, a planet of which we are a part but which we do not possess.

THE PLANET ON THE TABLE

Ariel was glad he had written his poems.
They were of a remembered time
Or of something seen that he liked.

Other makings of the sun
Were waste and welter
And the ripe shrub writhed.

His self and the sun were one
And his poems, although makings of his self,
Were no less makings of the sun.

It was not important that they survive.
What mattered was that they should bear
Some lineament or character,

Some affluence, if only half-perceived,
In the poverty of their words,
Of the planet of which they were part.

If mortals dwell in that they save the earth and if poetry is the original admission of dwelling, then poetry is the place where we save the earth.

Notes

page 2 'the years, the years': Hardy, 'During Wind and Rain', in *Moments of Vision* (1917).

5 'The considerable slope': *Emma*, published 1816, vol. 3, chap. 6.

6 'revert to wildwood': See Oliver Rackham, *The History of the Countryside* (1986; repr. London: Phoenix, 1997), p. 328.

6 'Going, Going . . . in 1972': A version was included in *How do you want to live?*, published that year by Her Majesty's Stationery Office. I quote the poem from Larkin's *High Windows* (London and Boston: Faber and Faber, 1974).

6 'ninety-seven per cent . . . gone': See Graham Harvey, *The Killing of the Countryside* (1997; repr. London: Vintage, 1998), p. 12.

7 'Raymond Williams': *The Country and the City* (1973; repr. London: Paladin, 1975), p. 135.

7 'a resident *native* gentry': Cobbett, *Rural Rides*, 'From Gloucester to Kensington', Burghclere, Wednesday 21 November 1821.

8 'The family of Dashwood': *Sense and Sensibility*, published 1811, vol. 1, chap. 1.

8–9 'The inclosure of Norland Common': vol. 2, chap. 11.

9 'nothing more than a room': Miles Hadfield, *A History of British Gardening* (1960; repr. Harmondsworth: Penguin, 1985), pp. 142–3.

10 'Who loves a garden': *The Task* (1785), book 3, 'The Garden', lines 565–87.

11 'work of landscape gardening': For a fine detailed treatment of this topic in Austen's novels, see Alistair M. Duckworth, *The Improvement of the Estate* (Baltimore and London: Johns Hopkins University Press, 1971, repr. 1994).

11 'The lake in front': *The Task*, 3. 773–4.

11 'Mansions once': *The Task*, 3. 745–7.

11 'Estates are landscaped': *The Task*, 3. 754–5.

11 'the ancestor of the Maypole': Richard Mabey, *Flora Britannica* (London: Sinclair-Stevenson, 1996), p. 209.

12 'Cut down an avenue!': *Mansfield Park*, published 1814, vol. 1, chap. 6, quoting *The Task*, 1. 338.

12 'the passions of men': Wordsworth, preface to *Lyrical Ballads* (1800).

13 'Novels of Character and Environment': The group includes *Under the Greenwood Tree* (1872), *Far from the Madding Crowd* (1874), *The Return of the Native* (1878), *The Mayor of Casterbridge* (1886), *The Woodlanders* (1887), *Wessex Tales* (1888), *Tess of the d'Urbervilles* (1891), *Life's Little Ironies* (1894), and *Jude the Obscure* (1896).

13 'The set of circumstances': *New Shorter Oxford English Dictionary*, ed. Lesley Brown (Oxford: Clarendon Press, 1993), sense 2. There had been an old, early seventeenth century, sense – 'being environed, encircled' – which was obsolete by Johnson's time.

14 'God made the country': *The Task*, 1. 749.

14 'thinkers who had most influenced him': See Gillian Beer, *Darwin's Plots: Evolutionary Narrative in Darwin, George Eliot and Nineteenth-Century Fiction* (London: Routledge and Kegan Paul, 1983, repr. 1985), p. 287. For the influence of Darwin on Hardy's novels, see chap. 8 of Beer's book, and also Perry Meisel, *Thomas Hardy: The Return of the Repressed* (New Haven and London: Yale University Press, 1972).

15 'suggestion of orchards': *The Woodlanders* (1887), chap. 5.

15–16 'They had a good crop': *Woodlanders*, chap. 6.

16 'It was true': *Woodlanders*, chap. 6.

17 'like a tropical plant': *Woodlanders*, chap. 6.

17 'He had a marvellous power': *Woodlanders*, chap. 8.

17 'the tongue of the trees': *Woodlanders*, chap. 44.

18 'coterminous with the margin': *Woodlanders*, chap. 19.

18 'know all about those': *Woodlanders*, chap. 17.

21 'Many teachers of English': Leavis and Thompson, *Culture and Environment: The Training of Critical Awareness* (London: Chatto and Windus, 1933), p. 1.

21 'The industrial England': Lawrence, *Lady Chatterley's Lover* (1928), chap. 11, quoted in Leavis and Thompson, p. 95.

23 'acknowledge that recognition of the crisis': Williams, *The Country and the City*, pp. 361–2.

23 'Wordsworth . . . network of National Parks': see chapter two of my *Romantic Ecology: Wordsworth and the Environmental Tradition* (London and New York: Routledge, 1991).

25 'Where indeed shall we go': Williams, *The Country and the City*, p. 21.

26 'Upended man': Ted Hughes, *Tales from Ovid: Twenty-four Passages from the 'Metamorphoses'* (London: Faber and Faber, 1997), p. 8.

28 'Moreover, with this model': this, and preceding quotations, from Hughes, 'The Environmental Revolution', repr. in his *Winter Pollen:*

Occasional Prose, ed. William Scammell (London and Boston: Faber and Faber, 1994), pp. 128–35.

28 'And the first age was Gold': *Tales from Ovid*, p. 10.

29 'The inward ear': *Tales from Ovid*, p. 12.

30 'pinpoint the moment': Rousseau, *Discourse on the Origin of Inequality*, trans. Franklin Philip (Oxford: Oxford University Press, The World's Classics, 1994), pp. 23–4. All quotations are from this translation.

31 'no longer exists . . . in order to judge': *Discourse*, p. 15.

31 'I shall, as it were': *Discourse*, p. 25.

31–2 'his protest is directed': Starobinksi, *Jean-Jacques Rousseau: Transparency and Obstruction*, trans. Arthur Goldhammer (Chicago: University of Chicago Press, 1988), p. 23.

32 'We are born with the use': Rousseau, *Emile or on Education*, trans. Allan Bloom (New York: Basic Books, 1979, repr. London: Penguin, 1991), p. 39. My following quotation is from the next paragraph.

33 'The creative and regulative': *New Shorter Oxford English Dictionary*, 'Nature', sense 5.

33–4 'Employed as a metaphysical concept': Kate Soper, *What is Nature? Culture, Politics and the Non-Human* (Oxford and Cambridge, Mass.: Blackwell, 1995), pp. 155–6.

35 'The subtly apotheosized': *Winter Pollen*, p. 129.

35 'voice of nature': 'La voix de la nature' – letter to M. Dupeyrou, 21 November 1768.

36 'As long as the face': Adorno, *Aesthetic Theory*, ed. Gretel Adorno and Rolf Tiedemann, trans. C. Lenhardt, London and Boston: (Routledge and Kegan Paul, 1984; original German, 1970), p. 95.

36 'Natural beauty is myth': *Aesthetic Theory*, p. 98.

36 'Green thinking': There are now many treatments of the different strands of green thinking. David Pepper, *Modern Environmentalism* (London and New York: Routledge, 1996) is a useful introduction, *The Green Reader*, ed. Andrew Dobson (London: André Deutsch and San Francisco: Mercury House, 1991) a valuable anthology, and Michael E. Zimmerman, *Contesting Earth's Future: Radical Ecology and Postmodernity* (Berkeley, Los Angeles and London: University of California Press, 1994) a more advanced critical treatment. An investigation of ecofeminism might begin with Val Plumwood, *Feminism and the Mastery of Nature* (London and New York: Routledge, 1993) or Janet Biehl, *Rethinking Ecofeminist Politics* (Boston: South End Press, 1991), of ecological socialism (more often known as 'social ecology') with Murray Bookchin, *The Philosophy of Social Ecology* (Montreal: Black Rose Books, 1990) or Andrew Ross, *The Chicago*

Gangster Theory of Life: Nature's Debt to Society (London and New York: Verso, 1994).

38–9 'This is the final stage': Rousseau, *Discourse*, p. 82.

40 'mutual aid': Kropotkin, *Mutual Aid: A Factor of Evolution* (1902, rev. edns. 1904, 1914), drawing together articles published in the *Nineteenth Century* between 1890 and 1896, in reaction against T. H. Huxley's 'The Struggle for Existence: A Programme' (*Nineteenth Century*, February 1888). Kropotkin developed his theory – that beside the law of mutual struggle in nature there is also a law of mutual aid – from a lecture delivered at a Russian Congress of Naturalists in January 1880 by Karl Fyodorovich Kessler, though he pointed out that the theory was 'in reality, nothing but a further development of the ideas expressed by Darwin himself in *The Descent of Man*' (*Mutual Aid*, ed. Paul Avrich [New York: New York University Press, 1972], p. 19).

40 'take the form': *Discourse*, p. 3.

41 'I have seen him travel': Quoted, Starobinski, p. 257.

41 'The more sensitive the soul': Rousseau, *Reveries of the Solitary Walker*, trans. Peter France (Harmondsworth: Penguin, 1979), p. 108.

42 'When I see the bright green': Merleau-Ponty, *Phenomenology of Perception*, trans. Colin Smith (London: Routledge and Kegan Paul, 1962), p. 330.

43 'The earth, left to its natural': Rousseau, *Discourse*, pp. 26–7.

43 'Because plants get their nourishment': Buffon, *Natural History*, as quoted by Rousseau, p. 89.

43 'the destruction of the topsoil': Rousseau, *Discourse*, p. 90.

44 'Vindication of the Natural Diet': On the importance of Shelley's vegetarianism, see Timothy Morton, *Shelley and the Revolution in Taste: The Body and the Natural World* (Cambridge: Cambridge University Press, 1994).

44–5 'It is not his understanding . . . an animal at the end': Rousseau, *Discourse*, p. 33.

45 'When we consider': *Discourse*, p. 94.

46 'Admire human society': *Discourse*, p. 94.

46 'Savage man': *Discourse*, p. 95.

46 'mental agonies . . . the numbers of unwholesome': *Discourse*, p. 98.

46–7 'I fear that it will occur': *Discourse*, p. 100.

47 'cry of nature': *Discourse*, p. 39.

47–8 'The true founder': *Discourse*, p. 54.

48 'scarcely profiting': *Discourse*, p. 55.

48 'from the moment . . . vast forests': *Discourse*, p. 62.

48 'Everything begins to take on': pp. 60, 64. Rousseau alludes here to the classical myth of fall: 'Ceres first gave laws', writes Ovid (*Metamorphoses*, 5. 343) of the goddess of agriculture who rules the silver age which begins after the end of the golden age of natural plenty presided over by Saturn. The progression then moves inexorably to the age of iron, which brings property lines, imperial expansion across the seas, and mining, conceived as mankind ripping out the bowels of the earth (see *Metamorphoses*, 1. 89–150).

50 'a savage inhabitant': Mary Shelley, *Frankenstein (The 1818 Text)*, ed. Marilyn Butler (Oxford: Oxford University Press, The World's Classics, 1994), pp. 12–15. All quotations from this edition.

50 'an acquaintance with the different relations': Quoted, Anne K. Mellor, *Mary Shelley: Her Life, Her Fiction, Her Monsters* (London and New York: Routledge, 1988), p. 93. The whole of Mellor's chap. 5, 'A Feminist Critique of Science' is relevant. See also Laura Crouch, 'Davy, *A Discourse*: a possible scientific source of *Frankenstein*', *Keats-Shelley Journal*, 27 (1978), 35–44.

51 'devouring *maladie*': *Frankenstein*, p. 154

51 'a new species': *Frankenstein*, p. 36.

51 'dull yellow eye': *Frankenstein*, p. 38.

51 'insensible to the charms': *Frankenstein*, p. 37.

52 'This was the order': Vico, *The New Science*, sec. 239, quoted, Robert Pogue Harrison, *Forests: The Shadow of Civilization* (Chicago and London: University of Chicago Press, 1992), p. xv.

52 'While I listened': *Frankenstein*, p. 96.

52 'There can be no': *Frankenstein*, p. 78.

53 'I shall not be': *Frankenstein*, p. 109.

53 'I placed a variety': *Frankenstein*, p. 113.

53 'If you consent': *Frankenstein*, p. 120.

54 'The idea that the sun': Lopez, *Arctic Dreams: Imagination and Desire in a Northern Landscape* (1986; repr. Toronto, New York, London, Sydney and Auckland: Bantam, 1987), p. 17.

55 'naturalist . . . travel writer . . . memoirist': Some examples of his work in these genres: *The Naturalist in La Plata* (1892), *Birds in London* (1898), *Birds and Man* (1901), *Adventures among Birds* (1913), *Idle Days in Patagonia* (1893), *Nature in Downland* (1900), *Hampshire Days* (1903), *A Shepherd's Life* (1910, an idealization of the small-holding yeomanry of Wiltshire), *A Crystal Age* (1887, a utopian/dystopian fiction of the conflict between industrialization and nature), and *Far Away and Long Ago* (1918, a fine memoir of the author's childhood in Argentina).

56 'The blue sky': W. H. Hudson, *Hampshire Days* (1903; repr. London: Dent, 1923), pp. 47–8.

56 'Ah yes, we are all': *The Purple Land* (1885; 8th impression, London: Duckworth, 1926), p. 254.

57 'Thou hast conquered': Swinburne, 'An Interlude'. In an excellent study, *The Nature Novel from Hardy to Lawrence* (London and Basingstoke: Macmillan, 1977), John Alcorn places Hudson in what he calls the 'naturist' tradition of late nineteenth and early twentieth century English writing, a tradition he characterizes as follows: 'The naturist world is a world of physical organism, where biology replaces theology as the source both of psychic health and of moral authority. The naturist is a child of Darwin; he sees man as part of an animal continuum; he reasserts the importance of instinct as a key to human happiness; he tends to be suspicious of the life of the mind; he is wary of abstractions. He is in revolt against Christian dogma, against conventional morality, against the ethic which reigns in a commercial society. His themes are inevitably utopian ... As a novelist, he is likely to prefer a loose plot structure, built around an elaborately described landscape' (p. x). The shorthand for this tradition might well be Rousseau + Romanticism + Darwin.

58 'its savage inhabitants': *Green Mansions* (1916 edn., repr. London: Robin Clark, 1990), p. 12. All quotations from this edition.

58 'the last act': *Mansions*, p. 14.

59 'With that luxuriant': *Mansions*, p. 39.

59 'my beloved green': *Mansions*, p. 84.

60 'Have you ever observed': *Mansions*, p. 108.

61 'She had begun': *Mansions*, p. 178.

61 'a period of moral': *Mansions*, p. 309.

62 'In Spanish ... Rima is "rhyme"': See Jason Wilson's excellent essay, *W. H. Hudson: The Colonial's Revenge*, University of London Institute of Latin American Studies Working Papers 5 (1981), p. 10.

62 'memorial to the life': On the controversy surrounding the supposed 'obscenity' of the bas-relief and the anti-semitic vandalising of it, see Stephen Gardiner, *Epstein: Artist against the Establishment* (1992; repr. London: Flamingo, 1993), pp. 232–40, 246–59.

63 'The Park throughout': Quoted, Simon Schama, *Landscape and Memory* (London: Fontana Press, 1996), p. 569.

64–5 'Januaries, Nature greets': Bishop, *The Complete Poems 1927–1979* (New York: Farrar Straus Giroux, 1983), p. 91.

65 'Florida': *Complete Poems*, p. 32.

67 'confess that the same': Lorrie Goldensohn, *Elizabeth Bishop: The Biography of a Poet* (New York: Columbia University Press, 1992), pp. 203–4.

68 'the very Shakspeare': *The Romantics on Shakespeare*, ed. Jonathan Bate (London: Penguin, 1992), p. 530.

71 'The perfect symmetry': Bruno Latour, *Nous n'avons jamais été modernes* (Paris: Editions La Découverte, 1991), trans. Catherine Porter (Cambridge, Mass.: Harvard University Press, 1993), pp. 8–9.

72 'book of explicitly ecological literary criticism': John Elder, *Imagining the Earth: Poetry and the Vision of Nature* (Urbana and Chicago: University of Illinois Press, 1985), a study of twentieth-century American poetry.

73 'The poets are everywhere': 'On Naïve and Sentimental Poetry', trans. Julius A. Elias, in *German Aesthetic and Literary Criticism*, ed. H. B. Nisbet (Cambridge: Cambridge University Press, 1985), pp. 196, 191, Schiller's emphasis in latter quotation.

74 'The poetic representation of innocent': 'On Naïve and Sentimental Poetry', p. 210.

74 'Along his infant veins': Wordsworth, *The Prelude 1799, 1805, 1850*, ed. Jonathan Wordsworth, M. H. Abrams, Stephen Gill (New York and London: Norton, 1979). 1805 text, 2. 262–4. See the whole sequence from lines 237 to 303.

75 'the owls do not respond': 1805 *Prelude*, 5. 389–413.

75 'What is the pastoral convention': Paul de Man, 'The Dead-End of Formalist Criticism', repr. in his *Blindness and Insight: Essays in the Rhetoric of Contemporary Criticism* (2nd edn, Minneapolis: University of Minnesota Press, 1983), p. 239.

76 'The program of the Enlightenment': Adorno and Horkheimer, *Dialectic of Enlightenment*, trans. John Cumming (London and New York: Verso, 1979), p. 3. Originally published as *Dialektik der Aufklärung* (1944). The phrase 'disenchantment of the world' was originally Max Weber's.

76–7 'Despite his lack': *Dialectic of Enlightenment*, p. 4.

77 'enslaves nature and exploits the masses': The critique of Enlightenment and the link between the technological exploitation of humankind and that of nature remain central to the work of later social theorists influenced by Adorno and Horkheimer, such as Herbert Marcuse and Jürgen Habermas. See Marcuse's *One Dimensional Man: Studies in the Ideology of Advanced Industrial Society* (Boston: Beacon Press, 1964) and Habermas' theory of the 'commodification' and 'colonization' of the 'lifeworld' – *The Theory of*

Communicative Action. Vol. 2: The Critique of Functionalist Reason
(Cambridge: Polity, 1987), pp. 303–403.

77 'the crystal ball': Davis, *City of Quartz: Excavating the Future in Los
    Angeles* (London: Verso, 1990, repr. Vintage, 1992), p. 48.

77 Leo Marx: *The Machine in the Garden: Technology and the Pastoral Ideal
    in America* (New York: Oxford University Press, 1964), chap. 2 (p. 72).

78 'Men pay for': *Dialectic of Enlightenment*, p. 9.

78 'Men have always': *Dialectic*, p. 32.

78 'The disenchantment': *Dialectic*, pp. 5, 28.

78 'With the progress': *Dialectic*, pp. 18–19.

79 'I am talking': Césaire, *Discourse on Colonialism*, trans. Joan Pinkham
    (New York: Monthly Review, 1972), p. 22.

79 'communal warmth': Senghor, *Poetry and Prose*, ed. and trans. John
    Reed and Clive Wake (London: Heinemann, 1976), p. 99.

79 'It evokes a traditional': Buell, *The Environmental Imagination: Thoreau,
    Nature Writing, and the Formation of American Culture* (Cambridge,
    Mass.: Harvard University Press, 1995), p. 64.

79 'Caliban is the man': Césaire, interviewed by S. Belhassen in *Radical
    Perspectives in the Arts*, ed. Lee Baxandall (Harmondsworth: Penguin,
    1972), p. 176.

79 'l'anti-Nature': Césaire, *Une tempête* (Paris: Seuil, 1969), p. 74.

80 'heard from afar': *Une tempête*, p. 92.

80 'New World Trilogy': Published together as *The Arrivants* (Oxford:
    Oxford University Press, 1973).

82 'writes back': Phrase borrowed from the title of Bill Ashcroft, Gareth
    Griffiths and Helen Tiffin, *The Empire Writes Back: Theory and Practice
    in Post-colonial Literatures* (London and New York: Routledge, 1989).

82 'British literature and literary forms': Brathwaite, *History of the Voice:
    The Development of Nation Language in Anglophone Caribbean Poetry*
    (London and Port of Spain: New Beacon, 1984), p. 8.

82 'the colonizing centers': Retamar, 'Caliban', *Massachusetts Review*, 15
    (1974), p. 7.

83 'the "classical", even *Prosperian* element': *History of the Voice*, p. 38.
    Previous quotations from pp. 10, 5, 13.

84–5 'a dance in which': *The Arrivants*, p. 274.

85 'Methought the billows . . . Thy dukedom': *The Tempest*, 3. 3. 96–9,
    5. 1. 120–1, quoted from Shakespeare's *Complete Works*, ed. Stanley
    Wells and Gary Taylor (Oxford: Oxford University Press, 1988).

87 'In his *Discourse on Method*': Harrison, *Forests: The Shadow of
    Civilization* (Chicago and London: University of Chicago Press, 1992),
    pp. 107–8.

88 'A sylvan fringe': *Forests*, p. ix.

89 'In *The Tempest*': Cheyfitz, *The Poetics of Imperialism: Translation and Colonization from 'The Tempest' to 'Tarzan'* (New York and Oxford: Oxford University Press, 1991), p. 26.

89 'Robert Browning': 'Caliban upon Setebos', published in *Dramatis Personae* (1864). The best reading of the poem remains C. R. Tracy, 'Caliban upon Setebos', *Studies in Philology*, 35 (1938), pp. 487–99.

90 'Ariel to Miranda': The poem was first published in 1832; I quote the text based on the original manuscript, repr. in *Shelley's Poetry and Prose*, ed. Donald H. Reiman and Sharon B. Powers (New York: Norton, 1977), pp. 449–51.

93 'Ariel': From Les Murray, *Dog Fox Field* (North Ryde, New South Wales: Angus and Robertson, 1976).

94–5 'I had a dream . . . The world was void': Lord Byron, *The Complete Poetical Works*, ed. Jerome J. McGann, vol. 4 (Oxford: Clarendon Press, 1986), pp. 40–1.

95 'possible literary sources': *Poetical Works*, 4. 459–60. The main substance of the note is taken from R. J. Dingley's '"I had a dream . . .": Byron's "Darkness"', *The Byron Journal*, 9 (1981), 20–33, an article that is strong on literary sources but silent on meteorology.

96 'we have had lately': *Byron's Letters and Journals*, ed. Leslie A. Marchand, 12 vols (London: John Murray, 1973–82), 5. 86.

96 'stress of weather': *Letters and Journals*, 5. 81.

96 'average temperature that July': John D. Post, *The Last Great Subsistence Crisis in the Western World* (Baltimore and London: Johns Hopkins, 1977), pp. 21, 9. Post is also my source for more general remarks about the weather at this time.

96–7 'temperature in London': Figures from W. Cary's monthly Meteorological Tables in *The Gentleman's Magazine*.

97 'It had nothing': 'Atmospheric Constitution of New York, from March to July 1816', *New York Medical Repository*, NS, 3 (1817), 301–7 (p. 301).

97 'volcanic vapour': Franklin, *Works*, ed. Jared Sparks, 10 vols (Boston, 1836–40), 6. 456–7.

98 'prophet of ecocide': Though he does not mention the weather, Timothy Morton sees 'Darkness' as 'demonstrating an ecological consciousness of famine as the death of nature and of cultural, political order' – *Shelley and the Revolution in Taste: The Body and the Natural World* (Cambridge: Cambridge University Press, 1994), pp. 220–1.

98 'establish a partition': Bruno Latour, *We Have Never Been Modern*,

trans. Catherine Porter (Cambridge, Mass.: Harvard University Press and Hemel Hempstead: Harvester Wheatsheaf, 1993), pp. 10–11.

99 'who, then, is inflicting': Michel Serres, *The Natural Contract*, trans. Elizabeth MacArthur and William Paulson (Ann Arbor: University of Michigan Press, 1995), pp. 31–2.

99 'working-over': Karl Marx, *Selected Writings*, ed. David McLellan (Oxford: Oxford University Press, 1977), p. 82.

99 'literary criticism of the Cold War': On Cold War criticism, see further the discussion at the beginning of chapter seven.

100 'the eighteenth century': Serres, *Hermès IV: la distribution* (Paris: Minuit, 1977), p. 229, quoted in Arden Reed, *Romantic Weather: The Climates of Coleridge and Baudelaire* (Hanover and London: University Press of New England, 1983), p. 38. See also Serres, *La naissance de la physique* (Paris: Minuit, 1977), p. 86. Reed's book is an attempt to reintroduce unstable weather into the discourse of Romanticism, but for a deconstructive purpose. His favourite weather is mist and cloud, which serve as metaphors of *aporia* and hermeneutic *abyme*. My reading of Romantic weather, in contrast, begins from actual meteorological conditions at a particular historical moment.

100 'imperialism . . . accompanied by ecological exploitation': See Alfred W. Crosby, *Ecological Imperialism: The Biological Expansion of Europe, 900–1900* (Cambridge: Cambridge University Press, 1986), but also the defence of early colonial 'environmental scientists' in Richard H. Grove, *Green Imperialism: Colonial Expansion, Tropical Island Edens, and the Origins of Environmentalism, 1600–1860* (Cambridge: Cambridge University Press, 1995).

100 'a matter of human agency': See especially *Spring*, lines 272ff. On Newton's mastery: 'Nature herself / Stood all subdued by him, and open laid / Her every latent glory to his view' ('To the Memory of Sir Isaac Newton', lines 36–8) – Nature here is female, passive, open to possession.

101 'it was the people': Luc Ferry, *The New Ecological Order*, trans. Carol Volk (Chicago: University of Chicago Press, 1995), p. 14. For a provocative study of the influence of climate on economic development, see Jayantanuka Bandyopahyaya, *Climate and World Order: An Inquiry into the Natural Cause of Underdevelopment* (Atlantic Heights NJ: Humanities Press, 1983).

102 'a delicate shuttle': *We Have Never Been Modern*, p. 5.

103 'late twentieth-century criticism': See, for example, Jerome J. McGann, 'Keats and the Historical Method in Literary Criticism,' in his *The Beauty of Inflections* (Oxford: Clarendon, 1985), p. 61.

104 'The delightful Weather': *The Letters of John Keats*, ed. Hyder E. Rollins, 2 vols (Cambridge, Mass.: Harvard University Press, 1958), 2. 148.

104 'discourses of sea-bathing': See further, Alain Corbin, *The Lure of the Sea: The Discovery of the Seaside 1750–1840*, trans. Jocelyn Phelps (London: Penguin, 1995), pp. 62, 71–2.

104 'Men who live together': *Letters*, 2. 208–9.

105 'How beautiful the season': *Letters*, 2. 167.

105 'Health': *Letters*, 2. 289, 306.

105 'they thought it the worst': Severn to Taylor, *Letters*, 2. 379.

106 'biodiversity is the key': See Edward O. Wilson, *The Diversity of Life* (Cambridge, Mass.: Harvard University Press; repr. London: Penguin, 1994), especially chap. 9. For further discussion, see my chapter eight.

108 'exploitation of women and the exploitation of the earth': Ortner's essay was published in *Women, Culture, and Society*, ed. Michelle Rosaldo and Louise Lamphere (Stanford: Stanford University Press, 1974), 67–87; Merchant, *The Death of Nature: Women, Ecology, and the Scientific Revolution* (San Francisco: Harper and Row, 1980). But see also the critique in Janet Biehl, *Rethinking Ecofeminist Politics* (Boston: South End Press, 1991).

109 'By chance or wisdom': Serres, *The Natural Contract*, p. 27.

110 'Therefore all seasons': Coleridge, *Poems*, ed. John Beer (London: Everyman, 1993), p. 190. The influence on 'Autumn' has often been noted; see, for example, Miriam Allott's notes to her edition of Keats's *Complete Poems* (London: Longman, 1970), pp. 651–4.

111 'this kind of topology': Serres, *Eclaircissements: cinq entretiens avec Bruno Latour* (Paris: Bourin, 1992, repr. Flammarion, 1994), pp. 92–3.

111 'voisinages': *Eclaircissements*, p. 93.

112 'In politics or economics': Serres, *Le contrat naturel* (Paris: François Bourin, 1990, repr. Flammarion, 1992), p. 71, my trans. and italics.

112–13 'Modernity neglects': *The Natural Contract*, p. 48.

113 'probably the greatest American poem': Yvor Winters, 'Wallace Stevens, or the Hedonist's Progress', originally publ. 1943, frequently repr., quoted from *Wallace Stevens: A Critical Anthology*, ed. Irvin Ehrenpreis (Harmondsworth and Baltimore: Penguin, 1972), pp. 121–2. I refer to Stevens's poems by their titles, quoting them from his *Collected Poems* (New York: Knopf, 1954 and London: Faber, 1955).

113 'wilderness forms': Vendler, 'Stevens and Keats' "To Autumn"', in *Wallace Stevens: A Celebration*, ed. Frank Doggett and Robert Buttel (Princeton: Princeton University Press, 1980), pp. 171–95 (pp. 173–4).

For a wide-ranging inquiry into Stevens and wilderness, see Gyorgyi
Voros's excellent study, *Notations of the Wild: Ecology in the Poetry of
Wallace Stevens* (Iowa City: University of Iowa Press, 1997).

115 'The mood of autumn': Letter to J. R. Feo, 25 October 1948, in
Collected Letters, ed. Holly Stevens (New York: Knopf, 1966).

116 'similar to the later Heidegger': For a rich comparison of poet and
philosopher, see Frank Kermode, 'Dwelling Poetically in
Connecticut', in *Wallace Stevens: A Celebration*, pp. 256–73. Also,
Thomas J. Hines, *The Later Poetry of Wallace Stevens: Phenomenological
Parallels with Husserl and Heidegger* (Lewisburg, Pa.: Bucknell
University Press, 1976).

117 'Notes toward a Supreme Fiction': 'It must give pleasure', section VII.

119 'Beginning with Schelling': Adorno, *Aesthetic Theory*, ed. Gretel
Adorno and Rolf Tiedemann, trans. C. Lenhardt (Routledge and
Kegan Paul: London and Boston, 1984; original German, 1970),
chap. 4, p. 91.

120 'all that is not': *Aesthetic Theory*, p. 92.

120 'What Art really reveals': Wilde, 'The Decay of Lying' (Vivian's first
two speeches), in *Intentions* (1891), quoted from *The Works of Oscar
Wilde* (London: Collins, 1992), p. 909.

121 'in their antithetical': *Aesthetic Theory*, p. 91.

122 'Delight in nature': *Aesthetic Theory*, p. 96.

122 'both legitimates . . . As long as': *Aesthetic Theory*, p. 96.

122 'Over long periods': *Aesthetic Theory*, p. 93.

122 'represents the recollection': *Aesthetic Theory*, p. 98.

122 'art is influenced': *Aesthetic Theory*, p. 97.

123 'Like every promise': *Aesthetic Theory*, p. 108.

123 'Just how inextricably': *Aesthetic Theory*, p. 97.

124 'However true': *Aesthetic Theory*, p. 106.

125 'Olives and vines': Anthony Trollope, *He Knew He Was Right*
(1869), ed. John Sutherland (Oxford: Oxford University Press, 1985),
p. 733.

125 'On a rock': *The Poems of Gray, Collins, and Goldsmith*, ed. Roger
Lonsdale (London: Longman, 1969), pp. 185–6.

126 'the thought': See Lonsdale's footnote to 'The Bard', citing letter
from Gray to Bedingfield, August 1756. Raphael's painting is now in
the Pitti Palace, Florence.

127 'a peculiar circularity': Andrews, *The Search for the Picturesque:
Landscape Aesthetics and Tourism in Britain, 1760–1800* (Stanford:
Stanford University Press, 1989), p. vii.

129 'A temple or palace': Price, *An Essay on the Picturesque* (1794), chap. 3.

130 'You must not inquire': *Sense and Sensibility*, chap. 18 – *The Novels of Jane Austen*, ed. R. W. Chapman, vol. 1 (Oxford: Oxford University Press, 1933), pp. 96–7.

130–1 'On the spot, no doubt': *Observations, Relative Chiefly to Picturesque Beauty, Made in the Year 1772, on Several Parts of England; Particularly the Mountains, and Lakes of Cumberland, and Westmoreland* [sic] (2 vols., 1786), quoted from 2nd edn., 1788, 1. 7–8.

131 'I am not fond of nettles': *Sense and Sensibility*, pp. 97–8.

133 ''Tis all in vain': William Combe, illus. Thomas Rowlandson, *The Tour of Dr Syntax in search of the Picturesque* (1809), pp. 10–11.

135 'proper arrangement of cattle': Plate 10 is from William Gilpin, *Observations, Relative Chiefly to Picturesque Beauty, Made in the Year 1772, on Several Parts of England; Particularly the Mountains, and Lakes of Cumberland, and Westmoreland*.

137 'the power and effects of fire . . . earth and all its commodities': Descartes, *Discourse on Method*, 6, trans. F. E. Sutcliffe, in *Discourse on Method and the Meditations* (Harmondsworth: Penguin, 1968), p. 78. This is the passage quoted by Robert Harrison in the section of his *Forests: The Shadow of Civilization*, which I cited in chapter three.

139 'obvious benefits . . . than to feel': 1805 text, 11. 121–37, quoted from *The Thirteen-Book Prelude*, ed. Mark L. Reed, 2 vols (Ithaca and London: Cornell University Press, 1991). Subsequent quotations are also from this text.

139–40 'The degree and kind of attachment': *The Prose Works of William Wordsworth*, ed. W. J. B. Owen and J. W. Smyser, 3 vols (Oxford: Clarendon Press, 1974), 3. 339.

140 'disliking here': *Prelude*, 11. 153–5.

140 'early works . . . in conventional picturesque language': On this, see Nicola Trott, 'Wordsworth and the Picturesque: A strong infection of the age', *The Wordsworth Circle*, 18 (1987), 114–21.

140 'giving way': *Prelude*, 11. 157–64.

141 'another cause': *Prelude*, 11. 166–70.

141 'In which the eye': *Prelude*, 11. 172.

141 'Yet was I often': *Prelude*, 11. 190–5.

142 'That had no interest': 'Lines written a few miles above Tintern Abbey, On revisiting the banks of the Wye during a tour, July 13, 1798. ' in *Lyrical Ballads, with a few other poems* (London, 1798), lines 82–4.

142 'read Gilpin's *Observations*': Wordsworth knew Gilpin's works on the picturesque well. Several allusions are listed in Duncan Wu's authoritative book on the young poet's reading (*Wordsworth's Reading*

1770–1799 (Cambridge: Cambridge University Press, 1993), pp. 64–6). A line in the early poem *An Evening Walk* includes the word 'sugh' and is furnished with a note saying that this is a Scottish word used by Burns and referring the reader to Gilpin's *Observations, Relative Chiefly to Picturesque Beauty, Made in the Year 1776, on Several Parts of Great Britain; Particularly the High-Lands of Scotland.* When Wordsworth left London for Racedown in August 1795, he left a number of books with Basil Montagu; in March 1796, he wrote a letter to William Mathews asking him to retrieve them: 'Gilpin's tour into Scotland, and his northern tour, each 2 vol., ought to be amongst the number'. The latter tour was the one that included Gilpin's account of the Lake District: *Observations, Relative Chiefly to Picturesque Beauty, Made in the Year 1772, on Several Parts of England; Particularly the Mountains, and Lakes of Cumberland, and Westmoreland.*

142 'We travel for various purposes': Gilpin, *Observations on the River Wye* (quoted from 2nd edn., London, 1789), p. 1.

143 'the ruins of abbeys': *Observations, Relative Chiefly to Picturesque Beauty, Made in the Year 1772, on Several Parts of England*, 1. 13.

143 'A more pleasing retreat': *Observations on the River Wye*, pp. 46–7.

143 'one great disadvantage': *River Wye*, p. 53.

144–5 'While it is true': Adorno, *Aesthetic Theory*, p. 96.

145 'Once again': 'Tintern Abbey', lines 4–8.

146 'These plots': 'Tintern Abbey', lines 11–15.

147 'And I have felt': 'Tintern Abbey', lines 94–103.

147–8 'Integrated in the commercial world': *Aesthetic Theory*, p. 101.

148–9 'This is the way in which he did his work': Quoted, Russell Noyes, *Wordsworth and the Art of Landscape* (Bloomington and London: Indiana University Press, 1968), pp. 198–9.

149–50 'Amid the turns': *Prelude*, 11. 196–214.

151 'If you exclaim': Adorno, *Aesthetic Theory*, p. 102. On this issue, see further Charlotte Klonk, *Science and the Perception of Nature: British Landscape Art in the late Eighteenth and early Nineteenth Centuries* (New Haven and London: Yale University Press, 1996), p. 152. Klonk offers a suggestive reading of early nineteenth-century English art as being motivated by a 'phenomenalism' that breaks down the subject/object barrier.

151–2 'As an indeterminate': *Aesthetic Theory*, p. 107.

153 'thing-experience': Husserl, *The Crisis of European Sciences and Transcendental Phenomenology*, trans. David Carr (Evanston, Ill.: Northwestern University Press, 1970), p. 138.

153–4 'The Hollow Tree': Where possible, quotations of Clare's poetry are from *John Clare: Selected Poetry*, ed. Geoffrey Summerfield (London: Penguin, 1990).

154 'the distant past resounds': Bachelard, *The Poetics of Space*, trans. Maria Jolas (1964, repr. Boston: Beacon Press, 1994), p. xvi. Brief comparison between the chapter on nests in Bachelard's book and John Clare's 'nesting instinct' is made by Hugh Haughton in one of the best single essays on Clare that I know: 'Progress and Rhyme: "The Nightingale's Nest" and Romantic poetry', in *John Clare in Context*, ed. Hugh Haughton, Adam Phillips and Geoffrey Summerfield (Cambridge: Cambridge University Press, 1994), pp. 51–86 (reference on pp. 71–2).

154 'the duality of subject and object': *Poetics of Space*, p. xix.

154 'In this orientation': *Poetics of Space*, p. xxxv.

154 'spaces which afford us protection': In a sense, the argument anticipates the 'prospect and refuge theory' of such landscape theorists as Jay Appleton, who argue that our love of, on the one hand, wide-open prospects seen from above, and, on the other, enclosed nooks such as caves and forest groves may be traced back to the self-protective instincts of early *homo sapiens* – Appleton, *The Experience of Landscape* (London and New York: Wiley, 1975). See further, the overview by Judith H. Heerwagen and Gordon H. Orians, 'Humans, Habitats, and Aesthetics', in *The Biophilia Hypothesis*, ed. Stephen R. Kellert and Edward O. Wilson (Washington DC: Island Press, 1993), chap. 4, and bibliographic references therein.

155 'with the presence': *Poetics of Space*, p. 79.

155 'he calls inhabiting . . . I call dwelling': I prefer the word 'dwelling' partly for its Heideggerian resonance, discussed in chapter nine, but also for the same reason as Robert Harrison in *Forests*. Harrison notes that Stanley Cavell, in his essay 'Thinking of Emerson', considers 'The substantive disagreement with Heidegger, shared by Emerson and Thoreau' to be 'that the achievement of the human requires not inhabitation and settlement, but abandonment, leaving'. It is this distinction which needs to be collapsed. Harrison writes: 'In my understanding, Heidegger's idea of dwelling is akin to what Cavell means by "abandonment" and to what [Frank Lloyd] Wright means by an "unfolding" as opposed to an "enfolding" architecture. Heidegger's early word for what is implied by Cavell's notion of "inhabitation" is "inauthenticity. " In essence, the problem lies with the word "inhabitation" . . . we do not "inhabit" the earth in the closed sense; rather, we *dwell*. I like the word "dwell" because its etymology contains the notion of abandonment. In Old English

dwellan means precisely "to lead or go astray," as in a forest. In other words, we inhabit our estrangement, our "abandonment," even when we stay put in one particular place – as long, that is, as we do not close ourselves off to the alien element that inhabits our finitude' (Robert Pogue Harrison, *Forests: The Shadow of Civilization* [Chicago: University of Chicago Press, 1992], p. 265).

155 'in one short': *Poetics of Space*, p. 90.
155 'Our house is': *Poetics of Space*, pp. 4–6.
155 'For a knowledge': *Poetics of Space*, p. 9.
155 'areas of being': *Poetics of Space*, p. 33.
155 'from the intensity': *Poetics of Space*, p. 32.
155 'a snail's shell . . . The shell': *Poetics of Space*, pp. 118, 112.
156–7 'A bird, for Michelet': *Poetics of Space*, pp. 237–9.
157 'Intimacy needs': *Poetics of Space*, p. 65.
157–8 'A beginning of': *Poetics of Space*, p. 93.
158 'It is living nests': *Poetics of Space*, pp. 94–5.
158 'When we examine': *Poetics of Space*, p. 103.
160 'one night I lay': 'Journey out of Essex', in *John Clare's Autobiographical Writings*, ed. Eric Robinson (Oxford: Oxford University Press, 1986), p. 158.
161 'The cleverer I am': *Poetics of Space*, p. 150.
164 'History is repeating itself': *John Clare in Context*, p. 14.
165 'It is the landscape as itself': Barrell, *The Idea of Landscape and the Sense of Place: An Approach to the Poetry of John Clare* (Cambridge: Cambridge University Press, 1972), pp. 115–16. A more sympathetic neo-Marxist reading of the correspondence between the voice of the labourer and the voice of the land in this poem is offered by Elizabeth K. Helsinger in *Rural Scenes and National Representation: Britain, 1815–1850* (Princeton: Princeton University Press, 1997), chap. 4 (pp. 148–50).
166 'In a forest . . . expiration of Being': 'L'Œil et l'esprit' (1961), trans. by Carleton Dallery as 'Eye and Mind', in Merleau-Ponty's *The Primacy of Perception and other Essays on Phenomenological Psychology, the Philosophy of Art, History and Politics*, ed. James M. Edie (Evanston: Northwestern University Press, 1964), p. 167. Klee is cited via André Marchand in G. Charbonnier's *Le monologue du peintre* (1959). Merleau-Ponty's essay also offers a powerful assertion of the anti-Cartesian power of the creative artist: 'A Cartesian can believe that the existing world is not visible, that the only light is that of the mind, and that all vision takes place in God. An artist cannot grant that our openness to the world is illusory or indirect, that what we see is not

the world itself, or that the mind has to do only with its thoughts or with another mind. He accepts with all its difficulties the myth of the windows of the soul ... We must take literally what vision teaches us: namely, that through it we come in contact with the sun and the stars, that we are everywhere all at once ... Vision alone makes us learn that beings that are different, "exterior," foreign to one another, are yet absolutely *together*, are simultaneity' (pp. 186-7).

166 'in Schiller's sense, naive': On this, see Juliet Sychrava, *Schiller to Derrida: Idealism in Aesthetics* (Cambridge: Cambridge University Press, 1989), chaps. 3 and 6.

167 'A house that has': *Poetics of Space*, p. 47.

167 'the Depressions that distress me': *The Letters of John Clare*, ed. Mark Storey (Oxford: Clarendon Press, 1985), p. 592.

167-8 'an organism has meaning': McKusick, '"A language that is ever green": the Ecological Vision of John Clare', *University of Toronto Quarterly*, 61 (1991-2), 226-49 (p. 237).

168 'And suppose he were to answer': Harrison, *Forests: The Shadow of Civilization*, p. 109.

168-9 'One of the ways': *Forests*, p. 108.

169 'exact policemanship': quoted, *Forests*, p. 126.

169 'Today we are witnessing': *Forests*, p. 259.

169 'a very fine work': Italo Calvino, *The Baron in the Trees*, trans. Archibald Colquhoun (London: William Collins, 1959), p. 205.

170 'but as he wrote': *Baron*, p. 142.

170 'You'll find an equal there': *The Oxford Authors: John Clare*, ed. Eric Robinson and David Powell (Oxford: Oxford University Press, 1984), p. 19.

170 'forcd to return home fearing': Journal for Thursday 9 September 1824, *The Natural History Prose Writings of John Clare*, ed. Margaret Grainger (Oxford: Clarendon Press, 1983), p. 174.

171 'I saw one of these': *Natural History Prose Writings*, p. 87; punctuation added.

172 'The Fallen Elm': *Selected Poetry*, pp. 167-9.

172 'my two favourite Elm trees': To Taylor, 7 March 1821, *Letters*, p. 161.

172 'things which were the landmarks': *Clare: The Critical Heritage*, ed. Mark Storey (London: Routledge and Kegan Paul, 1973), p. 138.

173 'Poets will help us to discover': *Poetics of Space*, pp. 199-201.

174 'I'll be free in a prison': *Selected Poetry*, p. 224.

174 'While on the perilous ridge': 1805 *Prelude*, 1. 333-50.

174 'where still they live': 'The Raven's Nest', *Selected Poetry*, pp. 102-3.

175 'The denomination of objects': Merleau-Ponty, *Phenomenology of Perception*, trans. Colin Smith (London: Routledge and Kegan Paul, 1962), pp. 177–8.

175 'The song that names the earth': Heidegger, 'What are poets for?', in *Holzwege* (Frankfurt am Main: Klostermann, 1950), p. 254, apropos of Rilke. Here Heidegger writes 'das Land', as opposed to his more habitual 'die Erde' – that 'land' carries connotations of *nation* as well as *earth* raises the difficult matter of his politics, alluded to in my preface and discussed in my closing chapter. This sentence from *Holzwege* is quoted as a chapter epigraph in Michel Haar, *Le chant de la terre: Heidegger et les assises de l'histoire de l'Etre* (Paris: Editions de l'Herne, 1987). My own title *The Song of the Earth* is intended not only as an echo of Heidegger, but also as an expression of allegiance to the long tradition of Romanticism which embraces Gustav Mahler's setting of ancient Chinese poems, *Das Lied von der Erde*.

176 'I see in every animal': Rousseau, *Discourse on the Origin of Inequality*, trans. Franklin Philip (Oxford: Oxford University Press, The World's Classics, 1994), pp. 32–3.

177 'Seeing the best, he can choose': Ferry, *The New Ecological Order*, trans. Carol Volk (Chicago: University of Chicago Press, 1995), p. 5.

177 'My long sickness': *Timon of Athens*, 5. 2. 71–3.

177 'and man is subject': *Discourse*, p. 18.

177 'Society for the Prevention of Cruelty to Animals': See further, Keith Thomas, *Man and the Natural World: Changing Attitudes in England 1500–1800* (Harmondsworth: Penguin, 1984), especially chap. 4.

178 'While he spoke': Homer, *The Odyssey*, trans. Robert Fitzgerald (New York: Doubleday, 1961, repr. 1963), 17. 375–92.

179 'the estrangement from nature': *Dialectic of Enlightenment*, p. 48.

179 'Iliad critics or Odyssey critics': Northrop Frye, *A Natural Perspective: The Development of Shakespearean Comedy and Romance* (New York: Columbia University Press, 1965), p. 1.

179–80 'springs from their common rootedness': Karl Kroeber, *Ecological Literary Criticism: Romantic Imagining and the Biology of Mind* (New York: Columbia University Press, 1994), p. 3.

181 'What a piece of work': *Hamlet*, 2. 2. 305–10.

182 'trainer at the local bear-pit': Live animals were a feature of the Elizabethan and Jacobean stage, but we cannot know whether the bear would have been one such. Mouse, the clown in the popular anonymous pastoral romance *Mucedorus*, wonders whether the bear he meets is a supernatural agency: 'Nay, sure it cannot be a bear, but some devil in the bear's doublet; for a bear could never have had that

agility to have frighted me' (1. 2. 2–4). Here 'doublet' suggests the possibility of a bear-costume and consequently familiarity with actor-bears as well as live animals.

182 'cut a figure': *The Letters of John Keats 1814–1821*, ed. H. E. Rollins, 2 vols (Cambridge, Mass.: Harvard University Press, 1958), 2. 67.

182 'Is it not *life*': *Byron's Letters and Journals*, ed. Leslie Marchand, 12 vols (London: John Murray, 1973–82), 6. 232.

182–3 'I have got a new friend': *Letters and Journals*, 1. 135–6.

183 'No slang dictionary': *Letters and Journals*, 1. 136n., where E. H. Coleridge's marginalia is also cited.

183 'Milton, Dryden, Pope': *English Bards and Scotch Reviewers*, quoted from *The Oxford Authors: Byron*, ed. Jerome J. McGann (Oxford: Oxford University Press, 1986), pp. 5–7. Where possible, all subsequent quotations from Byron's poetry are from this edition, cited by line or canto and stanza reference.

184 'Man is the only animal': *The Complete Works of William Hazlitt*, ed. P. P. Howe, 21 vols (London: Dent, 1930–4), 6. 5.

184 'We weep at': Hazlitt, *Works*, 6. 5.

184 'To explain the nature': Hazlitt, *Works*, 6. 5.

184 'And if I laugh': *Don Juan*, canto 4, stanza 4.

185 'I have got two monkeys': *Letters and Journals*, 6. 108.

185 'took this Time': 'A Letter from Artemiza in the Town to Chloe in the Country', passage quoted and discussed by Anne Barton in 'John Wilmot, Earl of Rochester', in *English Poets: British Academy Chatterton Lectures* (Oxford: Oxford Unviersity Press, 1988), p. 64. For the comparison of Byron and Rochester, see pp. 57–9. The 1974 reprint of Graham Greene's biography, *Lord Rochester's Monkey*, has as frontispiece a fine colour reproduction of the portrait of Rochester and a monkey, attributed to Jacob Huysmans; the book's two epigraphs are a passage from a letter of Rochester's to Henry Savile suggesting that the nonsensicality of human affairs makes it 'a fault to laugh at the monkey we have here, when I compare his condition with mankind', and some lines from the 'Satyr against Reason and Mankind', including 'I'd be a dog, a monkey or a bear, / Or any thing but that vain animal, / Who is so proud of being rational'.

185 'all scratching': *Letters and Journals*, 6. 171.

186 'What is the reason': *Letters and Journals*, 8. 15.

186 'they perfectly understand . . . it may sulk': Darwin, *The Expression of the Emotions* (1872; repr. Chicago: University of Chicago Press, 1965), pp. 60–1, 131–8.

186 'I have just been scolding': *Letters and Journals*, 7. 105.

186 'Miss Edgeworth's cat': 'To J. H. Reynolds Esq. ', line 10.

186 'little curly-headed . . . A monkey': *Don Juan*, 1. 25; 3. 18.

186 'the artist and his ape': *Childe Harold*, 4. 53.

187 'he'd ape': *Don Juan*, 3. 86.

187 'they are such liars': *Don Juan*, 3. 87.

187 'fun & poetry': *Letters and Journals*, 6. 101.

187 'The question is not': Bentham, *An Introduction to the Principles of Morals and Legislation*, 1789, quoted, Thomas, *Man and the Natural World*, p. 176. One of the many paradoxes of the Green movement is that Bentham is a hero to animal rights activists, a villain to deep ecological critics of techno-utilitarianism. On the uneasy relationship between the 'animal' and the 'earth' wings of the Green advance guard, see Mark Sagoff, 'Animal Liberation and Environmental Ethics: Bad Marriage, Quick Divorce', in *Environmental Philosophy: from Animal Rights to Radical Ecology*, ed. M. E. Zimmerman (Englewood Cliffs, NJ: Prentice Hall, 1992), pp. 84–94.

187–8 'Kant suggests a path': Ferry, *The New Ecological Order*, p. 54.

188 'The simple pastimes': Wordsworth, *The Excursion* (1814), 2. 111–63.

189 'of eggs, coffee': *Don Juan*, 2. 133.

189 'made a most': *Don Juan*, 2. 123.

189 'tragedy does not tell the whole truth': Huxley, 'Tragedy and the Whole Truth', in his *Music at Night and other Essays* (London: Chatto and Windus, 1931), pp. 3–18 (p. 7).

189–90 'o'er the beauty': *Don Juan*, 4. 72–4.

190 'pure principle of love': *The Excursion*, 4. 1213.

191 'The power of his mind preys': 'Observations on Mr Wordsworth's Poem The Excursion', in *The Round Table, Complete Works of Hazlitt*, 4. 113. This review, probably known to Byron from its first publication in Leigh Hunt's *Examiner*, is the seminal critique of Romanticism's 'intense intellectual egotism [which] swallows up every thing'. Byron was also familiar with the similar account of Wordsworth in Hazlitt's lecture 'On the Living Poets'.

191 'What a sublime': *Don Juan*, 11. 2.

191 'the wordsworthian or egotistical sublime': Keats, *Letters*, 1. 387.

191 'Tuism': *Don Juan*, 16. 13.

192 'Erotic perception is not': Merleau-Ponty, *Phenomenology of Perception*, trans. Colin Smith (London: Routledge and Kegan Paul, 1962), p. 157.

192 'She look'd as if': *Don Juan*, 15. 45.

192 'her frolic Grace': *Don Juan*, 16. 123.

192 'And Wordsworth': *Don Juan*, Dedication, stanza 4.

192 'When a man talks of system': *Letters and Journals*, 6. 46.

193 'And then you overstrain': *Don Juan*, Dedication, stanza 3.

193 'A drowsy': *Don Juan*, 3. 94.

193 'builds up a': *Don Juan*, 3. 95.

193 'the drollery is in the utter discontinuity': *Spirit of the Age* essay on Byron, *Complete Works of Hazlitt*, 11. 75.

193 'cabin'd, cribb'd': *Macbeth*, 3. 4. 24; *Don Juan*, 4. 75.

194 'The pun on "cabined"': Beatty, *Don Juan and other Poems: A Critical Study* (Harmondsworth: Penguin, 1987), p. 93.

194 'Lord Byron told Captain Medwin': *The Halliford Edition of the Works of Thomas Love Peacock*, ed. H. F. B. Brett-Smith and C. E. Jones, 10 vols (London: Constable, 1924–34), 8. 500–1. Quotations from *Melincourt* itself (originally publ. 1817) are from this edition, but are followed by chapter reference. Byron's original remark – 'There was, by the bye, rather a witty satire founded on my bear' – is recorded in Medwin's *Conversations of Lord Byron*, ed. Ernest J. Lovell Jr (Princeton: Princeton University Press, 1966), p. 67.

194 'could not have failed to think': Byron read and admired *Melincourt* in 1820 or 1821, after obtaining his pet monkeys – for his admiration, see Shelley's letter to Peacock of 10[?] Aug. 1821, in *Letters of P. B. Shelley*, ed. F. L. Jones, 2 vols (Oxford: Clarendon Press, 1964), 2. 331. The Shelleys asked Maria Gisborne to bring them copies of *Headlong Hall* and *Melincourt* in July 1820. Peacock was on Byron's mind in June 1821: on the 22nd he included in a letter to Tom Moore the epigram, 'The world is a bundle of hay, / Mankind are the asses who pull; / Each tugs it a different way, / And the greatest of all is John Bull' (*Letters and Journals*, 8. 141), which looks as if it is adapted from Mr Derrydown's stave in chap. 16 of *Melincourt* on the theme 'Every man for himself': 'This world is a well-furnished table, / Where guests are promiscuously set: / We all fare as well as we're able, / And scramble for what we can get' (the parallel is not recorded by the editors of either *Letters and Journals* or *Complete Poetical Works*). A letter of 29 June 1821 refers to Peacock as 'a very clever fellow' (8. 145). Forester is generally regarded as a portrait more of Shelley than of Byron, but Marilyn Butler warns against a reading in terms of crude one-on-one correspondences in her excellent book, *Peacock Displayed: A Satirist in his Context* (London: Routledge and Kegan Paul, 1979), pp. 75–7 – as she points out, the obvious 'source' for Forester's ideas, made explicit in the footnotes, is Monboddo.

195 'among the *singes*': *Melincourt*, chap. 6.

195 'scene of origin': Haraway, *Primate Visions: Gender, Race, and Nature in the World of Modern Science* (London and New York: Routledge, 1989), p. 10.

196 'established his humanity': James Burnett, Lord Monboddo, *Ancient Metaphysics*, vol. 3, p. 40, quoted by Peacock in one of his footnotes to *Melincourt*, chap. 6.

196 '*with dignity and composure*': *Melincourt*, chap. 6, italics indicating quotation from Monboddo.

196 'our genome': for these percentages, see Jared Diamond, *The Rise and Fall of the Third Chimpanzee* (London: Radius, 1991, repr. Vintage, 1992), chap. 1.

197 'They discovered': *Melincourt*, chap. 42.

198 'elements of Sir Oran's': for example his ability to fell a tree, which gives the means of his first rescue of Anthelia. Also his tears: in chap. 33, when he can't find Anthelia, 'throwing himself into a chair [he] began to shed tears in great abundance' – Monboddo reports a gentleman who attested 'that an oran outang on board his ship conceived such an affection for the cook, that when upon some occasion he left the ship to go ashore, the gentleman saw the oran outang shed tears in great abundance' (*Origin and Progress of Language*, bk. 2, chap. 4, cited by Peacock in a note to chap. 6 of *Melincourt*).

198 'poeticopolitical': *Melincourt*, chap. 31.

199 'Brazil says': From *Turtle Island*, repr. in Snyder, *No Nature: New and Selected Poems* (New York and San Francisco: Pantheon, 1992), p. 236.

201 'At last we have someone who knows': Review of *North and South*, *The Nation*, 28 September 1946, repr. in Moore, *Complete Prose*, ed. Patricia C. Willis (London: Faber and Faber, 1987).

201–2 'In her "animiles" Moore': Rotella, *Reading and Writing Nature: The Poetry of Robert Frost, Wallace Stevens, Marianne Moore, and Elizabeth Bishop* (Boston: Northeastern University Press, 1991), p. 183.

203 'Travelling south': Heaney, *Seeing Things* (London and Boston: Faber and Faber, 1991), p. 83.

203 'Suicidal, at one': Plath, 'Ariel', in *Collected Poems*, ed. Ted Hughes (London and Boston: Faber and Faber, 1981), p. 240.

205–6 'In the cottage of Town End': Fenwick note, in *The Poetical Works of William Wordsworth*, ed. E. de Selincourt and Helen Darbishire, 5 vols (Oxford: Clarendon Press, 1940–9; 2nd edn. of vols. 2–3, 1952–4), 3. 417.

206 'discovers a new form on a particular afternoon': In fact it is not strictly true that he only wrote one sonnet as a younger man: see *Poetical Works*, vol. 1, pp. 3, 265, 269, 296, 308. But, as always with

Wordsworth, the self-made myth of the poet's career has more force than does the minute history of his development.

207 'harmony . . . republican austerity': Letter of 20 April 1822, in *The Letters of William and Dorothy Wordsworth*, 2nd edn, 7 vols (Oxford: Clarendon Press, 1967–88), *The Later Years Part I: 1821–1826*, ed. Alan G. Hill (1978), pp. 125–6.

208 'not see for nearly ten years': This is to assume that he did not see Annette and the baby Caroline on the brief return visit to Paris which he seems to have made in the autumn of 1793.

209 'I who with the breeze': 1805 *Prelude*, 10. 253–8, quoted from reading text in *The Thirteen-Book 'Prelude'*, ed. Mark L. Reed, The Cornell Wordsworth, 2 vols (Ithaca and London: Cornell University Press, 1992).

209 'and thus did soon': *Prelude*, 9. 124–6. On the complexity of the word 'patriot', especially in the 1790s, see chap. 1 of Peter Swaab, 'Wordsworth and Patriotism', unpubl. Ph.D. diss. (Cambridge University, 1989).

209–10 'It was a grief': 1805 *Prelude*, 10. 263–74.

210 'O Liberty!': Coleridge, *Poems*, ed. John Beer (London: Everyman, 1993), p. 283.

211 'sonnets political . . . and sonnets topographic': *Poems*, pp. 44ff., p. 125.

211 'Vane . . . Waldenses': Vane is cited in Wordsworth's *Liberty* sonnets (no. 15) and the Waldenses in his Ecclesiastical ones (2. 14).

211 'We had delightful walks': Entry in 'Grasmere Journal', Aug. 1802, quoted in *Poetical Works*, 3. 452.

211–12 'Fair Star of Evening': quoted from reading text in *Poems, in Two Volumes, and Other Poems, 1800–1807*, ed. Jared Curtis, The Cornell Wordsworth (Ithaca: Cornell University Press, 1983). Subsequent quotations from the 'Sonnets dedicated to Liberty' are also from this text.

213 'much mocked at the time': As in Gillray's caricature 'Introduction of Citizen Volpone [Fox] and his Suite, at Paris'. Wordsworth's poem was first published in January 1803 in the *Morning Post*, which, partly under the influence of Coleridge, had swung in the autumn of 1802 from an anti-Pitt and anti-war position to an anti-Fox and anti-peace one.

213 'Jones! When from Calais': This poem was heavily revised in 1815 (see the text in *Poetical Works*, 3. 110). It was a revision for the worse, introducing ponderous phrases like 'vernal coverts'. Most notably, the third line was altered to read 'Streamed with the pomp of a too-credulous day', the pontificating adjective distancing

Wordsworth utterly from his revolutionary youth and destroying the subtlety whereby the spirit of 1790 is rekindled in the very regret for its loss.

216 'may well be construed as Burkean': For the argument that there is a perennial Burkeanism in Wordsworth, see James K. Chandler, *Wordsworth's Second Nature: A Study of the Poetry and Politics* (Chicago: University of Chicago Press, 1984).

217 'writing in Elizabethan England': See Richard Helgerson, *Forms of Nationhood: The Elizabethan Writing of England* (Chicago: University of Chicago Press, 1992).

217 '*Britain*, called also *Albion*': *Britain*, p. i, quoted from *Camden's Britannia, Newly Translated into English*, publ. Edmund Gibson (London, 1695), which I have used because it is a more accurate translation of Camden's Latin than is Holland's.

217 'to restore Britain': Preface, sig. d2v. The opening of Camden's text implies that Britain is one nation, if with several names, played off against 'the continent of Europe'. But his title-page presented a more complicated picture. Philemon Holland translated it as follows: *Britain, or a Chorographicall Description of the most flourishing Kingdomes, England, Scotland, and Ireland, and the Ilands adjoyning, out of the depth of Antiquitie* ('chorographical' means 'the writing of regions', as opposed to 'geography', the writing of the whole earth). The county-by-county survey begins with Cornwall in the extreme south-west, goes across to Kent in the extreme south-east, then criss-crosses northward until it reaches Cheshire, at which point Camden digresses into Wales, where, he says, the ancient Britons still had their abode. Wales is thus subsumed into England, though with the recognition on the one hand that it is marginal – you must turn a little aside to acknowledge it – and on the other hand that it is special, since the Celtic or ancient British heritage remains unusually alive there. The latter acknowledgment might look to a Welshman like condescension masked as flattery. From Wales, Camden proceeds through the northernmost counties of England and into Scotland, which he says that he will willingly enter into, but lightly pass over, since he does not know its customs well and will not presume to trespass upon them. His text passes over Scotland in a score of leaves, whereas it has dwelt in England for hundreds of pages. The tone with regard to the Scots is strikingly deferential, suggesting awareness that they constitute a proud and independent nation. One senses that Camden was a little uneasy about subsuming them into his treatment of England-as-implicitly-Britain, as he has subsumed the Welsh. His task

became much easier after King James united the thrones of Scotland and England in 1603: he added to his 1607 edition several passages celebrating the union of the two crowns and invoking a rhetoric of 'one nation'.

217 'Neither be they here': *A Perambulation of Kent* (1570), quoted from 1826 reprint of the second edition, repr. with an introduction by Richard Church (Bath: Adams and Dart, 1970), p. 7.

218 'O noble *Kent*': Song XVIII, 729–38, in Drayton's *Works*, ed. J. William Hebel, 5 vols (Oxford: Shakespeare Head Press, 1933), 4. 381. Selden's 'Illustrations' to this Song specifically cite Lambarde's *Perambulation* as a source for information about Kent (p. 386).

221 'Was it for this': quoted from text in *The Thirteen-Book 'Prelude'*, 1. 272–80.

221 'river and the course of human life': On this, see chap. 5 of Lee M. Johnson, *Wordsworth and the Sonnet*, Anglistica XIX (Copenhagen: Rosenkilde and Bagger, 1973).

221–2 'Foster-mother . . . mingle with Eternity': Quotations and citations in this sentence are from sonnets III, IV, IX, XIII, XV, XVI, XVII, XIX, XXIV, XXXIII of the *Duddon* sequence.

222 'I thought of Thee': Sonnet XXXIV, text from *Poetical Works*, 3. 261.

222 'Surfactants, ammonia': Hughes, from the collection *River*, in *Three Books* (London and Boston: Faber and Faber, 1993), p. 118. The allusion in the poem's title is to Henry Williamson's *Tarka the Otter*, one of the books which most inspired Hughes in his youth. Williamson's combination of ecological and fascist sympathies are interestingly discussed by Anna Bramwell in her *Ecology in the Twentieth Century: A History* (New Haven: Yale University Press, 1989).

223 'What is a river?': Wyman H. Herendeen, *From Landscape to Literature: The River and the Myth of Geography* (Pittsburgh: Duquesne University Press, 1986), pp. 3–4.

223 '"Return" . . . "Seathwaite Chapel"': In a long note, Wordsworth makes it clear that these two sonnets may be considered as a single poem; he then gives his 'Memoir of the Rev. Robert Walker', the exemplary pastor of Seathwaite Chapel.

223 'a prose account of the Duddon': *Poetical Works*, 3. 508.

224 '*Guide to the Lakes*': In this edition it had the title *A Topographical Description of the Country of the Lakes, in the North of England*.

224 'It is with the little River Duddon': *Poetical Works*, 3. 504.

225 'learnt by Drayton from Spenser's': Thames and Medway are married in *The Faerie Queene*, 4. 11; 'Epithalamion Thamesis' was a

versification of Leland, anticipating Drayton's versification of Camden.

226 'buildings in Wordsworth's sonnets': See John Kerrigan's deeply thoughtful essay, 'Wordsworth and the Sonnet: Building, Dwelling, Thinking', *Essays in Criticism*, 35 (1985), pp. 45–75.

226–7 'Critical regionalism': Steven C. Bourassa, *The Aesthetics of Landscape* (London: Belhaven Press, 1991), pp. 137–9. See further, K. Frampton, 'Towards a critical regionalism: six points for an architecture of resistance', in *Postmodern Culture*, ed. Hal Foster (London: Pluto, 1985).

227 'I, who accompanied': Sonnet I. 1. All quotations are from *The Ecclesiastical Sonnets of William Wordsworth: A Critical Edition*, ed. Abbie Findlay Potts (New Haven and London: Yale University Press, 1922).

227 'Floating at ease': *Ecclesiastical Sonnets*, 3. 47.

228 'Troubles of Charles': *Ecclesiastical Sonnets*, 2. 44.

228 'rootedness of ecclesiastical buildings': See especially 'Places of Worship', 'New Churches' and 'Church to be Erected' (3. 17, 38, 39).

228 'Where holy ground begins': Text from original version in Manuscript F of *Ecclesiastical Sonnets*, Potts's edn, p. 107. Wordsworth seems deliberately to eschew the punctuation that would 'distinguish', or divide, the lines.

229 'Rose at five o'clock': quoted in *Poetical Works*, 3. 432.

229 'The ultimate irony of organic evolution': *The Diversity of Life* (Cambridge, Mass.: Harvard University Press, 1992, repr. London: Penguin, 1994), p. 328.

230 'Life in a local site': *Diversity of Life*, p. 13.

232 'We must somehow live': Kirkpatrick Sale, 'Mother of All', *The Schumacher Lectures Vol. 2*, ed. Satish Kumar (London: Abacus, 1974), p. 224. Repr. with other comparable material in *The Green Reader*, ed. Andrew Dobson (London: Deutsch and San Francisco: Mercury House, 1991).

232 'The little nations of the past': Snyder, 'The Place, the Region, and the Commons', in his *The Practice of the Wild* (New York: North Point Press, 1990), p. 37.

233 'North and South': The title of her first collection of poetry, which was then followed by the equally ecologically suggestive *A Cold Spring*, *Questions of Travel* and *Geography III*. In a wonderful essay, Tom Paulin has read Elizabeth Bishop against Heidegger, finding in her the embodiment of 'Dwelling without Roots': Paulin, *Minotaur: Poetry and the Nation State* (London: Faber and Faber, 1992), pp. 190–203. For good political reasons, Paulin is deeply sceptical of the Heideggerian

language of dwelling in which the poem is the equivalent of a Black Forest cottage: 'Is it possible to contemplate such an image without smelling the burnt flesh that clings to certain German place-names?' (p. 191).

233 'Mapped waters are more quiet': 'The Map', in Elizabeth Bishop, *The Complete Poems 1927–1979* (New York: Farrar Straus Giroux, 1983), p. 3.

234 'Did you always think': P. Craven and M. Heyward, 'An Interview with Basil Bunting', *Scripsi*, 1 (1982), p. 31.

234–5 'the abandoning of the North . . . an ecology of fox': Makin, *Bunting: The Shaping of his Verse* (Oxford: Oxford University Press, 1992), pp. 134, 16.

235 'Columba, Columbanus': Bunting, *Collected Poems* (Oxford: Oxford University Press, 1978), p. 53.

235 'I have been talking': quoted, Makin, p. 146.

236 'that impels / All thinking things': 'Tintern Abbey', lines 101–3.

236–7 'Conger skimped at the ebb': *Collected Poems*, p. 56.

237 'Both are given': 'Poetry and Religion', in Murray's *Collected Poems* (North Ryde, New South Wales: Angus and Robertson, new edn., 1991), p. 236.

237–8 'In the native religion of Japan': Murray, *Persistence in Folly* (Sydney and Melbourne: Angus and Robertson, 1984), p. 112.

238 'was for us a remote and unreal form': *Persistence in Folly*, p. 168.

239 'wild sound': *Persistence in Folly*, p. 21.

239 'Forests and State Forests': 'The Buladelah-Taree Holiday Song Cycle', section 8, *Collected Poems*, p. 126.

240 'Both Coolongolook River': 'The Human-Hair Thread', Murray's important essay on the Aboriginal influence on his work, in *Persistence in Folly*, p. 16.

240–1 'the Ancestors had been poets': Chatwin, *The Songlines* (London: Cape, 1987, repr. Picador, 1988), p. 16.

241 'by what right do you claim to own': *Discourse on Inequality*, p. 67.

241 'Watching from the barn': *Collected Poems*, p. 83. See the discussion of this poem in 'The Human-Hair Thread', *Persistence in Folly*, p. 17.

243 'the only goods in the world': Rousseau, *Discourse on the Origin of Inequality*, trans. Franklin Philip (Oxford: Oxford University Press, The World's Classics, 1994), pp. 34–5.

243 'vervet monkeys use different vocalizations': See Dorothy L. Cheney and Robert M. Seyfarth, *How Monkeys See the World: Inside the Mind of another Species* (Chicago: University of Chicago Press, 1990), chaps. 4–5, 10.

246-7 'The communities of creatures . . . and its poetry are not two': Gary
Snyder, *The Real Work: Interviews and Talks 1964-1979*, ed. W. Scott
McLean (New York: New Directions, 1980), pp. 173-4.

248 'To the extent that hermeneutics': 'Writing as a Problem for Literary
Criticism and Philosophical Hermeneutics', *Philosophic Exchange*, 2 no.
3 (Summer 1977), 3-15, repr. in *A Ricoeur Reader: Reflection and
Imagination*, ed. Mario J. Valdés (New York and London: Harvester
Wheatsheaf, 1991), pp. 320-37 (p. 320). For the argument that
writing is itself a cause of ecological estrangement, see David Abrams,
The Spell of the Sensuous (New York: Vintage, 1997).

248 'For contemporary philosophy': Ricoeur, 'Mimesis and
Representation' (1980), repr. in *A Ricoeur Reader*, p. 137.

249-50 'Thanks to writing': 'Writing as a Problem', p. 330.

250 'restructure for their readers': 'Writing as a Problem', p. 330.

250 'In one manner . . . The effacement': 'Writing as a Problem', p. 331.

250 'not another person': 'Writing as a Problem', p. 332.

251 'I like very much this notion of Heidegger': 'Poetry and Possibility', in
A Ricoeur Reader, p. 453.

252 'We shall never experience our relationship': 'The Question
concerning Technology', trans. William Lovitt, repr. in Heidegger,
Basic Writings, ed. David Farrell Krell (San Francisco:
HarperSanFrancisco, 1977, repr. 1993), p. 311.

253 'It is of utmost importance': 'Question concerning Technology',
p. 317, glossing *Symposium*, 205b.

253 'The possibility of all': 'Question concerning Technology', p. 318.

253 'comes to presence': 'Question concerning Technology', p. 319.

254 'the revealing that holds sway': 'Question concerning Technology',
p. 320.

254 'does not unlock': 'Question concerning Technology', p. 320, my
italics.

254 'What the river is . . . In no other way': 'Question concerning
Technology', p. 321.

255 'The forester who measures': 'Question concerning Technology',
p. 323.

255 'Above all, enframing conceals': 'Question concerning Technology',
pp. 332-3.

256 'The need that': Bruce V. Foltz, *Inhabiting the Earth: Heidegger,
Environmental Ethics, and the Metaphysics of Nature* (Atlantic Heights,
New Jersey: Humanities Press, 1995), p. 98.

256-7 'Once through Christianity': *Hölderlins Hymnen 'Germanien' und
'Der Rhein'*, trans. Foltz, *Inhabiting the Earth*, p. 63. The critique of

Christianity anticipates an essay which has had great influence on radical ecology, Lynn White Jr's 'The Historical Roots of our Ecologic Crisis', *Science*, 155 (1967), pp. 1203–7.

257 'The threat to man': 'Question concerning Technology', p. 333, my emphasis.

257 'There was a time': 'Question concerning Technology', pp. 339–40.

258 'We can say "yes"': *Discourse on Thinking*, trans. John M. Anderson and E. Hans Freund (New York: Harper and Row, 1966), p. 54.

258 'through language that unconcealment takes place': For a lucid analysis of this complex idea, see Charles Taylor, 'Heidegger, Language, and Ecology', in *Heidegger: A Critical Reader*, ed. Hubert Dreyfus and Harrison Hall (Oxford UK and Cambridge USA: Blackwell, 1992), chap. 13.

258 'In a letter of June 4': Zimmerman, *Heidegger's Confrontation with Modernity: Technology, Politics, Art* (Bloomington and Indianapolis: Indiana University Press, 1990), p. 125.

259 'In lovely blue': Translated by Richard Sieburth in *Hymns and Fragments by Friedrich Hölderlin* (Princeton: Princeton University Press, 1984), p. 249.

261 'dwelling occurs only when poetry': '. . . Poetically Man Dwells . . .', in Martin Heidegger, *Poetry, Language, Thought*, trans. Albert Hofstadter (New York, Hagerstown, San Francisco, London: Harper and Row, 1971), p. 227.

262 '*Only if we are capable of dwelling*': 'Building Dwelling Thinking', in *Poetry, Language, Thought*, p. 160.

262 'Mortals dwell in that they save': 'Building Dwelling Thinking', p. 150.

263 'what is *here* seen': *Letters of Rainer Maria Rilke 1910–1926*, trans. Jane Bannard Greene and M. D. Herter Norton (New York and London: Norton, 1945, repr. 1969), p. 374.

263 'uninterrupted space': to Lou Andreas-Salomé, *Letters 1910–1926*, p. 369. Compare Bachelard on Rilke quoted p. 173, above.

264 'And this activity': *Letters 1910–1926*, pp. 374–5, Rilke's ellipsis.

265 'Things that we might': Rilke, 9th Duino Elegy, in *Selected Poetry of Rainer Maria Rilke*, trans. Stephen Mitchell (London: Picador, 1987), p. 201.

265 'For when the traveler': 9th Elegy, *Selected Poetry of Rilke*, p. 199.

265 'apparently needs us': 9th Elegy, p. 199.

267 'In the domain of poetic phenomenology': Bachelard, *The Poetics of Space*, trans. Maria Jolas (1964, repr. Boston: Beacon Press, 1994), pp. 187–8.

267 'Bramwell has demonstrated . . . Ferry's assault': Bramwell, *Blood and Soil: Richard Walther Darré and Hitler's 'Green Party'* (Bourne End, Bucks.: Kensal, 1985) and *Ecology in the Twentieth Century: A History* (New Haven and London: Yale University Press, 1989). Ferry, *The New Ecological Order*, trans. Carol Volk (Chicago: Chicago University Press, 1995).

268 'Wherever man opens his eyes': 'The Question concerning Technology', p. 324.

269 'death is a master': 'Todesfuge', in Celan, *Mohn und Gedächtnis* (1952), trans. Michael Hamburger in Celan's *Selected Poems* (London: Penguin, 1990), pp. 61–3.

269 'de poser et d'imposer': Philippe Lacoue-Labarthe, *La poésie comme expérience* (Paris: Christian Bourgois, 1986), p. 151.

269–70 'Todtnauberg': in *Lichtzwang* (1970), trans. Hamburger, in *Selected Poems*, p. 293.

271 'The Jew and nature': Paul Celan, *Collected Prose*, trans. Rosmarie Waldrop (Manchester: Carcanet, 1986), p. 18.

271 'What is earthy and material': Françoise Meltzer, *Hot Property: The Stakes and Claims of Literary Originality* (Chicago: Chicago University Press, 1994), p. 55.

271 'Paul de Man's swerve': Noteworthy here is a moment in de Man's early (1954) essay, 'Heidegger's Exegeses of Hölderlin': 'Heidegger's commentaries were thought out just before and during World War II, and are directly linked to an anguished meditation upon the historical destiny of Germany, a meditation that finds an echo in the "national" poems of Hölderlin. But that is a side issue that would take us away from our topic' (trans. Wlad Godzich, in de Man, *Blindness and Insight: Essays in the Rhetoric of Contemporary History*, 2nd edn [Minneapolis: University of Minnesota Press, 1983], p. 254). Might the subtext of the latter sentence be: 'but this is all too central an issue that would take us too uncomfortably close to my own complicity with the historical destiny of Germany'?

271 'that in the Black Forest': Gadamer, *Wer bin Ich und wer bist du?: Ein Kommentar zu Paul Celans Gedichtfolge 'Atemkristall'* (Frankfurt, 1973), p. 15. I owe this reference, and recognition of the poem's possible allusion to the yellow star of the Jew, to John Felstiner's excellent *Paul Celan: Poet, Survivor, Jew* (New Haven and London: Yale University Press, 1995), chap. 15.

273 'Home': 'Home [2]', *The Collected Poems of Edward Thomas*, ed. R. George Thomas (Oxford: Oxford University Press, 1978, repr. 1981), p. 59.

274 'In his loneliness': Marginal gloss to 'The moving Moon' stanza in 'The Ancient Mariner', part IV.

274 'Home [1]': *Collected Poems*, p. 39.

275 'Mortals dwell in that they receive': 'Building Dwelling Thinking', p. 150.

275 'A craft which': 'Building Dwelling Thinking', p. 160.

277 'This policy appears to me': Edmund Burke, *Reflections on the Revolution in France* (1790), ed. Conor Cruise O'Brien (Harmondsworth: Penguin, 1968), pp. 119–20.

278 'Volney links geological catastrophe theory to revolution': Volney began developing his theory of the decay of empires in his *Voyage en Syrie et en Egypte*, published in 1787, four years before *Les ruines*; when travelling in Egypt and Asia, he made a close study of geology, an interest developed when he visited America – his *Tableau du climat et sol des Etats Unis* (1803) was the first comprehensive geological and climatological survey of the United States.

279 'in modern civilized society': Thoreau, *Walden* (New York: The Library of America, 1985), p. 346.

280 'The cabinetmaker's craft was chosen': *What is called Thinking?*, trans. Fred D. Wieck and J. Glenn Gray (New York: Harper and Row, 1968), p. 23.

281 'like those of a wind over a sea': 'A Defence of Poetry', in *Shelley's Poetry and Prose*, ed. Donald H. Reiman and Sharon B. Powers (New York and London: Norton, 1977), p. 504.

281 'Evening of misty stillness': Quoted, *Collected Poems*, p. 144.

281 'ecological in two senses': I am grateful to Greg Garrard for clarification on many points, but this one in particular.

281–2 'Precisely because finitude': Robert Pogue Harrison, *Forests: The Shadow of Civilization* (Chicago and London: University of Chicago Press, 1992), p. 249.

Suggestions for Further Reading

What follows is not a comprehensive bibliography but a list of about fifty books which the reader may find especially helpful in thinking further about ecopoetics.

On the idea of dwelling and the natural contract

David Abram, *The Spell of the Sensuous: Perception and Language in a More-than-Human World* (New York: Vintage, 1997)

Bruce V. Foltz, *Inhabiting the Earth: Heidegger, Environmental Ethics, and the Metaphysics of Nature* (Atlantic Heights, NJ: Humanities Press, 1995)

Robert Pogue Harrison, *Forests: The Shadow of Civilization* (Chicago: University of Chicago Press, 1992)

Martin Heidegger, 'The Question concerning Technology', trans. William Lovitt, repr. in Heidegger, *Basic Writings*, ed. David Farrell Krell (San Francisco: HarperSanFrancisco, 1977, repr. 1993); 'What are Poets for?', 'Building Dwelling Thinking' and '. . . Poetically Man Dwells . . .' in his *Poetry, Language, Thought*, trans. Albert Hofstadter (New York, Hagerstown, San Francisco, London: Harper and Row, 1971)

Michel Serres, *The Natural Contract*, trans. Elizabeth MacArthur and William Paulson (Ann Arbor: University of Michigan Press, 1995)

Michael E. Zimmerman, *Heidegger's Confrontation with Modernity: Technology, Politics, Art* (Bloomington and Indianapolis: Indiana University Press, 1990)

On the Romantic tradition

Malcolm Andrews, *The Search for the Picturesque: Landscape Aesthetics and Tourism in Britain, 1760–1800* (Stanford: Stanford University Press, 1989)

Jonathan Bate, *Romantic Ecology: Wordsworth and the Environmental Tradition* (London and New York: Routledge, 1991)

'Green Romanticism': special issue of *Studies in Romanticism*, 35 (Fall 1996)

Karl Kroeber, *Ecological Literary Criticism: Romantic Imagining and the Biology of Mind* (New York: Columbia University Press, 1994)

Timothy Morton, *Shelley and the Revolution in Taste: The Body and the Natural World* (Cambridge: Cambridge University Press, 1994)

'Romanticism and Ecology': special issue of *The Wordsworth Circle*, 28 (Summer 1997)

Anna D. Wallace, *Walking, Literature, and English Culture: The Origins and Uses of Peripatetic in the Nineteenth Century* (Oxford: Clarendon Press, 1993)

On the history and ideas of the environmental movement

Anna Bramwell, *Ecology in the Twentieth Century: A History* (New Haven: Yale University Press, 1989)

Andrew Dobson, ed., *The Green Reader* (London: André Deutsch and San Francisco: Mercury House, 1991)

Luc Ferry, *The New Ecological Order*, trans. Carol Volk (Chicago: University of Chicago Press, 1995)

David Pepper, *Modern Environmentalism: An Introduction* (London and New York: Routledge, 1996)

Kate Soper, *What is Nature? Culture, Politics and the Non-Human* (Oxford and Cambridge, Mass.: Blackwell, 1995)

Donald Worster, *Nature's Economy: A History of Ecological Ideas* (Cambridge: Cambridge University Press, 1985)

Michael E. Zimmerman, *Contesting Earth's Future: Radical Ecology and Postmodernity* (Berkeley, Los Angeles and London: University of California Press, 1994)

On representations and transformations of nature in history and literature

William Cronon, *Changes in the Land: Indians, Colonists, and the Ecology of New England* (New York: Hill and Wang, 1983)

Neil Evernden, *The Social Creation of Nature* (Baltimore: Johns Hopkins University Press, 1992)

Clarence Glacken, *Traces on the Rhodian Shore: Nature and Culture in*

Western Thought from Ancient Times to the end of the Eighteenth Century (Berkeley: University of California Press, 1967)

Richard H. Grove, *Green Imperialism: Colonial Expansion, Tropical Island Edens, and the Origins of Environmentalism, 1600–1860* (Cambridge: Cambridge University Press, 1995)

Richard Kerridge and Neil Sammells, eds., *Writing the Environment: Ecocriticism and Literature* (London and New York: Zed Books, 1998)

Joseph Meeker, *The Comedy of Survival: Studies in Literary Ecology* (New York: Scribner's, 1974)

Max Oelschlaeger, *The Idea of Wilderness: from Prehistory to the Age of Ecology* (New Haven: Yale University Press, 1991)

Simon Schama, *Landscape and Memory* (London: HarperCollins, 1995)

Keith Thomas, *Man and the Natural World: Changing Attitudes in England 1500–1800* (Harmondsworth: Penguin, 1984)

Raymond Williams, *The Country and the City* (1973; repr. London: Hogarth, 1993)

On the American environmental literary tradition

Lawrence Buell, *The Environmental Imagination: Thoreau, Nature Writing, and the Formation of American Culture* (Cambridge, Mass.: Harvard University Press, 1995)

John Elder, *Imagining the Earth: Poetry and the Vision of Nature* (Urbana and Chicago: University of Illinois Press, 1985)

Cheryll Glotfelty and Harold Fromm, eds., *The Ecocriticism Reader: Landmarks in Literary Ecology* (Athens, Ga.: University of Georgia Press, 1996)

Leo Marx, *The Machine in the Garden: Technology and the Pastoral Idea in America* (Oxford University Press: New York and Oxford, 1964)

Roderick Nash, *Wilderness and the American Mind* (New Haven: Yale University Press, 3rd edn, 1982)

On ecofeminism and ecological socialism

Murray Bookchin, *The Philosophy of Social Ecology* (Montreal: Black Rose Books, 1990)

Annette Kolodny, *The Lay of the Land: Metaphor as Experience and History in American Life and Literature* (Chapel Hill: University of North Carolina Press, 1975)

Carolyn Merchant, *The Death of Nature: Women, Ecology, and the Scientific Revolution* (San Francisco: Harper and Row, 1980)

——, *Earthcare: Women and the Environment* (London and New York: Routledge, 1996)

Val Plumwood, *Feminism and the Mastery of Nature* (London and New York: Routledge, 1993)

Andrew Ross, *The Chicago Gangster Theory of Life: Nature's Debt to Society* (London and New York: Verso, 1994)

On love of nature and our responsibility towards animals

Donna Haraway, *Primate Visions: Gender, Race, and Nature in the World of Modern Science* (London and New York: Routledge, 1989)

Stephen R. Kellert and Edward O. Wilson, eds., *The Biophilia Hypothesis* (Washington DC: Island Press, 1993)

John Passmore, *Man's Responsibility to Nature* (London: Duckworth, 1980)

Edward O. Wilson, *Biophilia: The Human Bond with other Species* (Cambridge, Mass.: Harvard University Press, 1984)

On biodiversity and bioregionalism

Kirkpatrick Sale, *Dwellers in the Land: The Bioregional Vision* (San Francisco: Sierra Club Books, 1985)

Gary Snyder, *The Practice of the Wild* (New York: North Point Press, 1990)

Edward O. Wilson, *The Diversity of Life* (London and New York: Penguin, 1994)

On reading space and place

Gaston Bachelard, *The Poetics of Space*, trans. Maria Jolas (1964; repr. Boston: Beacon Press, 1994)

Mike Davis, *Ecology of Fear: Los Angeles and the Imagination of Disaster* (New York: Vintage, 1999).

Yi Fu Tuan, *Topophilia: A Study of Environmental Perception, Attitudes and Values* (Englewood Cliffs, NJ: Prentice Hall, 1974)

John Urry, *Consuming Places* (London and New York: Routledge, 1995)

Patrick Wright, *On Living in an Old Country* (London: Verso, 1985)

Acknowledgements

The initial thinking for this book was made possible by a British Academy Research Readership and the final preparation of it for the press by a Leverhulme Personal Research Professorship: I am deeply grateful for both awards. My second home during the writing of several chapters was the Huntington Library and Gardens, San Marino, California – thanks to Roy Ritchie and all the staff.

Acknowledgements are due to the editors of the following publications for permission to reproduce, in extensively revised form, those parts of my argument which have been given preliminary airings in other contexts: *English Comedy* (Cambridge University Press, special thanks to John Kerrigan), *John Clare Society Journal*, *London Review of Books*, *New Literary History* (special thanks to Herbert Tucker), *Shakespeare Survey* (Cambridge University Press), *Studies in Romanticism* (special thanks to David Wagenknecht), *Writing and the Environment* (Zed Books).

For invitations to give lectures which gave me the opportunity to test out material, I would like to thank David Amigoni, Alan Brissenden, Peter Browning, Sir Cyril Chantler, Simon Dentith, Greg Garrard, Catherine Golden, Sarah Goodwin, Jerry Hogle, Richard Kerridge, Michael John Kooy, Grevel Lindop, Mark Lussier, James McKusick, Jem Poster, Julie Sanders, Jon Stallworthy and Wynn Thomas. I have benefited from Bernard Beatty's incisive reading of the typescript, and from valuable discussions with two colleagues, Ralph Pite and Gillian Rudd, and my graduate student Greg Garrard (who taught me more than I could possibly teach him); also from the comments of Alan Hurd, John Kerrigan and Christopher Ridgway on an early draft introduction. David Pirie kindly nudged me towards a better title than my working one. My thanks to Ian Qualtrough and Suzanne Yee for their photographic work.

Peter Straus at Picador and David Godwin, my agent, had faith in what must have seemed an eccentric, uncommercial project. The American edition owes its life to Lindsay Waters at Harvard University Press.

Two of the Press Syndics at Harvard, Larry Buell and Judith Ryan, saved me from errors and suggested valuable improvements. The book was helped through production by the talents of Mary Mount and Nicholas Blake. Paula Byrne shared everything, as always.

Index

Visit **www.picador.com** to read more about all our books and to buy them. You will also find features, author interviews and news of any author events, and you can sign up for e-newsletters so that you're always first to hear about our new releases.

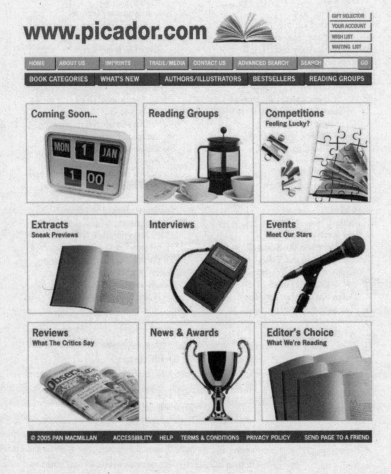